Communicating with pattern

Circles and dots

Mark Hampshire & Keith Stephenson

EAT
WITH LOVE FROM ME TO
Ringo Starr
12
11
1
10
2
9
3
8
4
7
5
6
HIGH TIDE

Communicating with pattern

Circles and dots

Published and distributed by RotoVision SA
Route Suisse 9, CH-1295, Mies, Switzerland
RotoVision SA, Sales and Editorial Office
Sheridan House, 114 Western Road, Hove
BN3 1DD, UK
Tel: + 44 (0) 1273 72 72 68
Fax: + 44 (0) 1273 72 72 69
E-mail: sales@rotovision.com
Web: www.rotovision.com

Copyright © RotoVision SA 2006
All rights reserved. No part of this publication may be reproduced, stored in a retrieval system or transmitted in any form or by any other means, electronic, mechanical, photocopying, recording or otherwise, without permission of the copyright holder.

10 9 8 7 6 5 4 3 2 1
ISBN 2-940361-16-9

Original book concept: Luke Herriott and Keith Stephenson.
Art direction: Tony Seddon
Design and artwork: Keith and Spike at Absolute Zero Degrees
Additional illustrations: Keith Stephenson

Reprographics in Singapore by Provision PTE
Printed in Singapore by Star Standard

002–003 Circles and dots

Contents

Introduction

Elemental yet elegant, the circle has forever mesmerized the creative eye with a simplicity that testifies to the writer Henry James' statement: "in art, economy is always beauty." Its symmetry has earned it a reputation for perfection, both esthetically and functionally, and given rise to its unique applications—with the wheel surely at the top of its list of achievements. In various hybrids, circles surround us in nature, art, architecture, and engineering: the sphere, a circle in 3D; the dome, half a sphere; the arch, a supporting semicircle; the spiral, an ever-decreasing circle; and the dot, a miniature circle.

The importance of the circle in society can be charted through representations of the sun in primitive art, the building of stone circles, and the medieval philosophical notion of Fortune's Wheel. From the Christian halo to the Buddhist Wheel of Life, circles feature in religious iconography to convey purity, wholeness, and fulfillment. Society has appropriated the circle for its sense of inclusiveness—Arthurian Knights sat at a Round Table so that no one should claim higher status—but with this inclusiveness comes the opposite idea of exclusivity, being outside the circle. In social hierarchy, the center of the circle represents the elite. Bullseye! We revere the dead center of the circle. It's where we set our sights; it carries the highest score.

Natural form or man-made? The circle splits opinion. Some assert the form is to be found everywhere in nature—in the shape of the sun and moon, in raindrops, bubbles, and flowers—and it is our desire to mirror its natural beauty that drives creative interpretations of the circle. Others maintain that the circle does not occur naturally, but is a man-made conceit that reflects the worlds of physics and mathematics—engineering tools that perpetuate the desire to create order from a chaotic world; awards and medals that commemorate human achievements.

001 *Circles are practical, everyday, individual, and inspiring. A collection of plates and bowls from Habitat, UK.*

If circles represent the big themes of life—the macro issues—dots represent detail, the minutiae, and the world in close-up. Think of halftone screen dots that make up the "big picture." Pointillist, Georges Seurat, realized the power of the dot when he experimented with juxtaposing dots of pure color on canvas—leaving the eye to mix the colors. The duality of dots means that, on one hand, they can communicate vital information—in the form of Morse code, Braille, and LED displays—yet they can also confuse. Like some other patterns, notably stripes, dots can be a chaotic surface pattern, causing a high degree of visual disorder. Spots are nature's way of warning—they indicate illness or poison—but they also offer a means of camouflage for animals that live in the dappled light of the forest.

Communicating with Pattern: Circles and Dots looks at the enduring appeal of the circle for artists, designers, and architects. It deals with the circles that evoke the big themes of life such as the solar system, social hierarchy, birth, and religion. Taking in expressions of membership and identity—from political causes to aircraft roundels—it then explores the huge array of themes and moods that can be communicated through the circle, including retro, nautical, glamor, and dynamism. Circles and dots that convey signals and information are covered—from Braille to commemorative plaques—and finally there are the hard-working circles of form and function, such as wheels, lenses, and perforated technical fabrics. Each of these distinct sections reveals another aspect of the circle, demonstrating the wealth of communication opportunities offered by this timeless form.

001

Life Circles

The Solar System
The Sun
The Halo
The Moon
The Earth
Stone Circles
Life

Life Circles

Compared to other patterns and forms, surely the circle has the most profound relationship with human existence. Our sun, moon, and the planets of our solar system are, after all, spheres, orbiting in near-circular motion. Prehistoric communities built stone circles for worship, social interaction, and burial. The circle constitutes part of the iconography of a diverse array of religions including the Pagan holly wreath, the Buddhist wheel, the yin yang symbol of Taoism, and the halo, witnessed in Christian religious art. Much of this symbolism can be seen to influence design work—think of the yin yang balance that is evoked by many well-being brands, or the way the halo represents purity.

The relationship between life, the universe, and the circle is examined here. Circles are present throughout the whole cycle of life—in the life-giving heat of the sun, the monthly lunation of the moon, the creation of plant life in biospheres, and the recycling of human waste. These are the circles that can be appropriated in the work of artists and designers to represent the great themes of life—birth, growth, rebirth, social structure, faith, and worship. From nurturing nest to age-indicating tree rings, they help us to create, sustain, and document human existence.

008

009

002 The setting sun never fails to inspire.
003 The development of maps and globes has helped us make sense of our existence.
004 The door of St John's Church, New York City, photographed by Carol Cotter, depicts the sunrise and the universe beyond.
005 The egg-like form of the Life Collection vase by Bahari, Thailand.
006 A mid-20th century wood carving based on sun motifs decorates this door in Barcelona, Spain.
007 A view of the earth from space, obtained in 1990 by the Galileo spacecraft, produced by NASA/JPL.
008 A Buddhist wheel painted on the ceiling of the Shrine of the Blissful, taken in Mongolia by Jannie Armstrong.
009 The Desert Dome at the Henry Doorly Zoo in Omaha, Nebraska, US.

The Solar System

Planets were formed from particles of gas and dust that clustered and grew like snowballs in space. On colliding, these particles became hot and molten and were pulled inward under the force of gravity. The sphere is what's left when everything has fallen into the center as far as it can. The solar system is in perpetual circular and elliptical motion. The gravitational pull of the sun keeps the planets orbiting around it. Satellites, asteroids, and comets orbit around the planets. This rotational energy is vital and life sustaining, and perhaps at the heart of our relationship with, and dependence on, the circle.

The planets are linked to Roman and Greek mythology and the visual language of astrology. Gustav Holst wrote *The Planets* in response to 19th century theories on the planets' influence on world affairs, and many artists, musicians, and designers have looked to the universe for the answers to the great unexplained themes of life.

010 *Calvin J. Hamilton produced this view of the solar system, based on images from Voyager, Mariner 10, and the Hubble Space Telescope, for his Web site, www.solarviews.com It shows (L-R): Sun, Mercury, Venus, Earth, Mars, Jupiter, Saturn, Uranus, Neptune, and Pluto, approximately to scale.*
011 *Photographer Chris George creates his own universe with his unique photographic technique, which captures 360º environments which he then displays on these spheres.*
012 *The symbols for the planets were developed for use in astronomy and are predominantly circular. Shown (L-R): Sun, Mercury, Venus, Earth, Moon, Mars, and Uranus. The symbol for Mercury represents the head and winged cap of the Roman god of the same name; the symbol for Venus, the goddess of love, is the same as the female symbol; the Earth symbol is a globe bisected by meridian lines; the symbol for the Moon is a crescent; the symbol for Mars, the god of war, is also used as the male symbol and depicts a shield and a spear.*

010

011

012

The Sun

As the ultimate source of life on earth, it's no wonder that the sun has been deified throughout history. When man started farming, he revered the fiery disc that regulated the seasons and sustained life. Ra, the sun god, was considered the first king of Egypt, the Pharaoh his son and representative on earth. In Mesopotamia the sun god Shamash, equated with justice, was a major deity. Although it had no institutionalized form of sun worship, Greece had two sun gods: Apollo and Helios. The influence of the sun in religious belief appears in Zoroastrianism, Mithraism, Hinduism, Buddhism, and among the Druids of the UK, the Aztecs of Mexico, the Incas of Peru, and many Native Americans. In Christian worship, a ring of sunrays adorns the Monstrance, used to display the round wafer of the host during Communion. Some modern day Pagans believe that Christmas customs evolved from Brumalia, meaning "rebirth" of the sun and celebrated just after the Winter Solstice, when presents would be exchanged to celebrate the return of the sun after the shortest day. France's Sun King, Louis XIV chose the sun and particularly Apollo as his emblem. Like Apollo, Louis XIV considered himself a peace-loving patron of the arts. He emphasized this comparison in the use of Apollo's symbols—the laurel leaf, lyre, and tripod—in the decoration of the palace of Versailles.

The sun continues to have relevance in modern design terms. Gilded representations of the sun can express luxury and exuberance, while its radiance is used to convey optimism and hope.

013 *The sun in all its fiery glory.*
014 *A naive representation of the sun is a fitting adornment for a plant pot, reminding us of our reliance on its power for growth.*
015 *An early evening view of the sun gives this Venetian view a romantic air.*
016 *SunDay, New York, identity by Lance Wyman, US.*
017 *Mimicking the Sun King: sunny shapes can bring an uplifting sense of light when used in interiors.*
018 *A Mexican mask with sunray motif.*
019 *Sam Phillips' Sun Records in Memphis, Tennessee, US, was the first label to release records by the unknown Elvis Presley in 1954.*
020 *A sunny welcome awaits guests at the Caleta Hotel, Acapulco, Mexico, courtesy of the identity designed by Lance Wyman, US.*
021 *The amber Solitaire light by Niche Modern, US.*

016

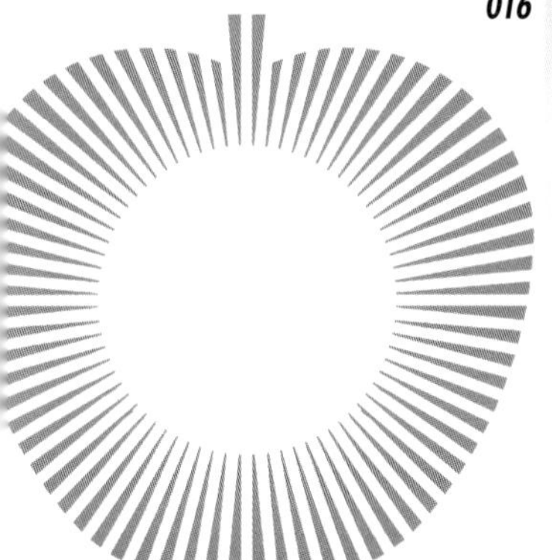

017

020

021

"The concept of the artificial light is man's attempt to mimic the sun. It started with a campfire. And progressively over the next few thousand years we've made light more interesting but have yet to harness the beauty and simplicity of the sun. Most attempts at artificial light get bogged down in their overcomplication of what should in fact be really simple. How do you improve upon what's already perfect?"

Jeremy Pyles,
Niche Modern, US

The Halo

Also referred to as a nimbus or aureole, a halo is a ring of light that surrounds an object. Its origins as an artistic device probably go back to the Greeks. Using the symbolism of light to represent spirituality, the Greek sun god Helios was depicted with a halo. Roman emperors elevated their standing by depicting themselves with halos. The motif is even found in 3rd century Indian Buddhist art, probably brought to the East by Greek invaders. Its Pagan origins meant that early Christian art eschewed the halo, but in the 4th century saints and angels started to be depicted with circles of golden light surrounding their heads to emphasize their holiness. Renaissance art, which placed more emphasis on perspective, transformed the halo from the aura surrounding the head, to an oval ring that floated above the subject's head.

022–024 *Various characters depicted with halos in stained glass from the St Joseph Catholic Church, Macon, Georgia, US Much of the church's stained glass was created at the Mayer workshops in Bavaria, Germany. Christian religious art adopte the halo in the 4th century, since when it has been used to depict the holiness of saints, angels, and the Messiah. The earliest surviving example of pictorial stained glass is a 10th century Head of Christ from Lorsch Abbey in Germany. Its popularity grew from the Romanesque period (12th century) through the Gothic period (13th–14th century) when narrative scenes in colorful stained glass became a popular way of relating the stories of the Bible to the illiterate masses*

These days, we tend to use the halo in more lighthearted applications—it has come to symbolize any person or thing that is pure and good intentioned, often appearing humorously above a character's head after a good deed or a pure thought. Innocent, the UK brand of fresh fruit drinks, has incorporated the halo into its friendly and engaging brand mark that depicts a saintly berry-like "dude" and its halo. The logo evokes the goodness of 100% fresh fruit, and there's a satisfying hint that you're being a bit of a saint by choosing something good for you. New York designers, intoto have rendered the halo in 3D to create the Halo stool. True to its name, there's a real sense of purity about the piece—in both its pared down, sculptural form and its pristine white lacquer finish.

025
028
029
NCIS
ASSISI

026

027

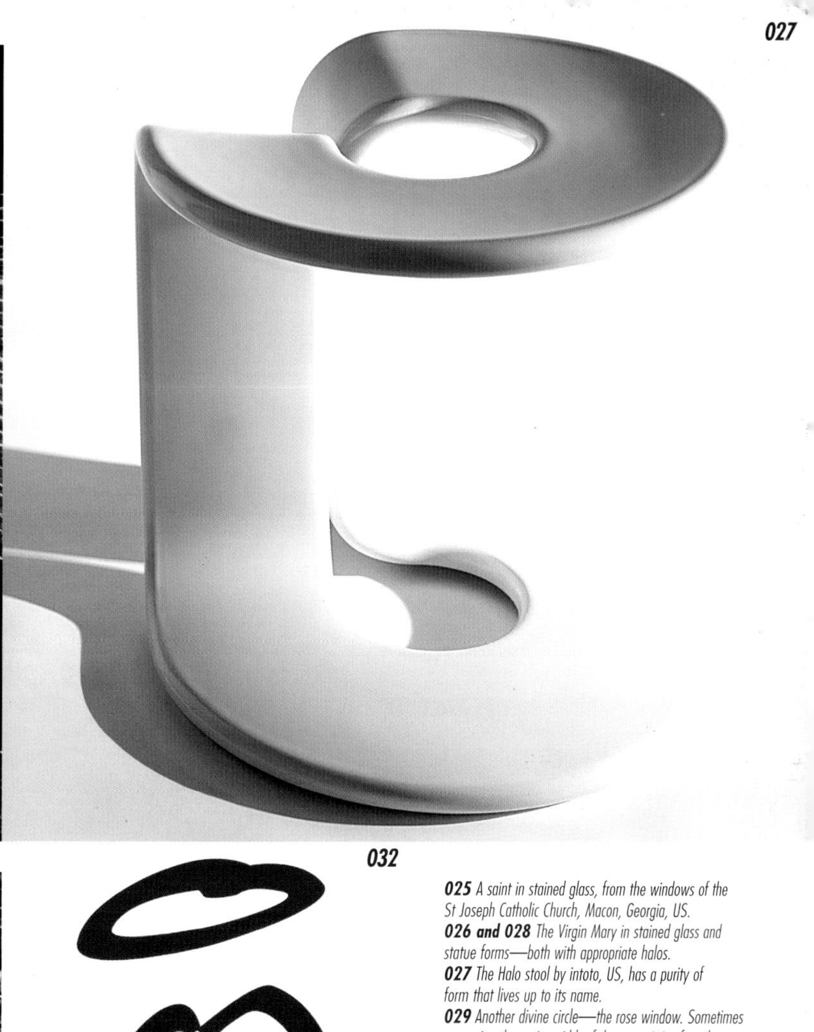

031

032

025 *A saint in stained glass, from the windows of the St Joseph Catholic Church, Macon, Georgia, US.*
026 and 028 *The Virgin Mary in stained glass and statue forms—both with appropriate halos.*
027 *The Halo stool by intoto, US, has a purity of form that lives up to its name.*
029 *Another divine circle—the rose window. Sometimes occupying the entire width of the nave, it is often the centerpiece of the church.*
030 *St Francis of Assisi bears a red halo.*
031 *Detail of the infant Jesus.*
032 *Fruit drink company, Innocent, uses a saintly halo as part of its brand iconography to promote the healthiness of its product.*

The Moon

The moon's appearance changes through eight phases of a lunation, starting with a new moon, when the unilluminated side is facing the earth and no moon is visible. The moon waxes as the crescent increases, becomes a full moon, and then wanes as the crescent decreases. The first waxing crescent moon marks the beginning of a month in the Islamic calendar and the crescent features in the flags of several Islamic countries.

Folklore and fiction evidence our love affair with the moon. Well before Neil Armstrong set foot on its surface, science fiction writers and movie makers fantasized about reaching the moon—epitomized by George Méliès' 1902 movie, *Le Voyage dans la Lune*, based on works by Jules Verne and H.G. Wells. We romanticize the full moon's influence on human behavior—linked to crime, suicide, mental illness (the term "lunatic" derives from the moon), birthrates, and fertility. Some people even buy and sell stocks according to phases of the moon. None of the theories has been proved, but the myths live on.

The moon's influence on tides is strangely enigmatic and in design terms we associate the moon with mystery and magic—think of ET cycling, silhouetted against a full moon—the icon that became the logo for Steven Spielberg's first production company, Amblin Entertainment. Spielberg clearly believes in the magic of the moon—the identity for his other company, DreamWorks, features a boy fishing, cradled by a crescent moon.

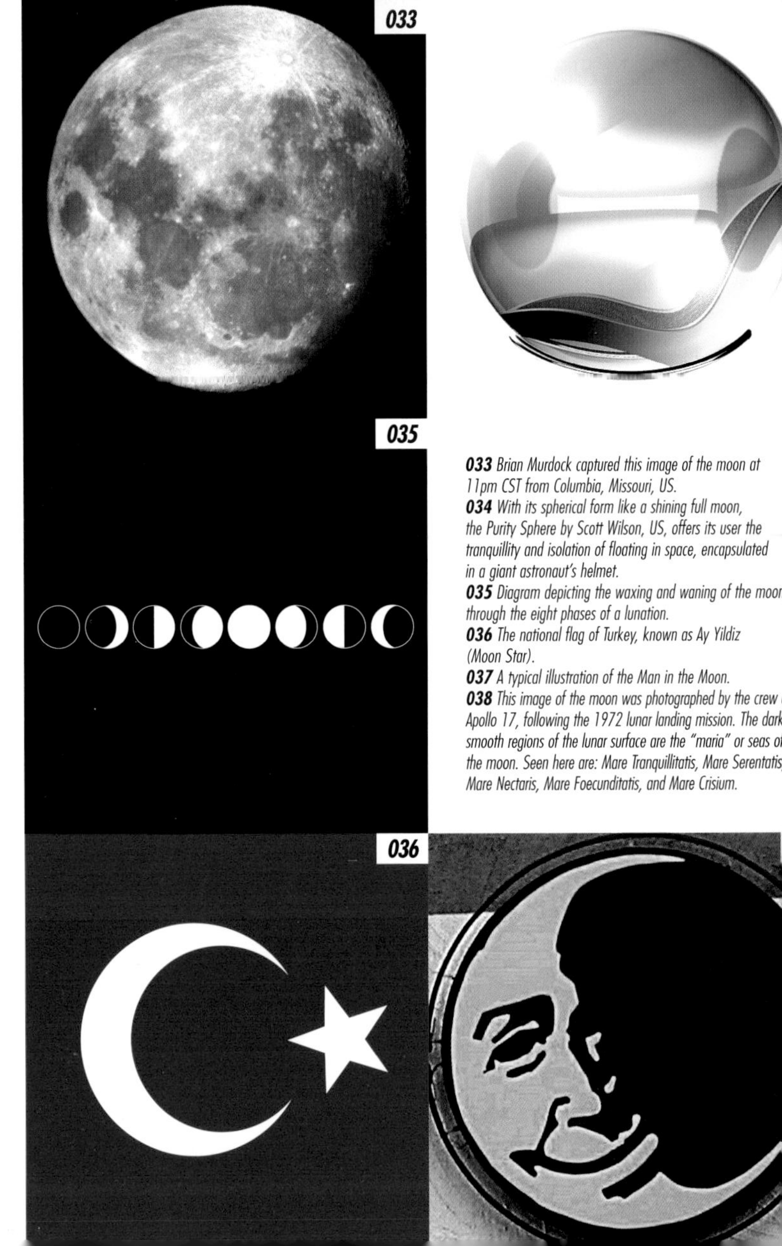

033 *Brian Murdock captured this image of the moon at 11pm CST from Columbia, Missouri, US.*
034 *With its spherical form like a shining full moon, the Purity Sphere by Scott Wilson, US, offers its user the tranquillity and isolation of floating in space, encapsulated in a giant astronaut's helmet.*
035 *Diagram depicting the waxing and waning of the moon through the eight phases of a lunation.*
036 *The national flag of Turkey, known as Ay Yildiz (Moon Star).*
037 *A typical illustration of the Man in the Moon.*
038 *This image of the moon was photographed by the crew of Apollo 17, following the 1972 lunar landing mission. The dark smooth regions of the lunar surface are the "maria" or seas of the moon. Seen here are: Mare Tranquillitatis, Mare Serentatis, Mare Nectaris, Mare Foecunditatis, and Mare Crisium.*

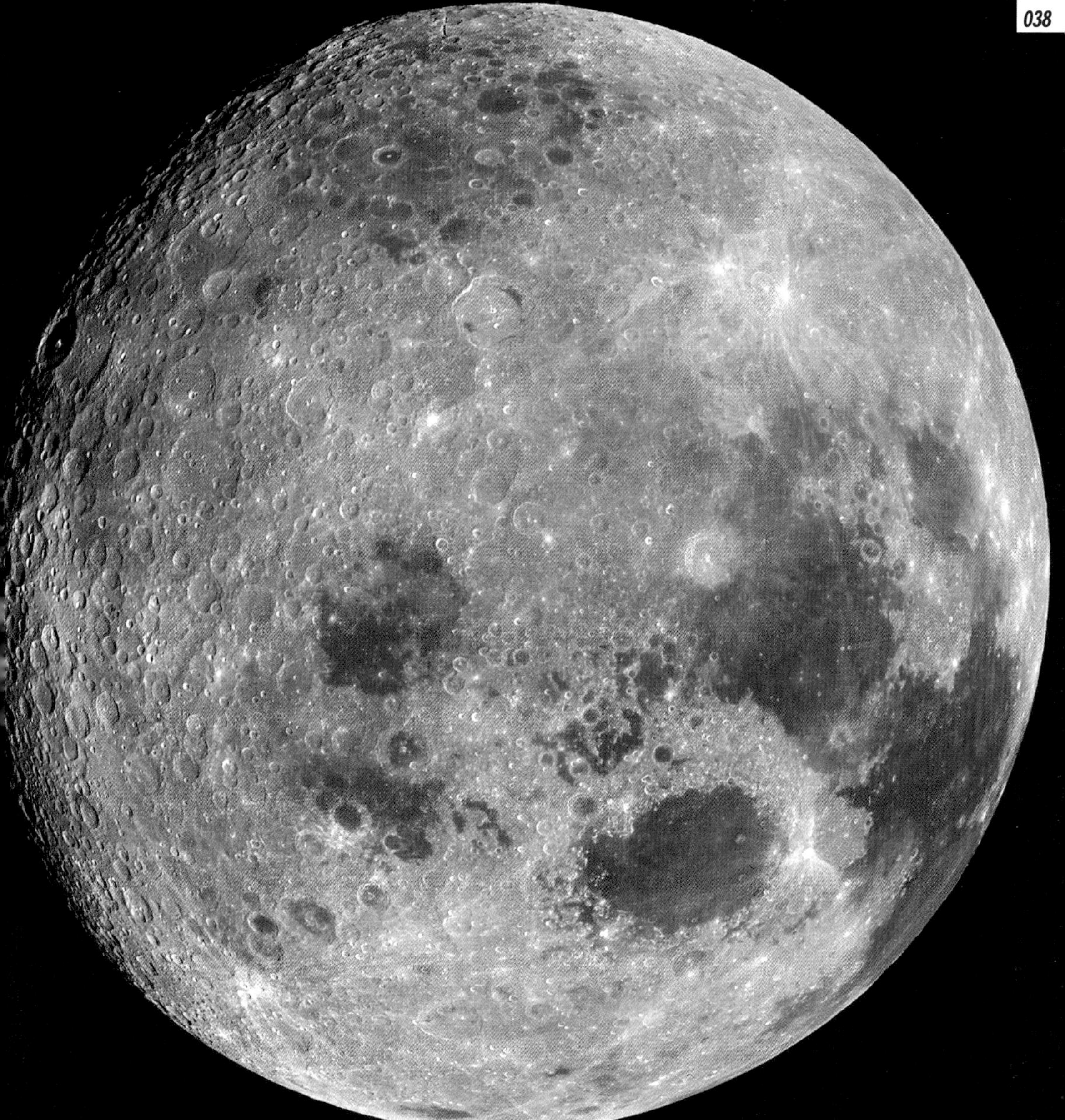
038

The Earth

According to the song, "they all laughed at Christopher Columbus when he said the world was round." Clearly, Gershwin used some artistic license because Aristotle had already found evidence for a spherical earth in the 4th century BC, based on observations such as the circular shadow of the earth on the moon during a lunar eclipse and ships disappearing over the horizon hull-first. There are even theories that the ancient Egyptians knew that the earth was a sphere as far back as 2600 BC. As for Columbus, he was probably more interested in discerning the earth's circumference, which he underestimated by about a quarter.

Nowadays we are familiar with the sight of the earth from space, but it's easy to imagine the excitement that gripped the world on April 12th, 1961 when Soviet cosmonaut, Yuri Gagarin, the first human to travel in space exclaimed "the earth is blue." Cultural observers have attributed our increased concern with the environment and the move toward global politics to the historic pictures of earth from space. From TV idents to corporate logos, organizations and brands use planet earth as visual shorthand for scale and globalism. Universal presents our planet glowing in space to create excitement and wonder. UK telecoms brand BT represents international connectivity through a globe abstracted into simple colored spherical shapes. So potent is the globe as a graphic device that it can be simplified to a minimal blue orb, like the One World logo, and still carry strong values and meaning.

UNIVERSAL

042

__039__ The Universal identity by brand consultancy Identica, UK, captures a sense of wonder and excitement.
__040__ Earth rising, taken from the Apollo 11 mission to the moon in 1969. Produced by NASA.
__041__ South America is visible in this view from the Galileo orbiter, taken when the spacecraft was about 1.3 million mile[s] from earth on its way to Jupiter in December 1990. Image produced by USGS Flagstaff.
__042__ Big idea, simple solution: the One World identity.
__043__ The Unisphere, constructed as the icon of the 1964 Ne[w] York World's Fair, designed by Gilmore D. Clarke, still stands impressively in Flushing Meadows Park, Queens, New York.
__044__ The abstract globe of BT's logo suggests connectivity.
__045__ An informative globe that switches the emphasis from land to sea, plotting marine life and their habitats.
__046__ Using the earth to highlight environmental issues.

040

041

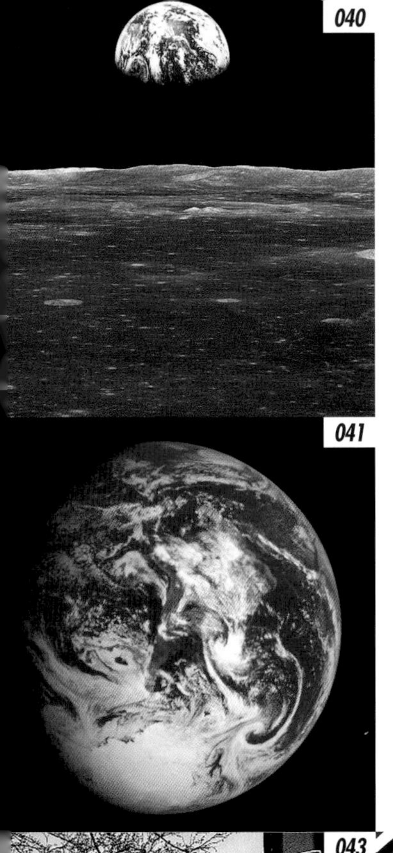

044

043

045

046

047

Stone Circles

Surely there can be no greater proof of the deep significance of circles to humanity than the ancient stone circle. As early as around 8,000 years ago, prehistoric people started creating circles in their landscape. Evidence exists of them all over the world, but particularly in Northern Europe and the UK. It's likely these circles were first built in wood (the post hole remains of Woodhenge near Stonehenge can still be seen) graduating to stone during the Stone Age, around 5,000–6,000 years ago. Alice Keens-Soper has made several documentaries about prehistoric people and remarks: "Archeologists generally believe that people were aware of the permanence of stone and wanted to leave a lasting mark on the earth that would outlive them." Circles have always held a deep significance and symbolism for people. But why? The earliest settled farming communities were formed in Europe from around 10,000 years ago in what has come to be known as the fertile crescent in modern day Turkey. →

048

047 *An entire village is enclosed within the henge at Avebury, Wiltshire, UK. A great ring of stones encloses two smaller rings, and one, possibly two, avenues of stones leading out from the henge. Its ditch is 30ft (9m) deep, rising to a bank over 15ft (4m) high. The site encloses 28 acres (11.5ha) and held 98 standing stones of local sarsen which are in their natural state, unlike the dressed stones of Stonehenge.*
048 *Believed to have originally contained 41 stones, 38 stones remain of the stone circle at Castlerigg, Cumbria, UK. Set among the mountains of the Lake District, 700ft (213m) above sea level, it is one of the earliest stone circles in the UK, dating from around 3200 BC.*
049 *Probably the most famous of all the stone circles is Stonehenge, UK.*

→ The most important stone circles, like Stonehenge, are perfectly aligned on the Midwinter and Midsummer Solstices (December 21st and June 21st)—key points in the farming year when people were desperate to ensure the repetition of the seasons so that life could begin again. In its circular form, representing the circular gods of the Sun and the Moon and having neither beginning nor end, the stone circle could have been considered fundamental to the continuance of life.

It also seems indisputable that the circular form was an early display of social hierarchy. Circles create a demarcation between those who are in the circle and those who are not. Even today we talk of an exclusive group being in the "inner circle." There's evidence from circular mound burials near to Stonehenge that chieftains—male leaders—may have used Stonehenge for ceremonial purposes. Some believe that these chieftains saw Stonehenge as a way of indicating their importance. Alice Keens-Soper remarks, "Compared to Avebury stone circle, some 30 miles from Stonehenge, 1,000 years older, and a far bigger, more inclusive monument, Stonehenge was a small circle, possibly meant for only a few exclusive people. If you stand inside the circle today there's no doubt that you feel important and in command of your landscape—you have a 360 degree view of your land."

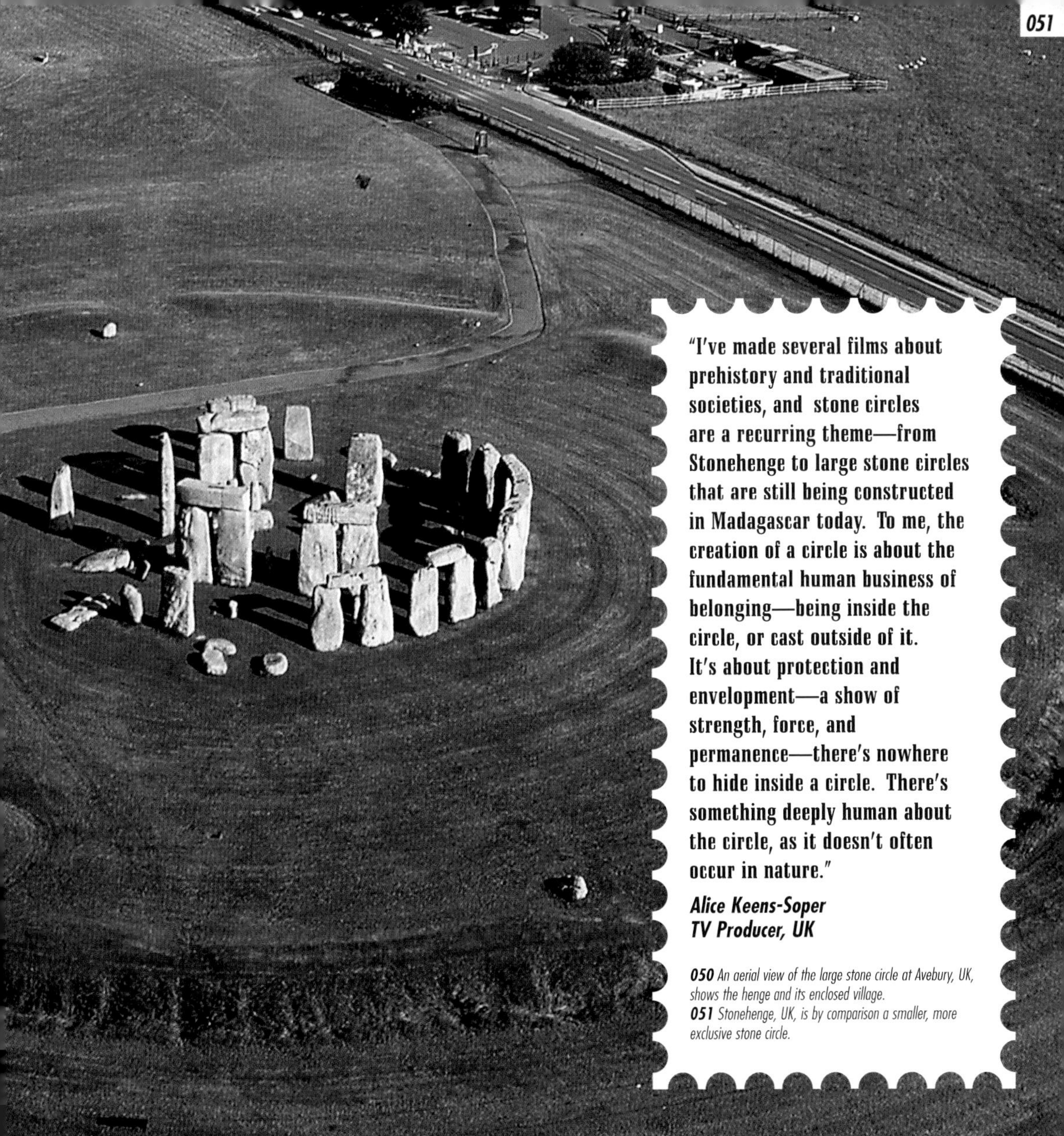

"I've made several films about prehistory and traditional societies, and stone circles are a recurring theme—from Stonehenge to large stone circles that are still being constructed in Madagascar today. To me, the creation of a circle is about the fundamental human business of belonging—being inside the circle, or cast outside of it. It's about protection and envelopment—a show of strength, force, and permanence—there's nowhere to hide inside a circle. There's something deeply human about the circle, as it doesn't often occur in nature."

Alice Keens-Soper
TV Producer, UK

050 *An aerial view of the large stone circle at Avebury, UK, shows the henge and its enclosed village.*
051 *Stonehenge, UK, is by comparison a smaller, more exclusive stone circle.*

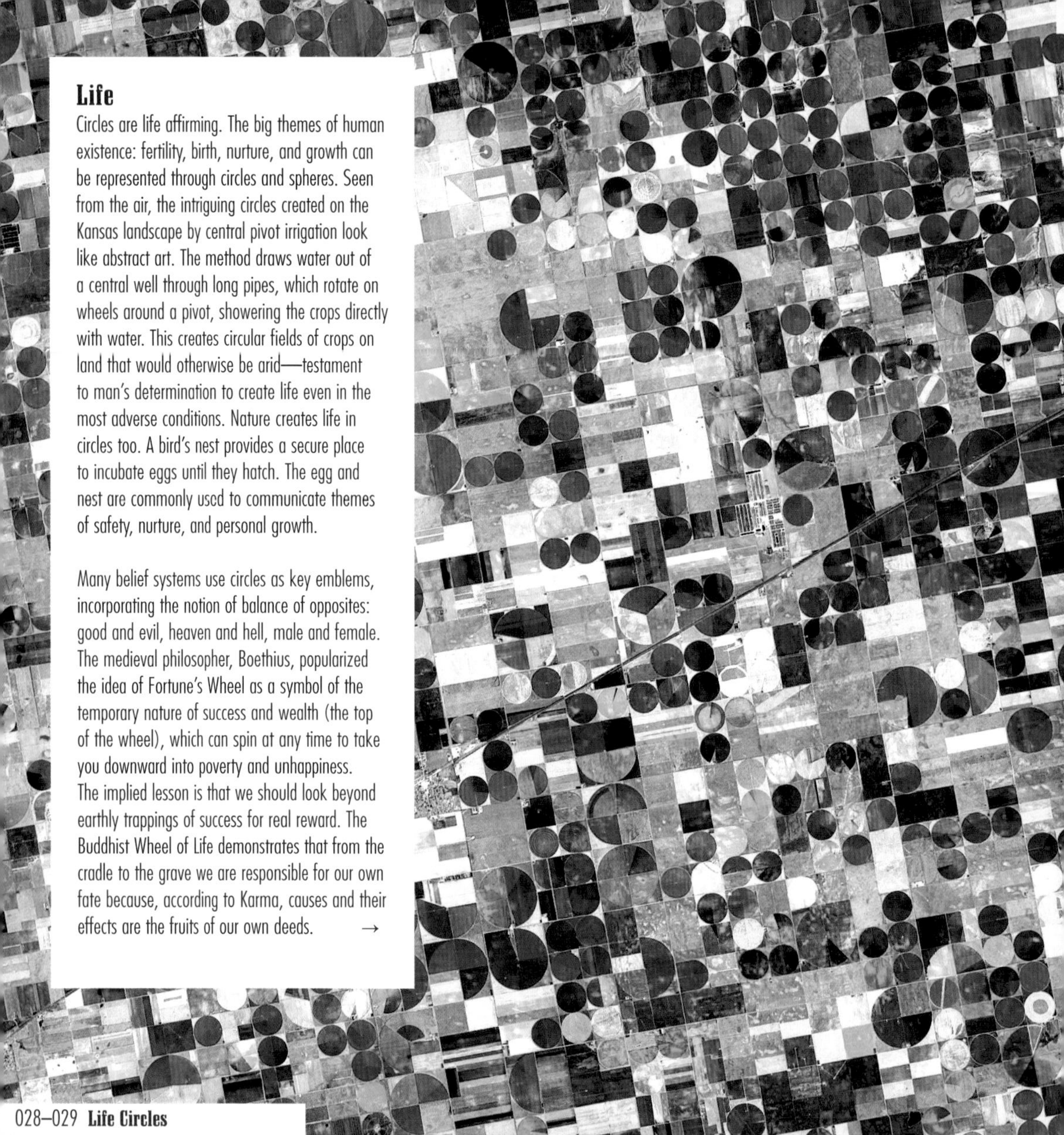

Life

Circles are life affirming. The big themes of human existence: fertility, birth, nurture, and growth can be represented through circles and spheres. Seen from the air, the intriguing circles created on the Kansas landscape by central pivot irrigation look like abstract art. The method draws water out of a central well through long pipes, which rotate on wheels around a pivot, showering the crops directly with water. This creates circular fields of crops on land that would otherwise be arid—testament to man's determination to create life even in the most adverse conditions. Nature creates life in circles too. A bird's nest provides a secure place to incubate eggs until they hatch. The egg and nest are commonly used to communicate themes of safety, nurture, and personal growth.

Many belief systems use circles as key emblems, incorporating the notion of balance of opposites: good and evil, heaven and hell, male and female. The medieval philosopher, Boethius, popularized the idea of Fortune's Wheel as a symbol of the temporary nature of success and wealth (the top of the wheel), which can spin at any time to take you downward into poverty and unhappiness. The implied lesson is that we should look beyond earthly trappings of success for real reward. The Buddhist Wheel of Life demonstrates that from the cradle to the grave we are responsible for our own fate because, according to Karma, causes and their effects are the fruits of our own deeds. →

053

052 *This image of crop circles in Kansas, US, is from NASA's Earth Observatory project and shows the various crops—corn, wheat, and sorghum—at different points of development.*
053 *Bales of corn—circles harvested from the land.*
054 *A closer view of circular crop irrigation.*
055 *Handblown glass terrariums by Paula Hayes, US.*
056 *Tom Chudleigh of Free Spirit Spheres, Canada, builds spherical tree houses in the same way as a cedar strip kayak. The suspended sphere is tethered to three separate trees, which distributes the load evenly. This triangle, formed by three trees, was called a sacred grove in druid tradition.*
057 *Eggs held within a protective circle, like a nest.*
058 *The breathtaking biospheres of the Eden project, UK.*
059 *Hatched egg, Life Collection vases by Bahari, Thailand.*
060 *Open Line, an internal staff support service, part of HSBC Bank plc, uses the egg and nest to create a sense of nurture and mentoring. Identity by Absolute Zero Degrees, UK.*

054

055

056

057

058

059

060

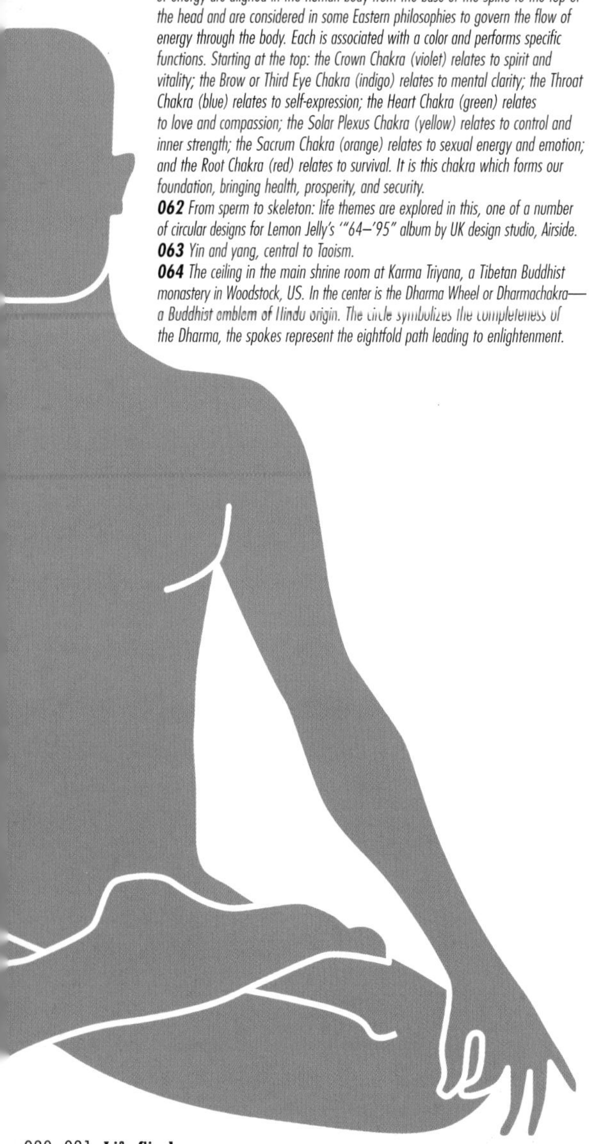

061 *The word "chakra" comes from the Sanskrit for "wheel." These seven nodes of energy are aligned in the human body from the base of the spine to the top of the head and are considered in some Eastern philosophies to govern the flow of energy through the body. Each is associated with a color and performs specific functions. Starting at the top: the Crown Chakra (violet) relates to spirit and vitality; the Brow or Third Eye Chakra (indigo) relates to mental clarity; the Throat Chakra (blue) relates to self-expression; the Heart Chakra (green) relates to love and compassion; the Solar Plexus Chakra (yellow) relates to control and inner strength; the Sacrum Chakra (orange) relates to sexual energy and emotion; and the Root Chakra (red) relates to survival. It is this chakra which forms our foundation, bringing health, prosperity, and security.*
062 *From sperm to skeleton: life themes are explored in this, one of a number of circular designs for Lemon Jelly's '"64–'95" album by UK design studio, Airside.*
063 *Yin and yang, central to Taoism.*
064 *The ceiling in the main shrine room at Karma Triyana, a Tibetan Buddhist monastery in Woodstock, US. In the center is the Dharma Wheel or Dharmachakra—a Buddhist emblem of Hindu origin. The circle symbolizes the completeness of the Dharma, the spokes represent the eightfold path leading to enlightenment.*

061

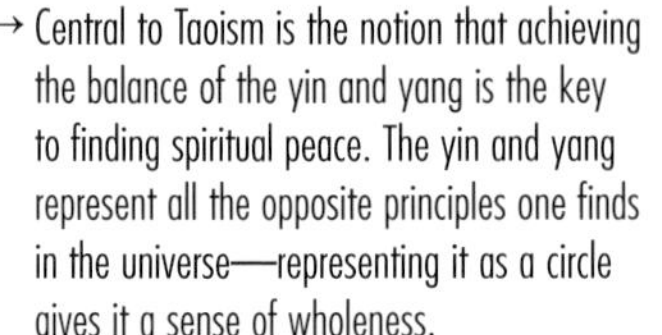

→ Central to Taoism is the notion that achieving the balance of the yin and yang is the key to finding spiritual peace. The yin and yang represent all the opposite principles one finds in the universe—representing it as a circle gives it a sense of wholeness.

As they can outlive many generations of humans, we venerate trees as inspiring symbols of permanence. As children we learn to count tree rings to indicate the age of the tree—a ring for each year. The rings both strengthen and nourish the tree, carrying water and minerals from the roots to the leaves. The widths of rings indicate what environmental conditions were like during the tree's lifetime—often narrower during droug years and wider when rainfall is plentiful. The representation of information through circles is mirrored by the ingenious Mongolian family tree, which indicates successive generations through concentric rings, bearing a striking resemblance to tree rings.

As we look for ways of cutting down on waste for the sake of the environment, the circle occurs regularly to promote the benefits of recycling. It's a bit like reincarnation for inanimate objects—s a tin can might come back in later life as part of a car. Having no beginning and no end, the circle represents continuity and sustainability, themes appropriate to recycling, without requiring words to explain the concept.

065 *Icons of life: the male and female symbols are also the symbols for the planets Mars and Venus.*
066 *A Mayan calendar at the National Museum of the Ameri Indian, Washington, DC. The top vertical segment indicates the date the museum officially opened, September 21st, 2004.*
067 *This Mongolian family tree echoes tree rings in assigning consecutive circles to each new generation—so the inner circ are the older generations and the outer circles indicate new family members.*

062
063
064
065
066
067

Today's Special

"Canada is known for its vast forests. Though it seems they are endless, conservation must be considered to protect this valuable resource. In today's modern society it is still surprising how wasteful we are with paper products. The connection to where paper products come from often seems to be forgotten. Stumpmat paper placemats remind their users of that connection."

Kirsten White
Cabin Project, Canada

070
071
072

073

074

075

076

068 *Stumpmat paper placemats by Kirsten White, Canada, remind users of the relationship between wood and paper.*
069 *A stack of logs showing their age-indicating rings.*
070–072 *Audrey Hayes, UK, produces outdoor furniture and sculptures, with many of her pieces being scorched. The carbon deposits are rubbed away and Danish oil is applied to the piece, offering a deep luster and enhancing the wood grain and its rings.*
073 *WE CAN is a non-profit organization in New York, dedicated to helping the poor and homeless help themselves through the collection and redemption of returnable deposit bottles and cans. Identity by Lance Wyman, US.*
074–076 *Various symbols on recycling bins have circular based symbols, reflecting the idea of the reusability of waste products. The most efficient form of recycling is "closed loop" recycling—making an old product into the same thing again, so that old aluminum cans are turned into new aluminum cans, old glass jars become new glass jars. This cuts out risk as manufacturers are assured that there is already a market for the recycled product. Ideally, organizations will be encouraged to collect their own waste products and have them recycled into the same products—effectively renting sustainable packaging.*

Membership and Identity

The Round Table
State and City Seals
House Plaques
Button Badges
Political Causes
Aircraft Roundels
Car Badges

Membership and Identity

The circle is an inclusive form that creates a sense of unity and acts as a perfect vehicle for communicating themes of membership and identity. The Round Table from the legend of King Arthur has proved such an enduring metaphor for equality and inclusiveness that it has entered common parlance—to have a roundtable means a meeting of peers for discussion and exchange of views. Central to the term is the powerful metaphor of the circle. Membership of clubs and political causes can be communicated through the circle—think of the UK's CND and Anarchy signs and statement button badges. The badge is the embodiment of both identity and membership. Badges on cars serve not only to identify the brand, but also to unite a circle of drivers with a shared passion.

As a means of identification, the circle is unsurpassed—from the round plaque that displays your house number to American state seals, the circle acts as a holding device for any number of icons and symbols. Now, imagine your country's flag simplified into a circle. That's the idea behind aircraft roundels—a military identification system that is both globally recognized and graphically captivating.

077 *Badges can convey beliefs or communicate snappy, sometimes very personal statements.*
078 *Seat numbers in circles at London's Royal Festival Hall.*
079 *A recruitment office in New York's Times Square displays the roundels of the army, navy, airforce, and marines.*
080 *A collection of button badges on a market stall.*
081 *The aircraft roundel for Sudan.*
082, 083, and 085 *House names and numbers in welcoming circles.*
084 *Designed for the UK's CND, this symbol now has a wider meaning—recognized as the symbol for peace.*
086–088 *Countries, states, cities, and organizations employ circular seals to identify themselves.*

079
S. ARMED FORCES
ECRUITING STATION
MY ★ NAVY ★ AIR FORCE ★ MARINES ★
080
HOT
Devil
081
084
085
12
088
CITY OF NORWICH
RIVER IDE WALK

The Round Table

Housed in Winchester Castle, UK, is an object that has become perhaps the greatest symbol of medieval mythology: The Round Table of King Arthur. There are many accounts of the legend of King Arthur, but not until Robert Wace's 1155 work, *Roman de Brut*, does the table enter the legend. The knights were made up of kings, princes, dukes, and barons, and they would fight over who should occupy the head of the table and take precedence at the King's council. In Wace's account, King Arthur commissioned the round table in an ingenious move to eradicate the head position, making all knights equal, regardless of birth. The Winchester table indicates places for 25 knights and was probably painted in its present form for Henry VIII, but it has been dated as far back as 1270, later than Wace's account and associating it with King Edward I—an Arthurian enthusiast who hosted tournaments that became known as "Round Tables."

The legend puts the number of Knights of the Round Table at anything from 25 to a staggering 1,600. This discrepancy serves to illustrate that the table's real significance is as a metaphor for membership, equality, and inclusiveness—key values of the modern day Round Table, a UK members' club that organizes events in the local community. The practical benefits of the round table are also apparent in modern life. Functions like weddings generally feature round tables because they're deemed more sociable than rectangular ones. Forward thinking corporates can take a lead from Arthurian wisdom and replace the traditional boardroom table with the more egalitarian round table to reflect a flat structured organization.

089

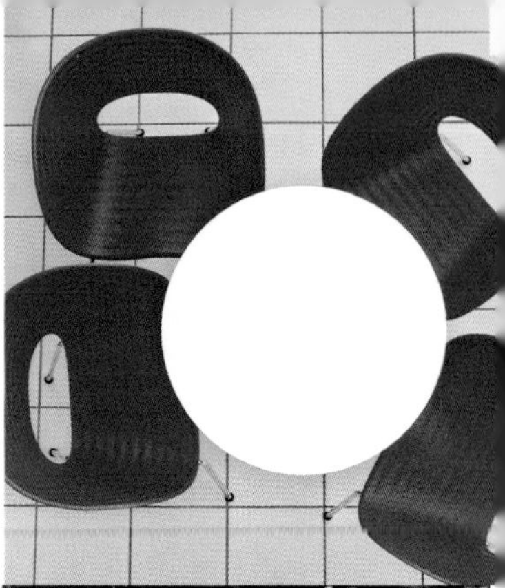

093

089 *Arthurian symbolism features in the identity of the Rou Table members' club, UK.*
090 *Circular tables in cafes enable us to gather round and interact with our friends in an informal manner.*
091 *The Round Table of King Arthur, Winchester Castle, UK, painted in its present form for King Henry VIII indicates plac for 25 knights.*
092 *Round tables make for better social interaction at weddings and functions.*
093 *The modern round table: Container table and chairs by Marcel Wanders, 2002, for Moooi, the Netherlands.*

kyng arthur

State and City Seals

The original city seals acted as a stamp of identity and approval—the medieval equivalent of a municipal credit card, used to authorize the city's financial transactions. Dating back to around 1170, the silver seal of the city of Exeter is the oldest surviving example in the UK. It bears an elaborate building between a pair of towers—symbols of wealth and security rather than depictions of specific buildings.

These days, the seal plays the role of location branding device, reflecting a city or state's uniqueness through imagery and a written motto, often rendered in relief as a plaque to be mounted in public places. City seals bear a strong resemblance to city coats of arms and serve a similar purpose, but it's a matter of geography and historic context whether the coat of arms or the seal becomes the official brand of the city. European cities often stick with the traditional shield devices of coats of arms, whereas in North America every city and state has a circular seal, designed to reflect the location's values and attributes.

Each seal is created according to the needs of the individual city or state and it is subject to revision and updating, just like corporate identity, so its styles can be very diverse. The current seal of Seattle was designed in 1937 by sculptor James A. When and clearly reflects both the history of Seattle and the esthetic of that period. As well as the profile of Suquamish Chief Sealth, it features two cones from an evergreen tree and what appear to be two dolphins or porpoises.

095

096

'94 New Orleans seal, photographed by Leo Reynolds.
'95 Kern County seal, photographed by Veronica Lynne.
'96 Suquamish Chief Sealth rendered in 1930s sculptural yle on the city seal of Seattle.
'97 A remnant of Soviet pride on the Moscow underground.
'98 City of Dartmouth, UK—the seal, granted by Edward III 1341, shows the king in a 14th century merchant cog.
'99 Seal of the city of Jackson.
00 The California State seal features Minerva, the Roman ›ddess of wisdom. A grizzly bear rests at her feet as a miner orks by the Sacramento River. The Sierra Nevada mountains n be seen in the background. The state motto, Eureka, refers the discovery of gold in California.
01 The original description of the 14th century city of orwich coat of arms: gules, a castle triple-towered argent, in ›se a lion passant gardant, meaning: on a red base, a silver stle of three towers with a walking lion, head facing out.

099

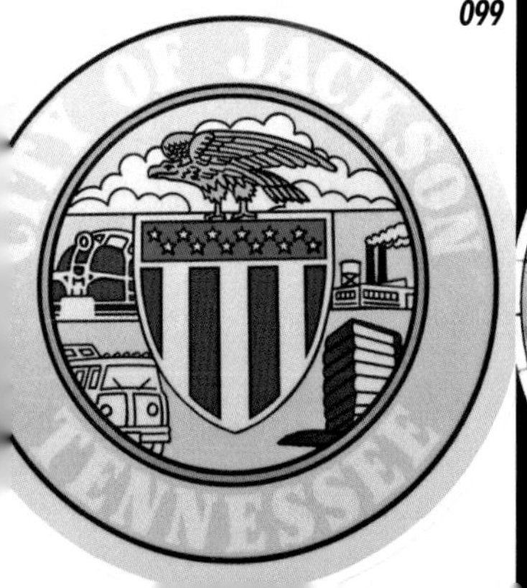

100

101

House Plaques

You could hang a simple number on your door to identify your house, but a number in a circle is much friendlier. The circle is an open, welcoming shape that communicates inclusiveness, softening the rectangular architectural details of doors and windows. In addition, numbers work well in circles. In polished brass, gleaming enamel, or fired porcelain, the circle acts as a containing device that draws attention to the number and offers it graphic standout.

If your house is distinguished enough to have a name, it deserves to have its identity proudly displayed in the form of a name plaque. The houses of the historic UK town of Rye have a tradition of displaying circular plaques outside their front doors. Local artist, David Sharp, made most of these plaques from the 1960s onward. The plaques became a familiar feature of the town and add to the sense of community and togetherness. Today, David Sharp's work is celebrated by collectors of 20th century studio pottery and the plaque company is still run by his family, who export these circular nameplates all round the world.

102–108 *In serif or sans serif face, a number in a circle can be subtle and elegant or big and bold, but always welcoming.*
109–118 *Take a trip to Rye, UK, and go house-plaque spotting. You'll find many like these, and can even commission your own at The David Sharp pottery, now run by his wife, Dot, and his son, Ben.*

No
8

WATCHBELL
DAVID SHARP CERAMICS . THE MINT. RYE.
HOUSE

110
HIGHER
DART
111
FLEETWOOD
COTTAGE
112
CATCHERS
EIGHT
113
THE OLD
TRADER
114
BAY
COTTAGE
115
CHRISTMAS
COTTAGE
116
NEPTUNE COTTAGE
117
ARBELLA
HOUSE
118
LITTLE
SUSSEX HOUSE
DAVID SHARP POTTERY - RYE

Button Badges

Invariably circular, the button badge is a mini-canvas of self-expression. Printed with slogans that are catchy, witty, or just bizarre, it can communicate political affiliation, sexual identity, and membership of clubs and causes. The disposable button badge became popular after WWII, quickly graduating from promotional giveaway to fashion accessory. Worn on the lapel, shoulder bag, or parka arm, it expressed the values and beliefs of several youth subgroups including hippies, mods, and punks. The politicized 1980s saw the button badge reach the peak of its popularity, but recently button badges have enjoyed a revival of interest from collectors and fashionistas alike—their quirky statements acting as cultural signposts, charting social history and the changing political mood from "Give Peas a Chance" to "Send Thatcher on a Cruise." →

***119–124** Button badges became popular in the 1950s as a cheaply produced promotional giveaway. They were quickly assimilated into youth culture, partly because their tiny surface area can express a surprisingly diverse range of political slogans and humorous messages.*

***125** The cover for the "Best of" album, "Supergrass is 10," designed by Blue Source, UK. The design appropriates the button badge, commonly found on children's birthday cards as well as badges with catchy slogans and images of the band. The reverse uses the button badge format to display song titles.*

LIFT OFF
45 R.P.M.
YOU INTEREST ME
ARE YOU ONE TOO?
Supergrass is 10
DRAFT BEER NOT STUDENTS
MAKE LOVE NOT WAR
GO NAKED
SUPPORT YOUR LOCAL BUTTON MERCHANT
AM I COOL?
SOCRATES EATS

WITH LOVE FROM ME TO YOU

Ringo Starr

The forerunner of the button badge was the enamel badge (and before that, the medal). Enamel badges were first produced in the 19th century and often used to mark achievements such as cycling proficiency or to indicate membership of clubs and organizations. British artist, Mark Titchner uses slogans and phrases borrowed from once avant-garde philosophies in his work. The phrases can be both arresting and puzzling when they appear in the public domain, such as advertising spaces. Teaming up with Trevor Pitt, curator at arts organization, The Public, the pair decided to create a piece of public art that would be affordable and ownable—an antidote to fixed art in public spaces. Trevor Pitt recalls, "At the time, Mark was making large poster work using the typography and esthetics of trade union banners. I was reminded of my dad and other workers who wore trade union badges. We both got excited about using enamel and creating a collaboration between artist and fabricator." An artist multiple of 150 were manufactured by Thomas Fattorini Ltd. The work formed part of the 2005 British Art Show and was available for the general public to buy—accessible art achieved through the medium of the button badge.

26 *Ringo Starr makes an appearance on this 1960s eatles button badge.*
27–129 *Badges of honor: derived from medals, enamel adges preceded button badges and were worn to signify embership of a club, society, or union.*
30 *Leo Reynolds' collection of vintage button badges.*
31 *Badges are commonly worn to show support for arities: vintage National Trust badge, UK.*
32 *"Take your hands off my button," one of the more cane button badges from Leo Reynolds' collection.*

"WHY NOT? are purported to be the last words of the late Dr Timothy Leary. The headlong leap into the void, suggested by those two powerful little words, in turn reminded me of a terrifying quote I came across a few years ago: IN ETERNITY ALL EYES ARE OPEN. So in this case the circle is the unblinking eye of infinity (and the pupil is dilated in reference to some of Dr Leary's famous activities). The eye is a motif I repeatedly use in various forms, itself analogous to the act of seeing and absorbing visual art—a mirror of our own gaze."
Mark Titchner, Artist, UK

133 *"Why Not?"—an artist multiple of 150 in enamel by UK artist, Mark Titchner.*
134 *The International Design Magazine, I.D., US, uses a button badge covered T-shirt on its cover to promote the feature, "50 designers/50 states." The badges bear slogans relevant to the state or the designer.*

he International Design Magazine

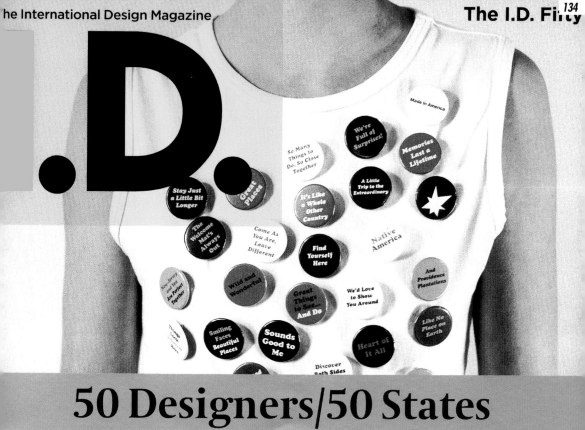

The I.D. Fifty

I.D.

50 Designers/50 States

Who Represents Yours?

Political Causes

Two symbols of political identity are the signs for Anarchy and CND. Both are instantly recognizable around the world without the need for words; both achieve graphic impact because they are circular. But they have very different backgrounds.

The symbol for the Campaign for Nuclear Disarmament was designed by RCA graduate, Gerald Holtom, and made its first appearance on the historic antinuclear march from London to Aldermaston over the 1958 Easter weekend—emblazoned on 500 circular protest signs in two colorways—black and white to be displayed on Good Friday and Saturday, green and white on Easter Sunday and Monday. A conscientious objector during WWII, Holtom explained the inspiration for the logo thus: "I drew myself: the representative of an individual in despair, with hands palm outstretched outward and downward in the manner of Goya's peasant before the firing squad. I formalized the drawing into a line and put a circle round it."

Less poignant, but no less prevalent is the Anarchy symbol. It has international appeal because the word for anarchy starts with "A" in many languages. Pierre-Joseph Proudhon first wrote about the concept of anarchy in the mid-19th century. Since then it has been much misappropriated, but the central notion is one of minimal government intervention—that "public and private consciousness… is alone sufficient to maintain order." The synthesis of the symbol can be explained as the "A" for "Anarchy" surrounded by the "O" for "Order."

135

138

141

135–144 *The success of these circular symbols is that they are both emotive and simple to draw—hence the amount of graffiti that uses them. In this way, they are truly democratic—their reproduction is governed by no particular body. Both symbols have moved beyond their original meaning—the symbol for the Campaign for Nuclear Disarmament standing more widely now for Peace, and the Anarchy sign having moved a long way from the 19th century treatise that first introduced the concept of self-governance.*

Aircraft Roundels

The roundel was first used as a means of identifying military aircraft during WWI. Early fighter planes had no markings, making it difficult for either side to know which planes to shoot at. So as to avoid confusion, planes of the Imperial German Air Service were painted with a black cross. It was the French who adopted the first roundel—reconfiguring the tricolor into concentric circles of blue, white, and red. The British soon switched from marking their planes with a Union Jack (which looked too much like the German cross) to a roundel similar to the French version, but with the colors reversed.

Great design solutions soon catch on, and it proved to be the French that set the world standard. With a few exceptions, most of the world's military aircraft still carry circular identities. In these roundels we witness the purity of the circle as a graphic device—taking national flag colors or cultural icons (the white cross of Switzerland, a kiwi for New Zealand) and distilling them into their simplest graphic form. Mostly, they benefit from a lack of formal design input and it's fascinating to examine the way that the elements of the flags have been incorporated: the rising sun of Japan's flag surrounded by a fine band of white; the swirl device that incorporates Ireland's national colors. →

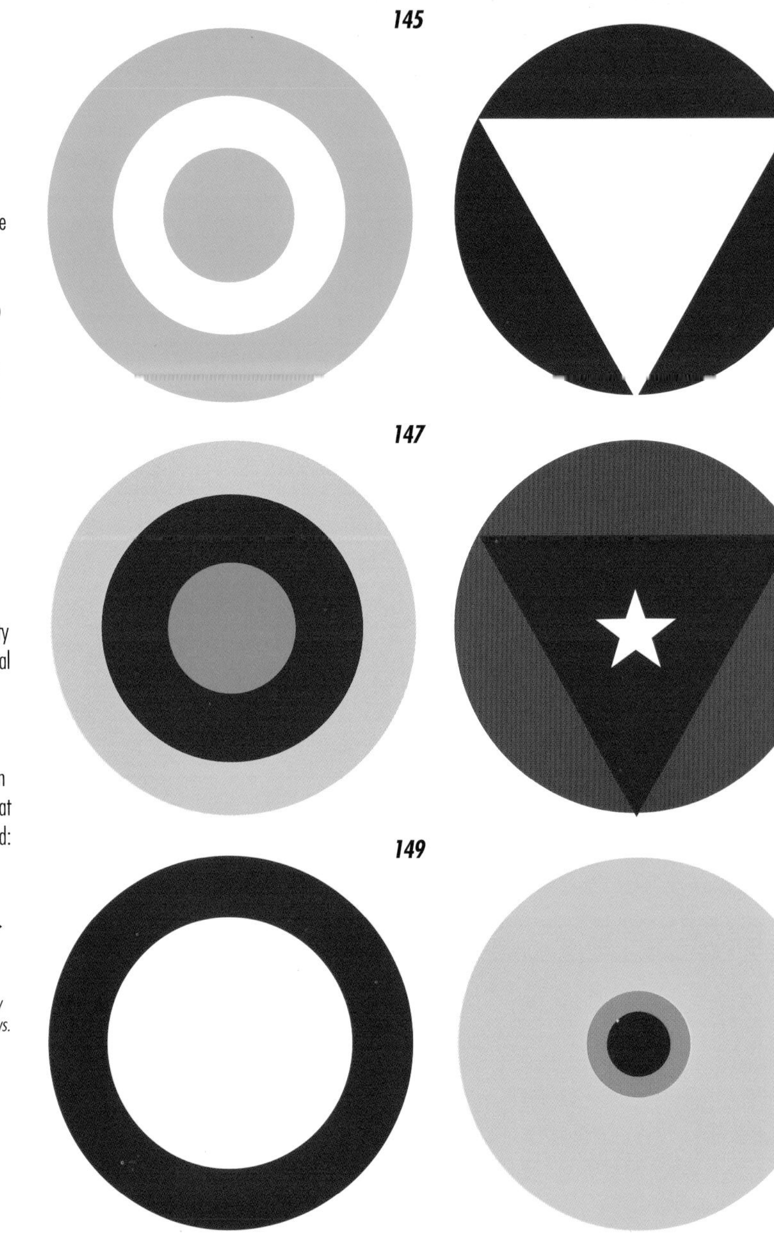

Aircraft roundels act like branding devices for countries. Many are distilled from the national flag as the selection here shows.
145 *Argentine Airforce.*
146 *Austria.*
147 *Cameroon.*
148 *Cuba.*
149 *Denmark.*
150 *Ecuador.*
151 *US Airforce star roundel, seen here by Mark Strozier.*

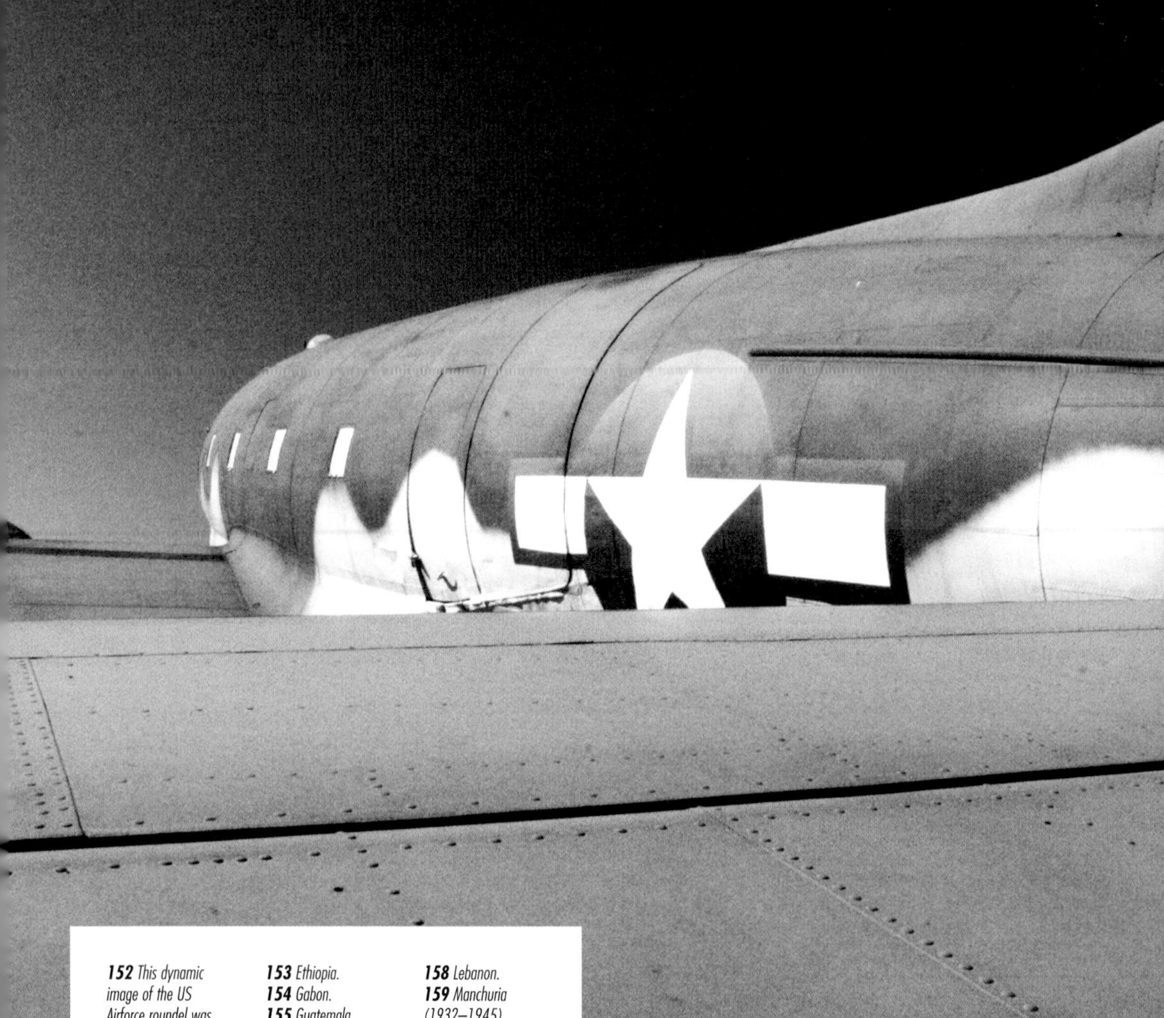

152 *This dynamic image of the US Airforce roundel was taken by Mark Strozier.*

153 *Ethiopia.*
154 *Gabon.*
155 *Guatemala.*
156 *India.*
157 *Japan.*

158 *Lebanon.*
159 *Manchuria (1932–1945).*
160 *New Zealand.*
161 *North Korea.*

153
154
155
156
157
158
159
160
161

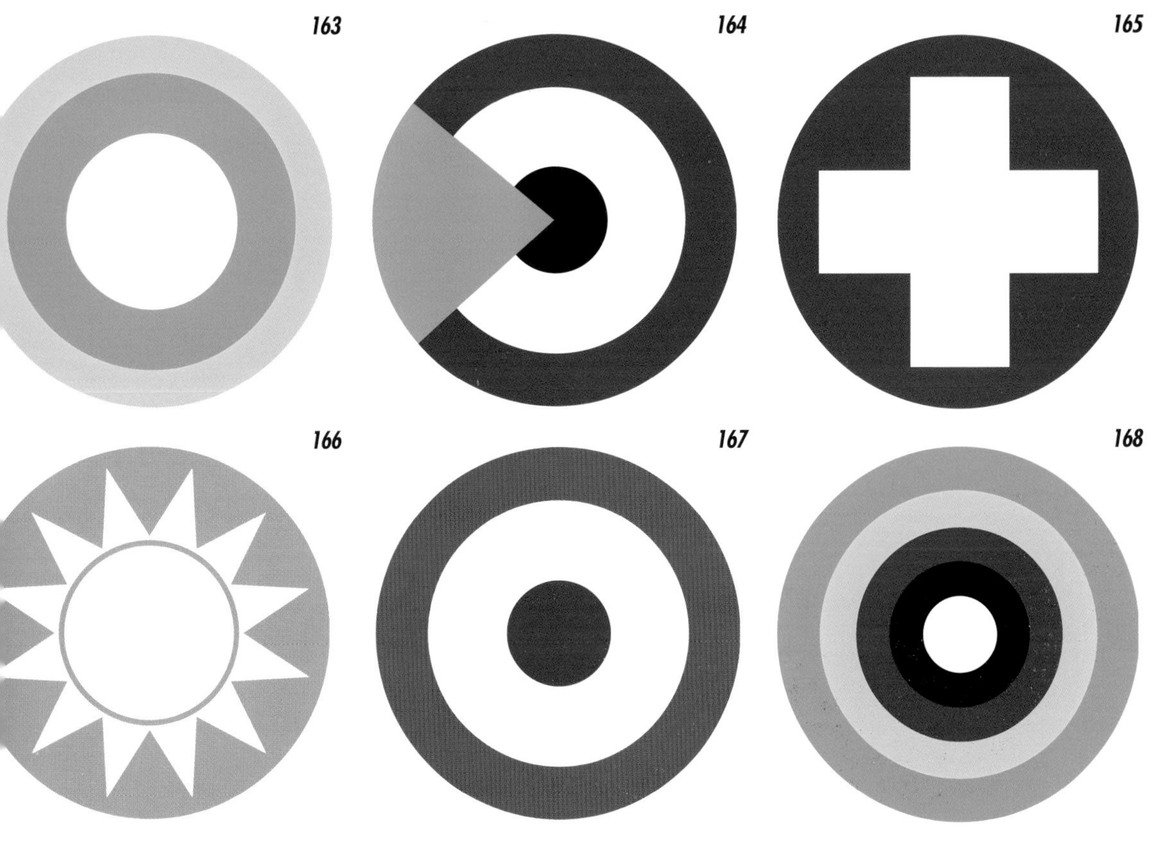

→ They also demonstrate how the circle offers the simplest form of identity system. Some countries have departed from the circular device—Estonia and Botswana both swap the circle for a triangle—but somehow, these variations don't have the impact of their circular counterparts.

Arguably, roundels make better national branding devices than the flags from which they are derived, perhaps because the circle is more visually arresting than the rectangle—it's more immediate and punchy. No surprise, then, that the roundel has since been adopted for many nonmilitary applications. Two particularly enduring examples of roundels as corporate branding devices are the UK's London Underground identity and Raymond Loewy's classic design for Lucky Strike.

162 *A stencil version of the US Airforce roundel.*
163 *Pakistan.*
164 *Sudan.*
165 *Switzerland.*
166 *Taiwan.*
167 *British Royal Air Force.*
168 *Zimbabwe.*

169 *BMW's distinctive roundel reflects the colors of the Bavarian flag—the German region where the company first started making aircraft engines.*
170 *The new Mini also has a shiny new circular badge.*
171 *Alfa Romeo's badge with its Milanese symbols—the company was originally called A.L.F.A.—Anonima Lombarda Fabbrica Automobili—until it was purchased by Nicola Romeo in 1918, when his name was added to the acronym.*
172 *Volkswagen's enduring logo.*
173 *Vauxhall's griffin configured as a circle.*

Car Badges

The car wears its identity front and rear in the form of a shiny badge, and many car owners metaphorically wear their car's badge as a status symbol and membership of an elite club. Many of the world's car brands have circular identities. Some, like Volkswagen, use simple initials contained within a circle; others, like Vauxhall, have reconfigured their traditional icon into a circle for a more contemporary appearance. Some companies, including Alfa Romeo, Mercedes-Benz, Cadillac, and Fiat, have used laurel wreaths to surround their badges—the symbol of motor sport champions.

Often the icons contained in the badge offer some insight into the car manufacturer's history. Alfa Romeo's badge is based on two key visual components: a red cross on the left and a man-eating serpent on the right. These are believed to have been the symbols of the two ruling families of medieval Milan,

ne birthplace of the company. Sometimes, a badge indicates the manufacturer's industrial heritage. The uartered circle of the BMW badge is an abstract rendering of a propeller, relating to the Bayerische Motoren Verke's roots as a manufacturer of military aircraft engines. The blue represents the sky and, combined with vhite, references the Bavarian coat of arms. Similarly, Mercedes-Benz's aspirational three-pointed star within circle signifies that the company made engines used in the air, on water, and on land.

or some cars, one circle isn't enough. Audi uses four interlocking circles in its identity, representing the four ompanies of the Auto-Union consortium of 1932—DKW, Horch, Wanderer, and Audi. After WWII the Audi ame disappeared, but was revived in 1965, using the four rings as its logo.

174 and 176 *Cadillac and Fiat both use the motor sport champions' symbol of the laurel wreath in their badges—a circular motif that suggests performance and quality.*
175 *The Mercedes-Benz three-pointed star was also originally surrounded by a laurel wreath, but was later simplified to the much-coveted star within a circle.*
177 *SAAB's crowned griffin was originally the symbol of the corporate entity, Saab-Scania, and was introduced onto cars in its current form in 2000.*

Themes and Moods

Retro
Science and Futuristic
Natural
Nautical
Decorative
Glamor
Sport and Leisure
Fantasy and Fun
Dynamism
Water and Air
Light and Heat

Themes and Moods

The diversity of ideas that can be expressed through the circular form is inspiring. Contemporary scientific circles bear a similarity to the optimism of the mid-20th century retro circle—proving that designers are always searching for new solutions. Circles in nature span all manner of flora and fauna, from the delicate seeds of a dandelion clock to a leopard's camouflage spots, whereas nautical circles are man-made—functional aids to the safe navigation of the sea. Circles are capable of communicating a host of visual moods—from the glamor of the glitter ball to the decorative kitsch of a paper doily. They're invaluable on the sporting field and they help us relax with a range of leisure pursuits. Dominos anyone? Surely no other pattern can express fun quite like dots and circles, or suggest dynamic energy as effectively as swirls and spirals. Bubbles and droplets are circular forms that act as graphic representations of air and water, while the spotlight and circle of flames are effective means of conveying light and heat.

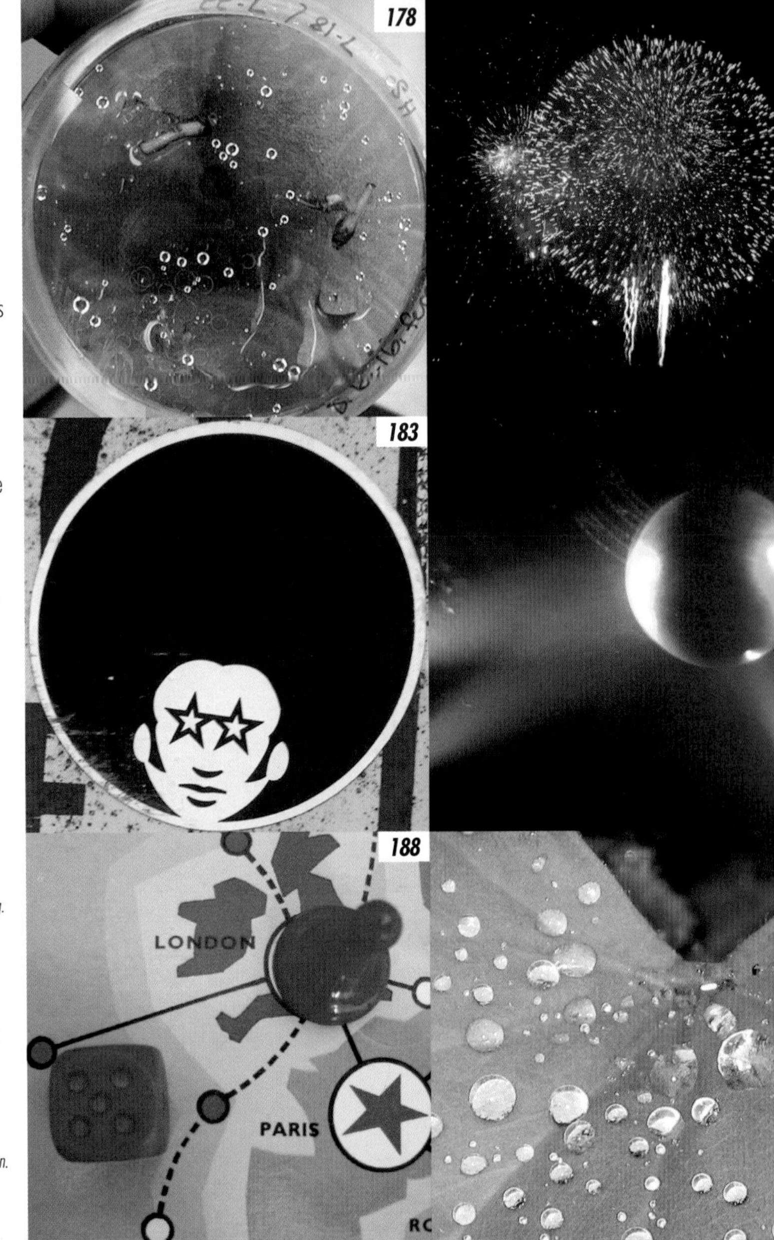

178 *Petri dish.*
179 *The excitement of a Fourth of July firework display.*
180 *André Waterkeyn's Atomium in Belgium.*
181 *A ship's wheel is a graphic shortcut to indicate seafaring.*
182 *The ideal 1970s' car accessory—furry dice.*
183 *This stylized Afro evokes a groovy retro mood.*
184 *The icon of glamorous disco days—the mirrored ball.*
185 *A traditional doily is a decorative way to present the results of an afternoon's baking.*
186 *The centrifuge is a vital piece of science lab equipment.*
187 *Racks of balls ready for gym class.*
188 *Die singular, dice plural.*
189 *Crystal-like dew drops on a leaf.*
190 *Fly Agaric mushrooms belong to a fantasy world.*
191 *Dominos.*
192 *An inspired view of a box of pipette tips by Esther Simpson.*

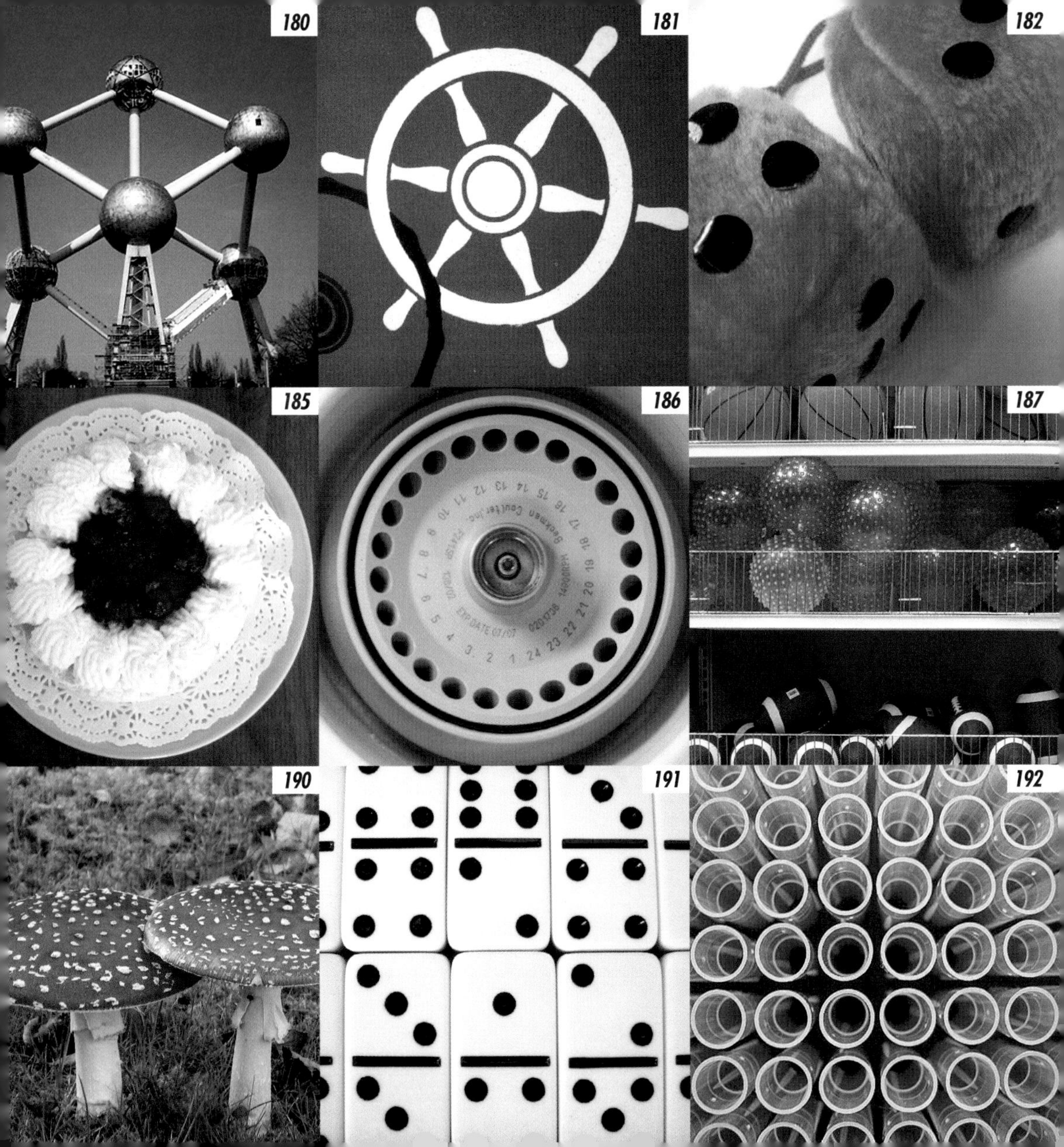
180
181
182
185
186
187
190
191
192

193

194

Retro

Perhaps it was due to experimentation with new materials like plastic, Perspex, and vinyl; surely it had a lot to do with the obsession with science fiction and all things futuristic. One way or another, design in the 1960s and 1970s went circle mad. It was a time of pushing barriers and defying conventions in fashion, art, and technology. A time defined by postwar optimism, sexual liberation, the space race, and technological advancement. So why settle for a brown rectangular boxy television when a white plastic sphere looked so much more spacey? Similarly furniture. Recline in a draylon armchair? Better to swivel, cocooned in a padded Perspex globe—cool!

And because of the prevalence of circles during these particularly bold times, the use of circles in contemporary design can often act as shorthand for a retro feel, either in faithful reproduction of classic retro styles or contemporary design that evokes the naive charm of the 1960s and 1970s. From the graphic impact of the op art movement through the disposable chic of pop art, into the dynamic swirls of psychedelia, circles, spirals, and spheres are core to retro styling.

193 and 195 *Starburst and Circles from the Wallter paintable wall applications collection by Fold Bedding, US.*

197

198

196

194 and 198 *Two graphic wallpapers, Ringo Circles and Matchsticks Circles by Hemingway Design, UK, for wallpaper producer Graham and Brown.*
196 *Ball Chair by Eero Aarnio 1966. This image shows the Finnish designer in the prototype of the chair with miniatures from Vitra. It is now available as part of the Adelta Collection, Germany.*
197 *Sgraffito canister, by Jonathan Adler, US.*
199 *Circles vases by Scabetti, UK.*
200 *Miss Pac light designed by Alvin Bagni for Habitat, UK.*
201 and 202 *Technology just feels groovier as a sphere.*

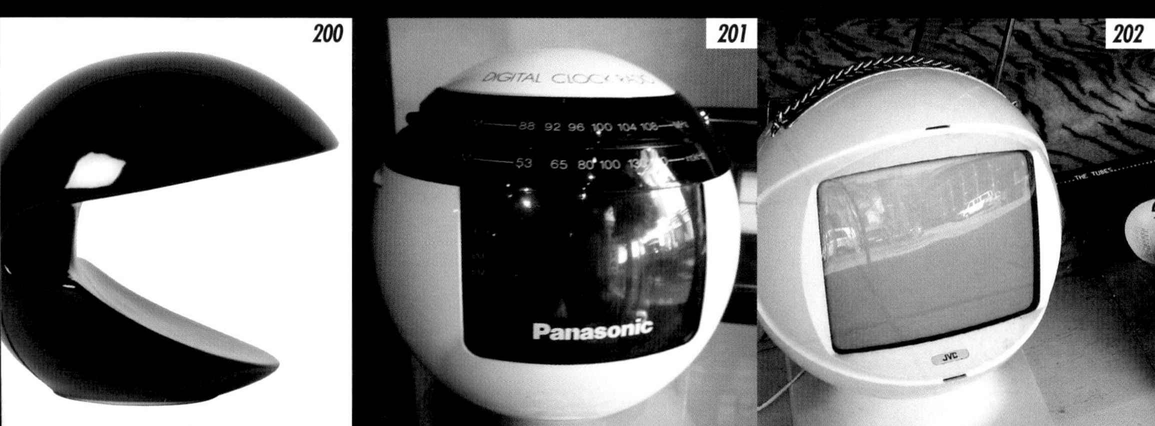

203
204
208
209
210
211

206

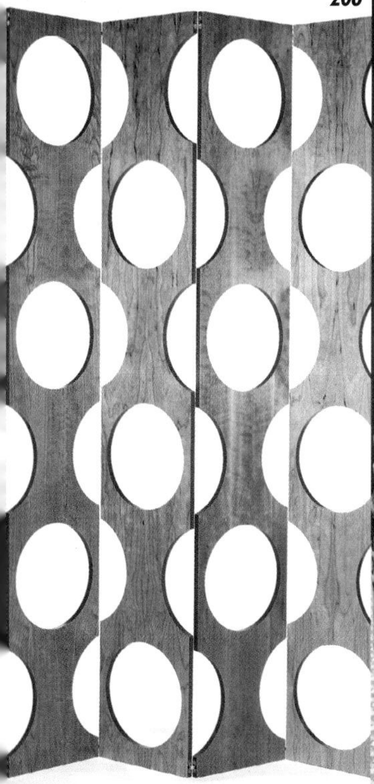

207

203 The Wallter wall applications from Fold bedding, US, allow the user to customize them with their own color choice.
204 Faux Wood wallpaper by Hemingway Design, UK, for Graham and Brown.
205 and 209 Circus fabric design, by Lebello, US.
206 This room divider by Moxbox, US, is aptly named Barbarella.
207 This Totem design dates from 1963, design by Susan Williams-Ellis, for Portmeirion Potteries, UK.
208 Clock by George Nelson, US.
210 Soda siphons would get any party swinging, especially when they look like this.
211 One of the 30 variants of tile designs used in the 1962, Gio Ponti designed, Parco dei Principi hotel in Sorrento, Italy.
212 Vintage Hornsea Pottery, UK.
213 The "net and ball" carpet was designed especially for the Royal Festival Hall in 1951, for the Festival of Britain.
214 and 215 The Plume series of pillows designed by Amy Ruppel, US, with Eleventwentyfive, available at Velocity Art and Design. They have a graphic simplicity, and strong, naive, retro colorways.

213

214

215

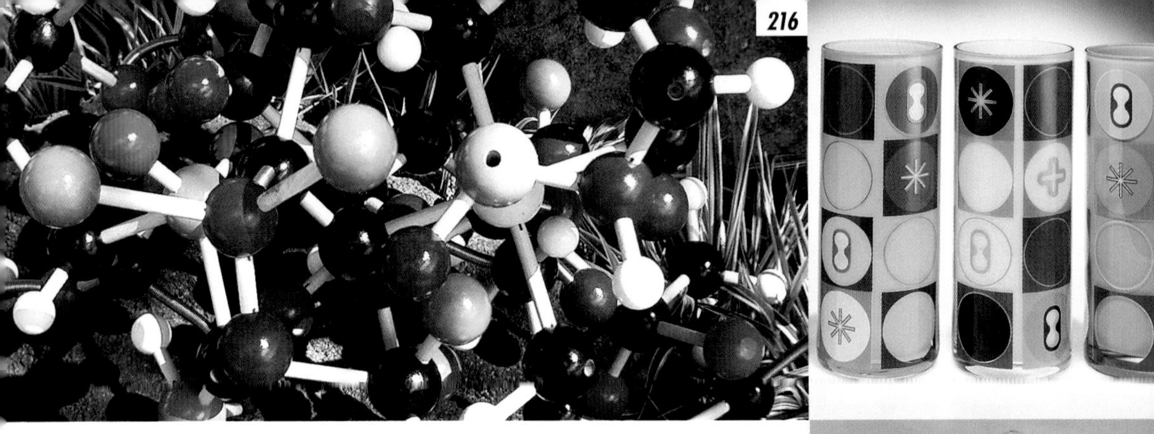

Science and Futuristic

Remember chemistry lessons? For some they offered an enlightening insight into the composition of matter. For the more esthetically minded, it was the diagrams that appealed. The visual language of science is largely circular. Atoms and molecules are represented by interconnected circles and spheres, often differentiated by bright candy colors. These diagrams and models have influenced art and design ever since the optimistic 1950s. Designers like Ray and Charles Eames and George Nelson based clocks, coat hooks, and fabrics on atomic motifs. Structures like André Waterkeyn's Atomium in Belgium replicate these geometric configurations in a futuristic blend of sculpture and architecture. Information graphics borrow from molecular structures to demonstrate organizational structures and related data. →

216 and 219 *Molecular structure models.*
217 *Komposition vases by Karim Rashid, US.*
218 *Sculpture meets architecture: the futuristic Atomium in Belgium.*
220 *A sculptural atom-like structure, captured by photographer Sam Judson.*
221–224 *"Elements of Graphic Design"—promotional material and interactive design for Nottingham Trent University graduate show by Matt Cooper, UK.*

221

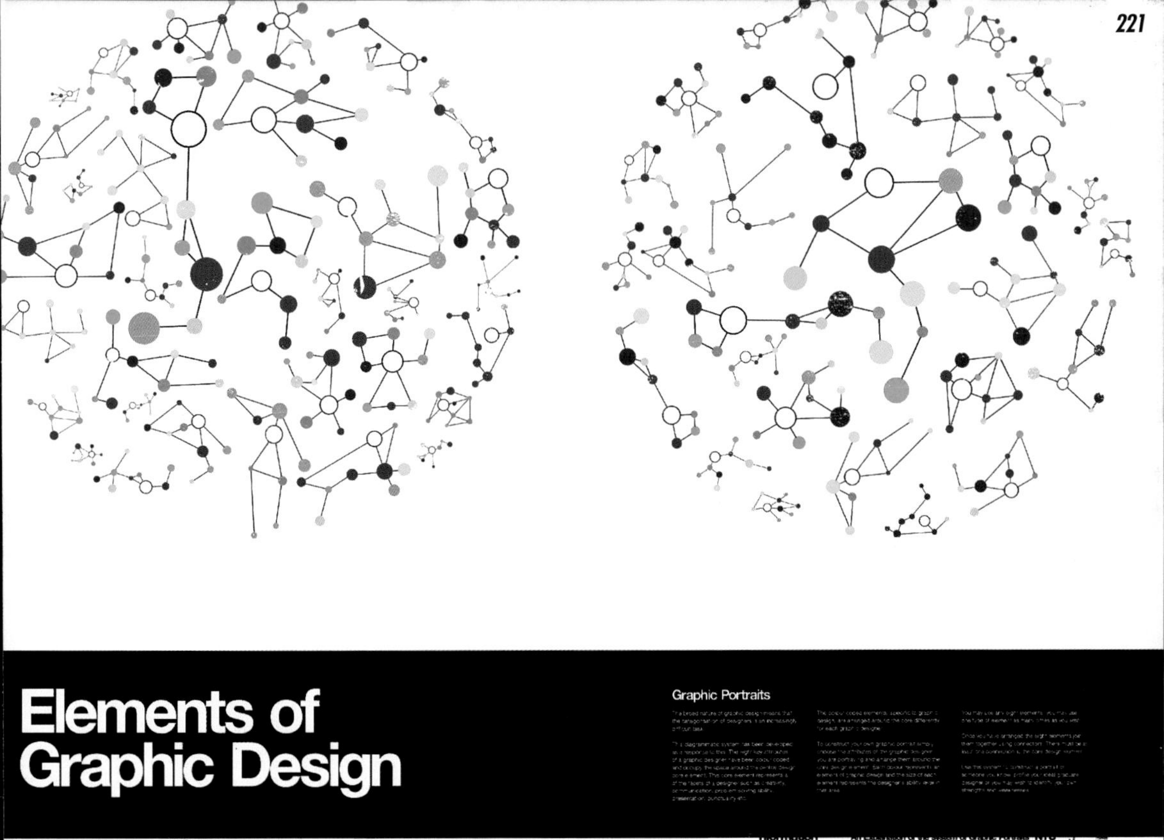

Graphic Portraits

222

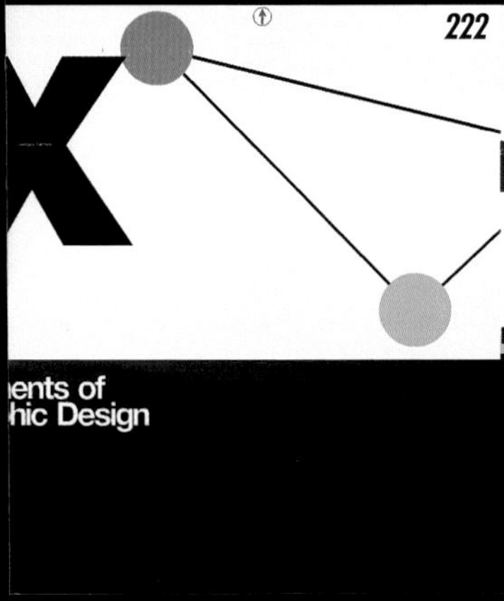

ents of
hic Design

223

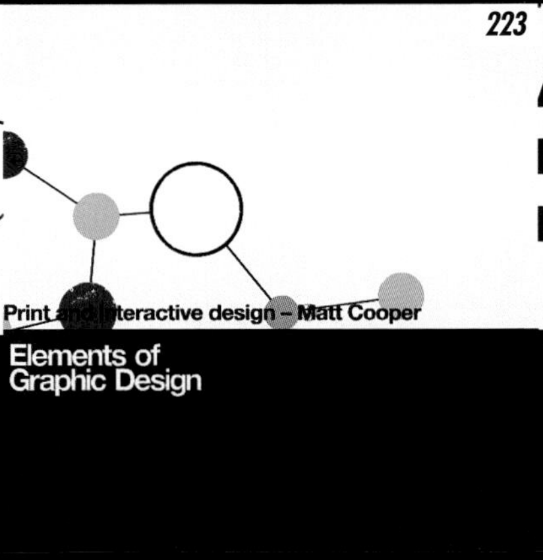

Print and Interactive design – Matt Cooper

Elements of
Graphic Design

ABC
DEFGHIJK
LMN PRST
UVW X

Elements of
Graphic Design

224

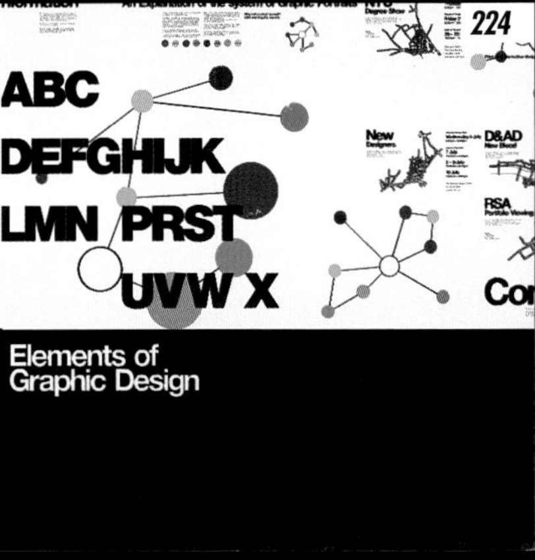

New Designers

D&AD New Blood

RSA

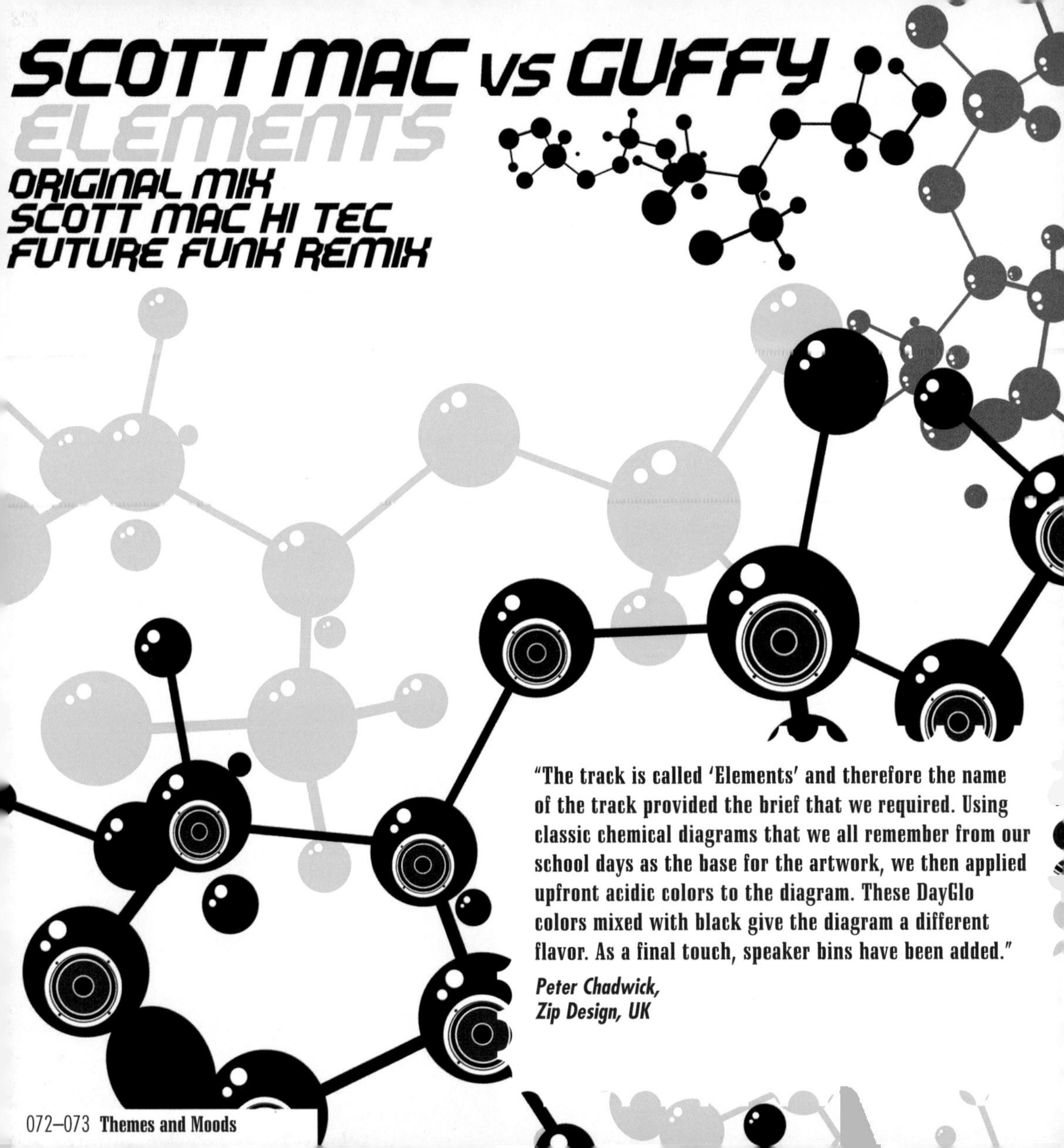

SCOTT MAC vs GUFFY
ELEMENTS
ORIGINAL MIX
SCOTT MAC HI TEC
FUTURE FUNK REMIX

"The track is called 'Elements' and therefore the name of the track provided the brief that we required. Using classic chemical diagrams that we all remember from our school days as the base for the artwork, we then applied upfront acidic colors to the diagram. These DayGlo colors mixed with black give the diagram a different flavor. As a final touch, speaker bins have been added."

Peter Chadwick, Zip Design, UK

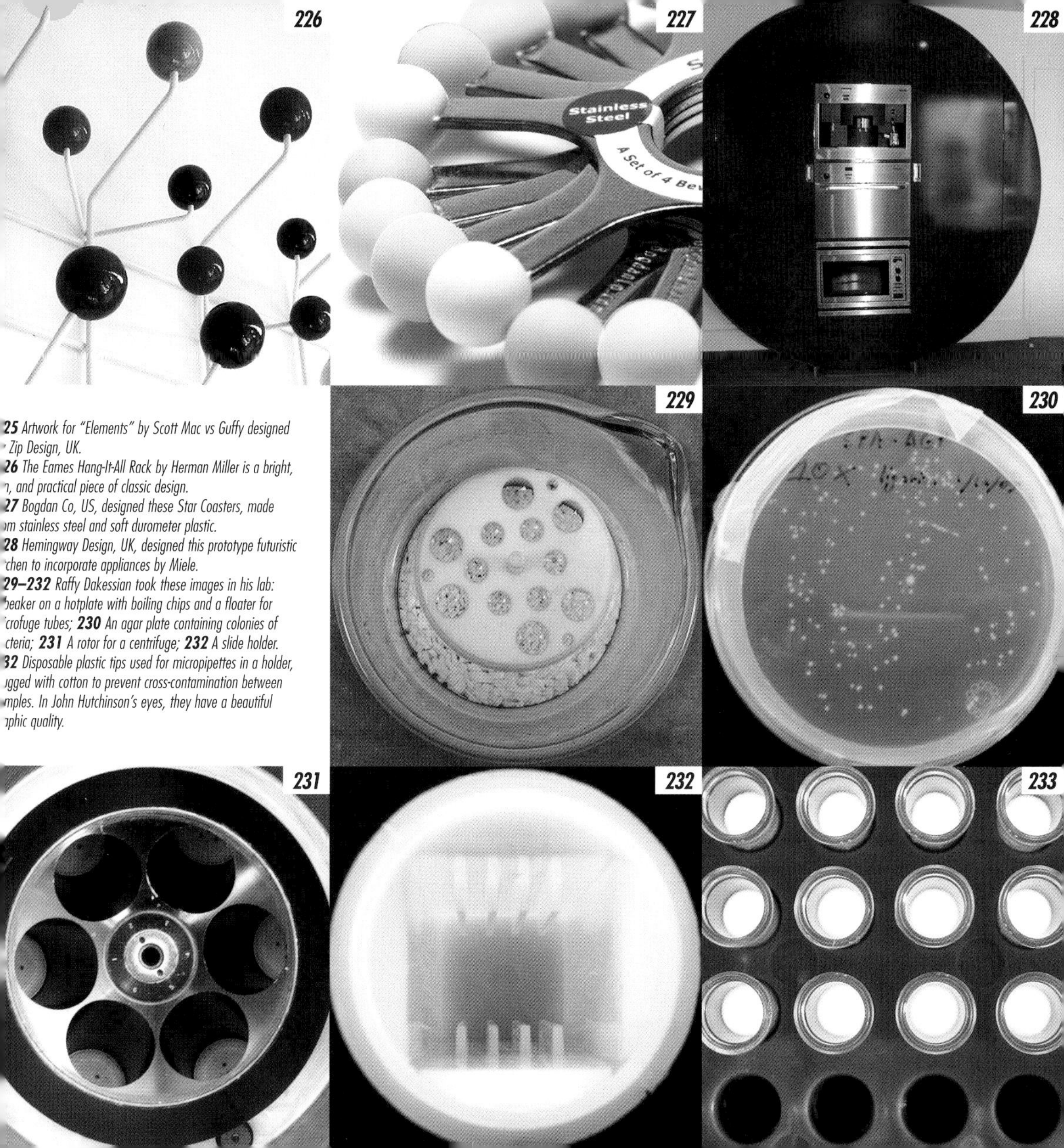

25 Artwork for "Elements" by Scott Mac vs Guffy designed
Zip Design, UK.
26 The Eames Hang-It-All Rack by Herman Miller is a bright,
n, and practical piece of classic design.
27 Bogdan Co, US, designed these Star Coasters, made
m stainless steel and soft durometer plastic.
28 Hemingway Design, UK, designed this prototype futuristic
chen to incorporate appliances by Miele.
29–232 Raffy Dakessian took these images in his lab:
beaker on a hotplate with boiling chips and a floater for
crofuge tubes; **230** An agar plate containing colonies of
cteria; **231** A rotor for a centrifuge; **232** A slide holder.
32 Disposable plastic tips used for micropipettes in a holder,
ugged with cotton to prevent cross-contamination between
mples. In John Hutchinson's eyes, they have a beautiful
aphic quality.

"My hope was to achieve an artificial environment. It is based on rigorous technology, used creatively to be functional. Icelandic craftsmanship is very good, especially in concrete and steel. I worked with a contractor responsible for the Blue Lagoon, a local geothermal pool. The atmosphere is one of surrealness, almost like stepping into the virtual. I used Corian to make all of the bar surfaces and shelves, which helped push that edge."

Michael Young,
Designer, Hong Kong

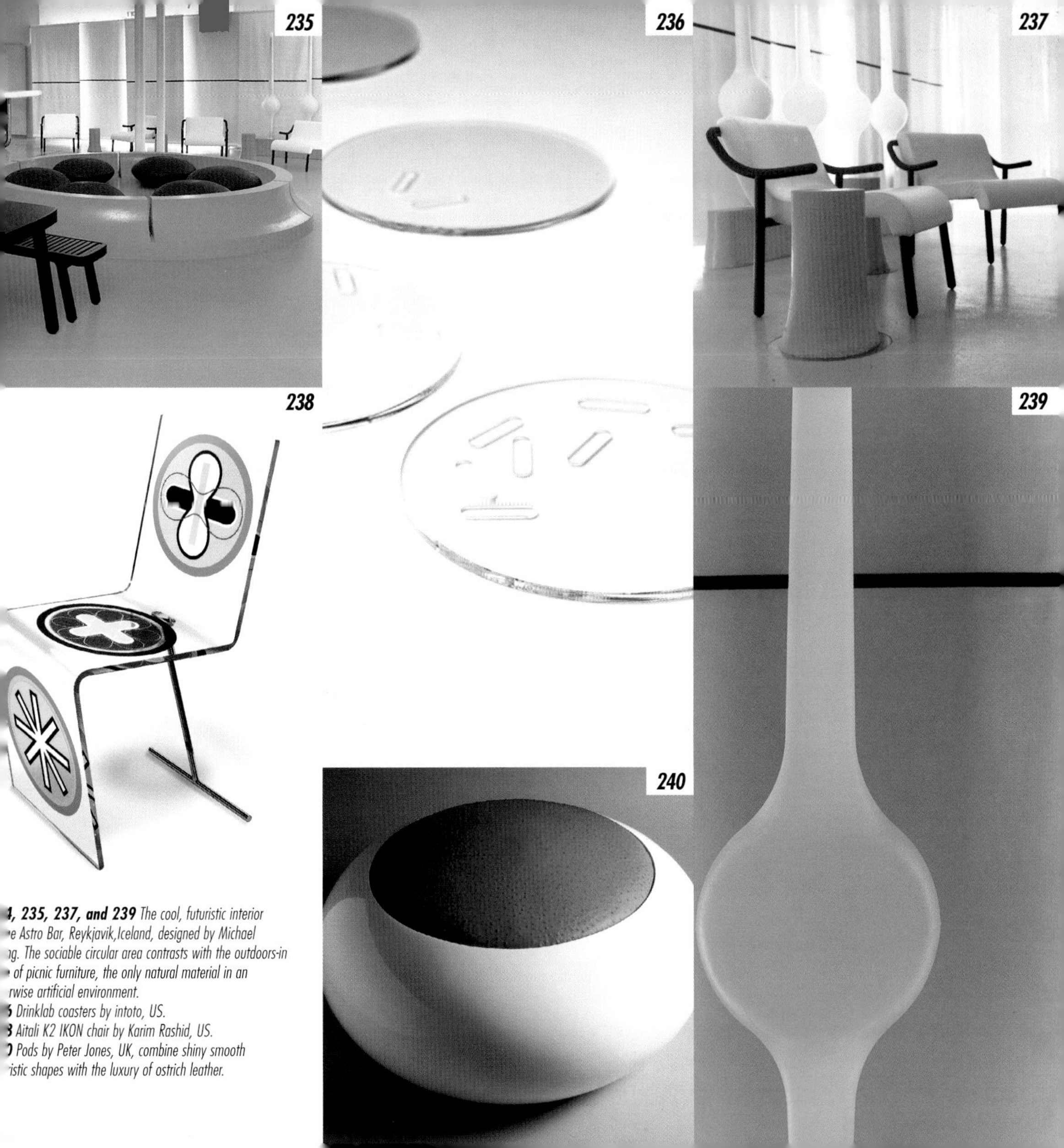

4, 235, 237, and 239 The cool, futuristic interior
e Astro Bar, Reykjavik,Iceland, designed by Michael
ng. The sociable circular area contrasts with the outdoors-in
of picnic furniture, the only natural material in an
rwise artificial environment.
6 Drinklab coasters by intoto, US.
8 Aitali K2 IKON chair by Karim Rashid, US.
0 Pods by Peter Jones, UK, combine shiny smooth
istic shapes with the luxury of ostrich leather.

→ The science lab is abundant with functional design. The circular forms of flasks, beakers, and test tubes in simple glass and ceramic have inspired pieces that bring the same clean, timeless design ethic into the domestic and commercial environment. We use test tubes as bud vases, oversized Petri dishes become fruit bowls, and we sip espresso from Pyrex coffee cups. All stylish circles inspired by science, shorthand for a futuristic style where form meets function. Contemporary design is once again finding spherical alternatives to traditionally square forms—like the Sheer kitchen by dragdesign and Michael Young's celebrated Astro Bar in Reykjavik. And in recognition of society's relationship with recreational and medical drugs, pill-shaped structures and symbols borrowed from the pharmaceutical industry feature in the work of British artist Damien Hirst and many contemporary fashion and graphic designers.

241 *The futuristic cladding of circular steel discs on the exterior of Selfridges in Birmingham, UK.*
242, 244, and 246 *Kitchen meets laboratory: the incredibly scientific looking Sheer kitchen by dragdesign, Italy.*

243 *Foil covered pill packaging.*
245 *This Bianca molded polyethylene table with an incorporated light has an almost pill-like look. Its central groove can be used as a magazine rack. Designed by Simon Pengelly, UK, for Habitat.*

247 and 248 *Pharmacy is the diffusion freeride range from White Stuff, UK, and its strength as a brand is its high technical specification. Scientific graphics emphasize this technical angle, seen here on this textile and brochure cover, designed by Absolute Zero Degrees, UK.*

Natural

Even if it could, the leopard really shouldn't change its spots. They act as vital camouflage, blending with the dappled light of its woodland habitat. The ladybug's spots also act as protection, but instead of hiding the creature, the high contrast of red and black, associated with poison, helps to ward away potential predators. For the peacock, spots act as the reverse of camouflage—it has brightly colored plumage featuring distinctive "eye" markings that it fans as a means of displaying itself to the peahen during courtship.

While rarely perfectly symmetrical, spots, dots, and circles are common in nature and can be used to communicate natural themes. Many flowers become complete circles once they are in full bloom—so the circle in nature can represent completion and perfection. But it is also tinged with fragility, as the flowering period has a time limit before the flower turns to seed. This process is best exemplified by the dandelion, whose rather ordinary flower head transforms into a globe of delicate seeds that are carried away on the wind.

Australian sculptor, Matthew Harding uses natural circles in his work as a "metaphor for the earth and the organic." His public art piece, *Symbiosis*, is reminiscent of the dandelion in its various stages of seed dispersion, and represents the circle not only as an organic shape, but also as "an esthetic classic within art and design."

→

249

255

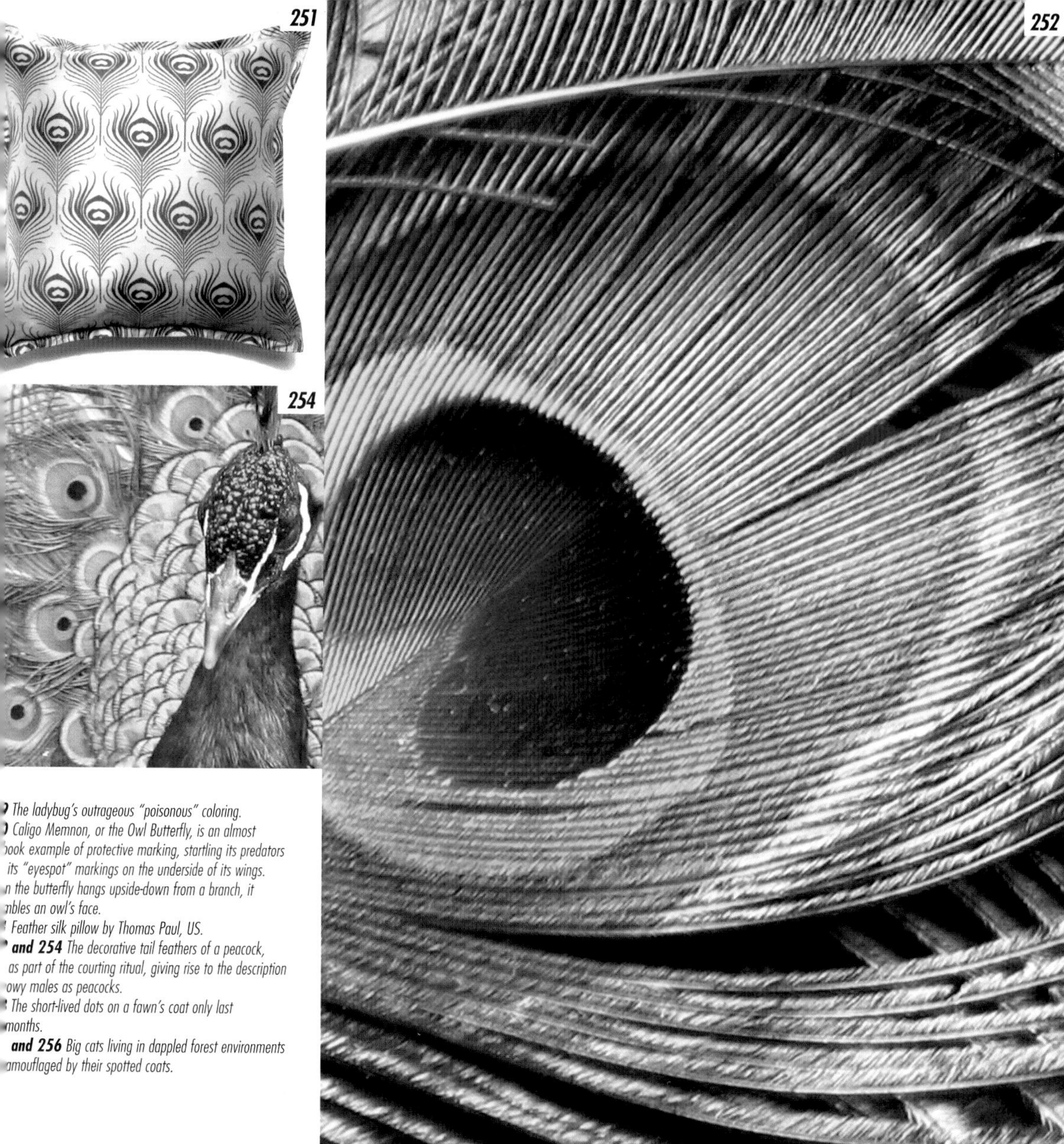

ʔ The ladybug's outrageous "poisonous" coloring.
ʔ Caligo Memnon, or the Owl Butterfly, is an almost
ɔook example of protective marking, startling its predators
its "eyespot" markings on the underside of its wings.
n the butterfly hangs upside-down from a branch, it
nbles an owl's face.
Feather silk pillow by Thomas Paul, US.
and 254 The decorative tail feathers of a peacock,
as part of the courting ritual, giving rise to the description
owy males as peacocks.
The short-lived dots on a fawn's coat only last
months.
and 256 Big cats living in dappled forest environments
amouflaged by their spotted coats.

257

260

257 and 260 Symbiosis, a sculpture exploring the sphere and organic erosion by Australian sculptor, Matthew Harding.
258, 259, and 261 Dandelions and the dandelion clock.
262 Dandelions wallpaper by Absolute Zero Degrees, UK, for Places and Spaces, uses a graphic motif of the dandelion clock exploding into dragonflies to create a light and airy but detailed pattern—contextualized in a typically English summer setting by Ian Rippington.

262

263 *A sunflower is always an uplifting sight.*
264, 266, and 267 *Daisies are some of the first flowers we identify as children.*
265, 268, and 269 *This vortex-shaped, outdoor installation by architects Benjamin Ball and Gaston Nogue is called Maximillian's Schell. Hovering over the courtyar of Materials and Applications (M&A) in Los Angeles, the structure is made of tinted Mylar, resembling stained glas. Looking as delicate as a circle of petals, its name reveals the inspiration behind the piece—the celestial black hole. Actor Maximillian Schell's character in Disney Studio's sci-fi thriller, "The Black Hole," was Dr Reinhardt, whose quest was to harness the power of the vortex.*

264
265
266
267
268
269

→ Other flowers that have become classics in art and design include the sunflower and the daisy. Loved by children, these are fun and uplifting flowers that can communicate a sense of naturalness and freshness, while their simple geometry belies an almost mathematically precise arrangement of petals.

At the beach, natural circles and spirals are again in abundance. The intricate detail, muted neutral color palette, and tactile feel of pebbles, seashells, sea urchins, and fossils make them a constant source of inspiration for artists and designers. These circles represent many thousands of years of evolution, unaffected by man's intervention. The pebble is smoothed by years of repeated tidal erosion. The intricate spirals of the ammonite fossil are all that remain of a sea creature long extinct, but considered related to the octopus and cuttlefish. It received its name because of its resemblance to a tightly coiled ram's horn—the Egyptian god Ammon being commonly depicted as a man with ram's horns. →

***270** A Spot of Nature, giclée fine art print on watercolor paper, by Sharon Elphick, UK. As the title wittily suggests, the piece uses spots to display a mesmerizing array of flowers and plants.*

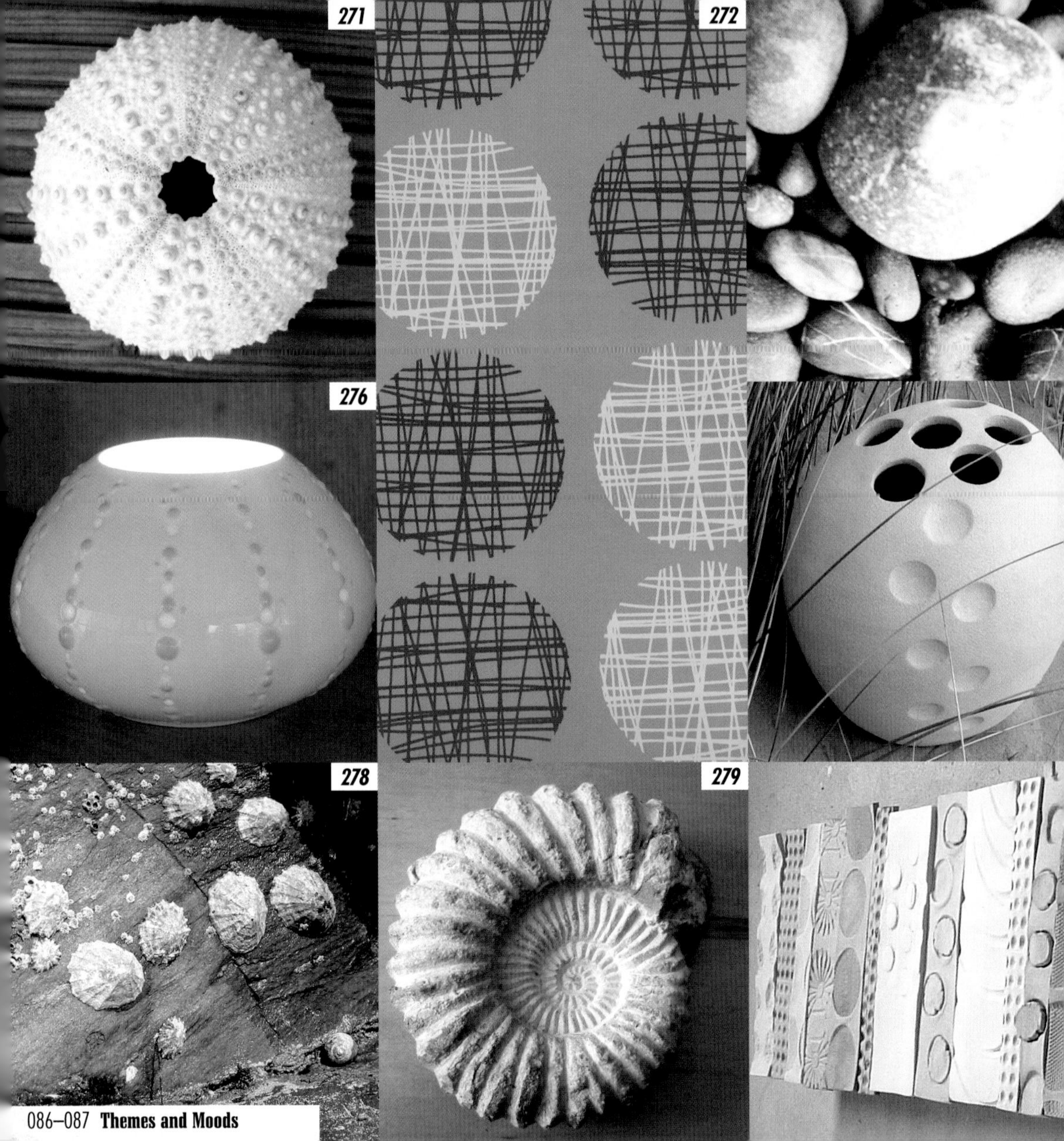
271
272
276
278
279

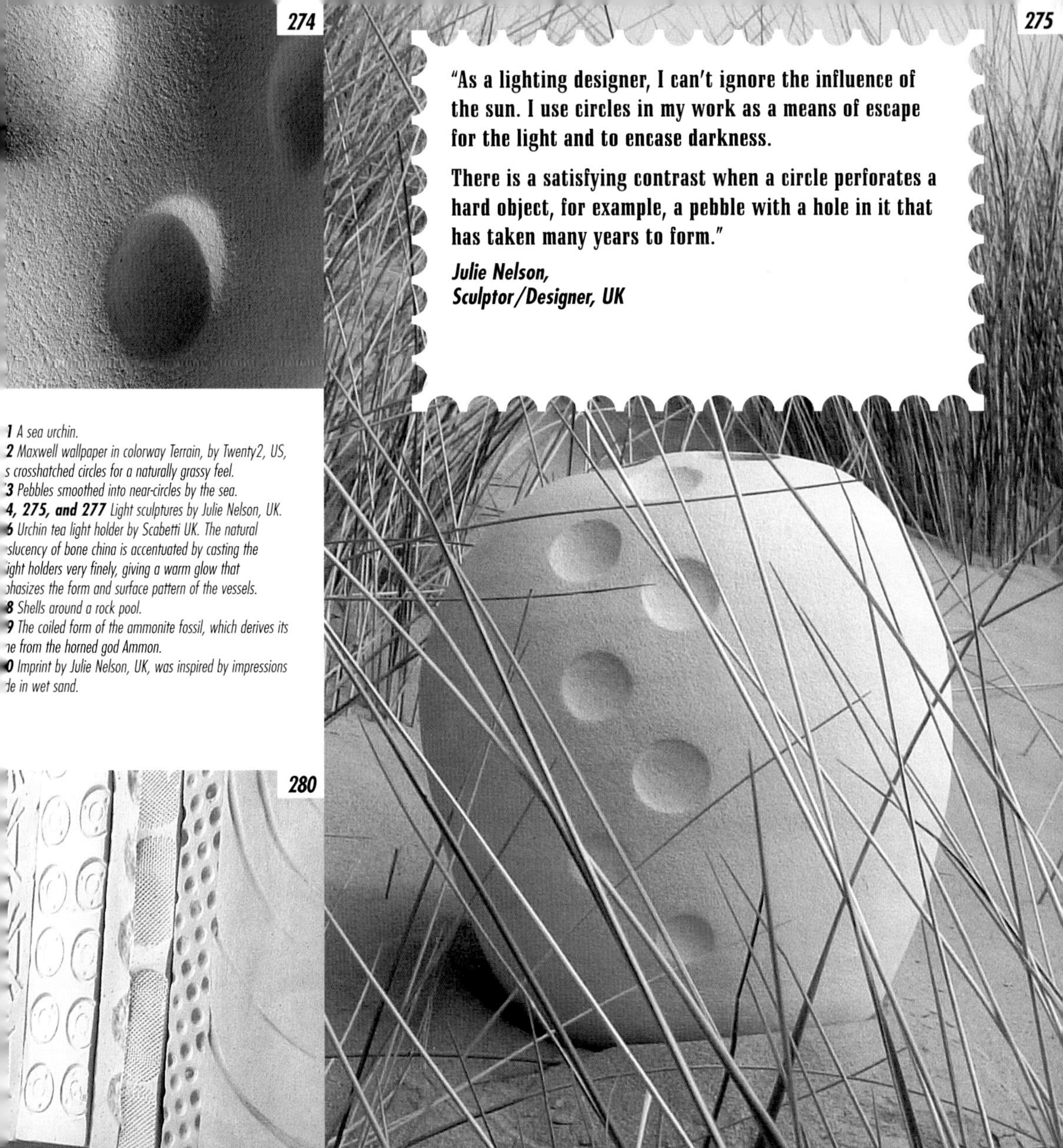

1 A sea urchin.
2 Maxwell wallpaper in colorway Terrain, by Twenty2, US, s crosshatched circles for a naturally grassy feel.
'3 Pebbles smoothed into near-circles by the sea.
***4, 275, and 277** Light sculptures by Julie Nelson, UK.*
6 Urchin tea light holder by Scabetti UK. The natural slucency of bone china is accentuated by casting the ight holders very finely, giving a warm glow that phasizes the form and surface pattern of the vessels.
'8 Shells around a rock pool.
9 The coiled form of the ammonite fossil, which derives its ne from the horned god Ammon.
0 Imprint by Julie Nelson, UK, was inspired by impressions de in wet sand.

"As a lighting designer, I can't ignore the influence of the sun. I use circles in my work as a means of escape for the light and to encase darkness.

There is a satisfying contrast when a circle perforates a hard object, for example, a pebble with a hole in it that has taken many years to form."

Julie Nelson,
Sculptor/Designer, UK

281
284
285

283

e sphere is a fitting shape to communicate
mes of fruition—and again, the basis for
s is in nature. Apples, tomatoes, peaches, and
ries are all spherical at the point of ripeness.
sty colors and graphic cross sections of
ncentric circles and segments make UK design
m Joseph Joseph's chopping boards the most
petizing kitchen accessories around—fresh,
ity, and natural.

1, 282, 284, and 286 *Roundness means ripeness.*
5 *Big, round portobello mushrooms are the most flavorsome.*
3 and 287–289 *Red Onion, Kiwi, Watermelon, and*
nge glass worktop savers by Joseph Joseph, UK. Their
ple circular form and bright colors abstract the natural into
d, functional cutting mats.

287 288 289

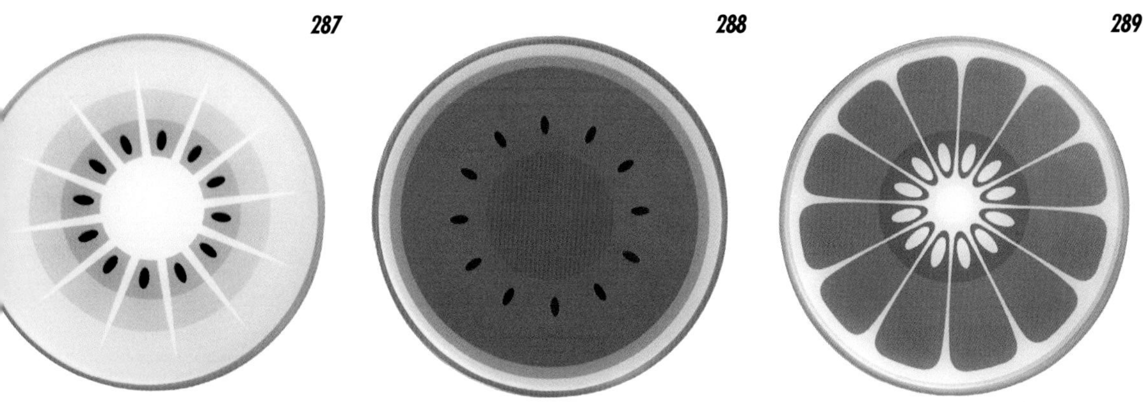

290

291

Nautical

Nautical circles are mostly functional and integral to sailing activity, from the compass that aids navigation to the spoked wheel that steers the ship. The circular porthole is quintessentially nautical but in decline as many modern ships are designed with more conventional sealed rectangular windows. Originally, though, the porthole, with its sturdy brass frame surrounded by hand adjustable nuts, allowed light and fresh air into the hull while keeping seawater out. A secondary brass flap could be secured in place to ensure the ship would remain watertight even if the glass broke. Round windows can be reminiscent of ship design and work particularly well when set into metal doors and walls. They have an industrial rather than a domestic feel and are often used in contemporary architecture to give a sense of precision engineering. →

290 and 295 *Situated on an estuary, much of Portmeirion, UK, has nautical architecture.* ***291*** *A docked ship, seen through a round opening.* ***292–294*** *Porthole-style windows can be used in lots of places from restrooms to restaurants.*
296 and 297 *Leo Reynolds took these two images on the steamship, Sir Walter Scott, Loch Katrine, Stirlingshire, UK.*

294

295

ed and white lifebuoys are also evocative of watery themes. Always to be found reassuringly at the water's dge at beaches, by harbors, or on ships' decks, the red and white hoop of the lifebuoy is graphic shorthand or safety. Even designs that have no seafaring function can take on a nautical look—like the Pop chair by erlea. Featuring an oversized padded ring design, seen in a palette of red and white, they'd look shipshape ither poolside or in the living room.

ircles help to define the nautical esthetic, though they're not always picturesque: old car tyres tied to the arbor wall sit alongside metal cleats, coils of rope in traditional jute or modern nylon, floating fluorescent uoys, and hooped fishing nets. These are working circles.

298 *Pop chairs, designed by Enzo Berti for Ferlea, Italy.*
299–302 and 304 *For safety's sake: a selection of lifebuoys, standing by at the water's edge in case of emergency.*
303 *Karim Rashid's bottle opener for Copco has a red rubber ring, offering a cushioned grip and giving it a striking likeness to a lifebuoy.*

305 and 306 *Engine order telegraphs were used to communicate orders from the bridge to the engine room.*
307 *A lone buoy on the beach.*
308 *Glazed pebble designs adorn the exterior of the Parco dei Principi hotel, Sorrento, Italy.*
309 and 314 *Coiled rope combines function and beauty.*
310 *The archetypal nautical circle—a ship's wheel.*
311 *Rope trimmed plaque with anchor icon.*
312 and 313 *Old tyres are put to a nautical use on the harbor wall.*
315 *You should have seen the one that got away.*
316 *Circular indicator on the plimsoll line.*
317 *Metal hoop on the harbor wall.*

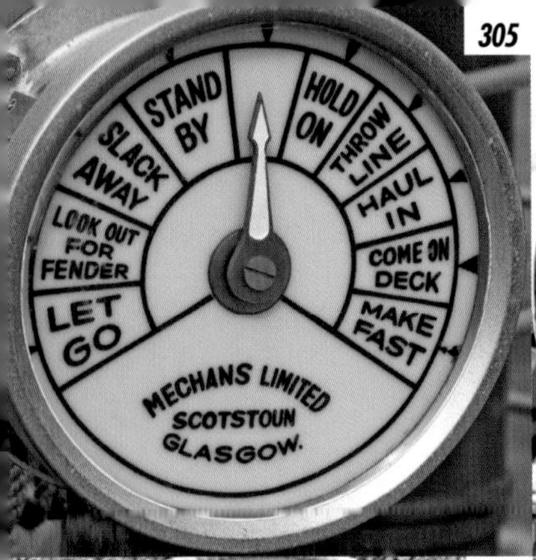

308
309
310
314
315
317

Decorative

As decoration and ornament make a comeback in the work of contemporary designers, decorative circles are finding their way into graphics, furniture, and fashion. Looking to the past for inspiration, designers evoke traditional styles, referencing romantic chintz, delicate lace, and even kitsch paper doilys. Championed by Northern European designers, this modern decorative style relies on unexpected, often humorous juxtapositions to create an antidote to mass-minimalism.

The key is the contemporary twist. So a swirl of pretty leaves morphs into circling swallows in high contrast black and white. Plain white dinner plates appear patterned when racked up behind Perspex, screen-printed with blue and white Delft style circles. Crisp contemporary table linen is embellished with pretty tea plate designs. The domestic becomes cutting edge and the hi-tech is softened with handcrafted touches. Even architecture can undergo the decorative treatment: witness the semicircular sweep of Klein Dytham's Leaf Chapel in Kobuchizawa, Japan, with its perforated metal design.

Once the height of bad taste, paper doilys only made an appearance on Sunday afternoons, bearing your grandmother's lemon drizzle cake. Nowadays, using laser-cutting techniques, intricate patterns can be replicated on the cake stand itself. In a style that might be dubbed "Granny Chic," tables and rugs also get the treatment, subverting the domesticity of the doily through surprising scale and unexpected materials like metal and felt.

"In my final year at the Royal College of Art inspiration came from the English Tea Room and my obsessive collection of plates. I created an installation with a fellow student with meters of dotty hand-printed greaseproof paper, dotty cakes, and cake cases. This led me to create my Tea Time Collection, which now sells commercially, consisting of tablecloths, tea towels, and napkins, printed with decorative plate images."

Lisa Stickley,
Designer, UK

318 *Lisa Stickley's Tea Time Collection was based on her self-confessed obsession with vintage plates.*
319 *The decorative style celebrates warmth and domesticity. That cake looks tasty.*

320 and 321 *Two of Leanne Doherty's designs, the Doily cake stand and Doily table are accomplished examples of conveying delicateness through the robustness of metal—the doily tabletop is intrinsic to its structure and holds the frame together.*

322 Donna Wilson, UK, designed this felt Doily Rug, a decorative circle that plays with proportion.
323 Delicate wood carving.
324 Craftsmanship is central to the decorative style—the twist with this Soma bowl by intoto, US, is that the effect is achieved by a robotic milling process, then finished by hand.
325 The delicately patterned steel "veil" of Klein Dytham's Leaf Chapel, Japan, lifts at the end of a wedding ceremony, revealing trees and mountains. Photography by Katsuhisa Kida.
326 Swallows textiles by Absolute Zero Degrees, UK, for Places and Spaces, UK.
327 Tea Time Collection by Lisa Stickley, UK.

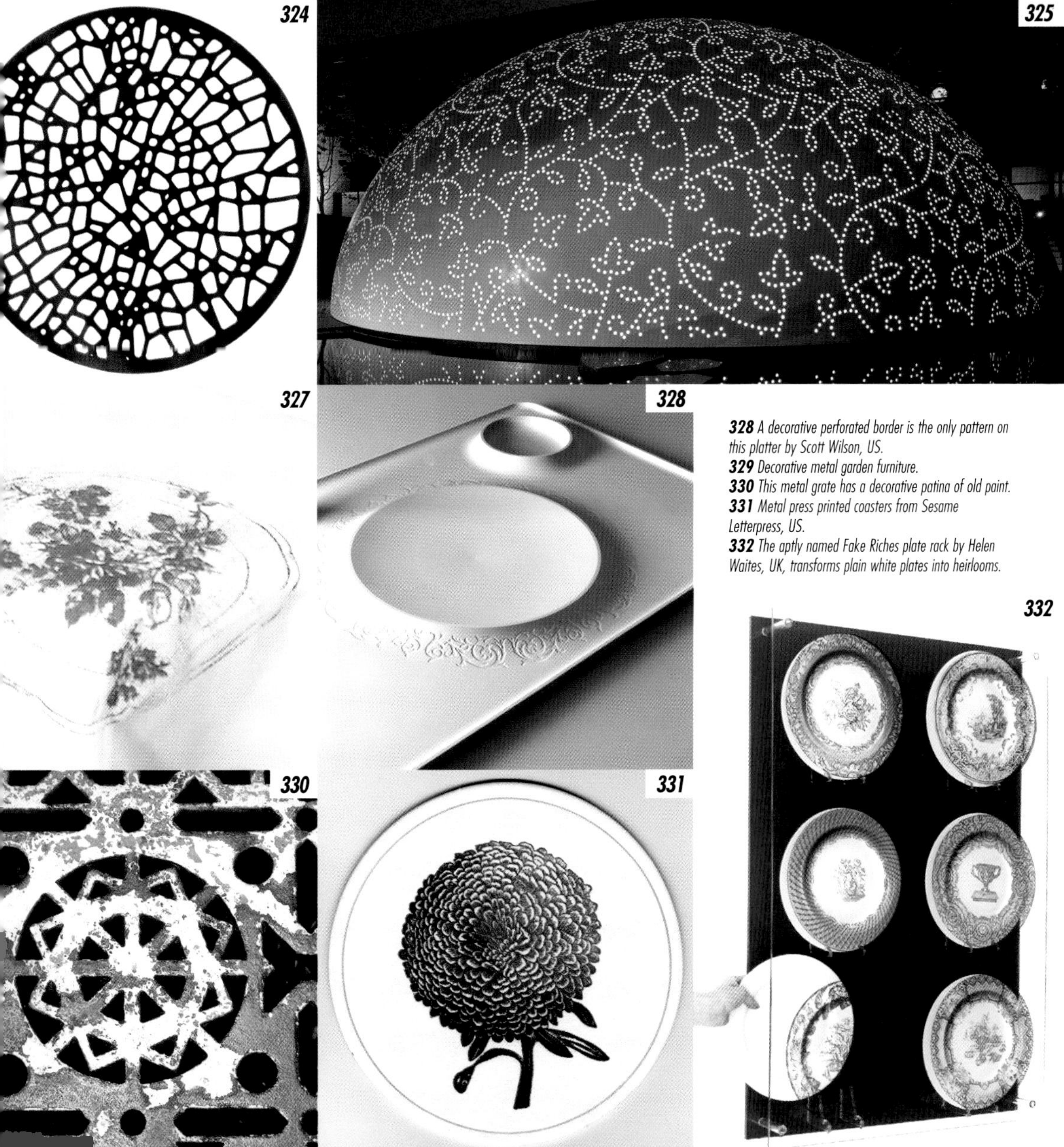

328 A decorative perforated border is the only pattern on this platter by Scott Wilson, US.
329 Decorative metal garden furniture.
330 This metal grate has a decorative patina of old paint.
331 Metal press printed coasters from Sesame Letterpress, US.
332 The aptly named Fake Riches plate rack by Helen Waites, UK, transforms plain white plates into heirlooms.

Glamor

The circle's association with glamor is nowhere more evident than in art deco designs of the 1920s and 1930s. Then, the emphasis was on decadence, and luxury and circles offered an exuberant foil to the chevrons, triangles, and waves that also adorned designs of the time. New York's Chrysler building, topped with diminishing arches of reflective chromium-nickel steel, exemplifies the style. The art deco style is evoked in the multitude of delicate sunray circles that make up Lara Bohinc's distinctive jewelry and accessories. Lavish gold combines with plush leather in powder pink and peacock blue to create individual pieces that are feminine, exotic, and undeniably glamorous. →

333 *Ball by Tom Dixon, UK, designed for Swarovski's Crystal Palace Collection.*
334 *Deco soap from Claus Porto.*
335, 337, and 338 *Deco-decadent jewellery and accessories by Lara Bohinc, UK.*
336 *The Euro chair by Matthew Harding, Australia, is constructed from exuberant concentric circles that have an art deco feel.*
339 *UK cosmetics brand, Pout, added sparkle to its Christmas packaging collection by producing packs with its jewel-encrusted logo on them.*
340 *Clusters of tiny gold rings make up the Circles pendant light by Habitat, UK.*

334
CLAUS PORTO
DECO
SABONETE AROMÁTICO
LIME BASIL BATH SOAP
335
336
337
LARA BOHINC 107
LARA BOHINC 107
338
339
Pout
340

→ Glamorous circles come out after dark in the form of diamond clusters and strings of lustrous pearls. They're about shiny surfaces and deluxe living. UK designer, Tom Dixon explores the glamor of the circle in two of his lighting designs. For crystal manufacturer, Swarovski, he has created Ball: an installation of thousands of individual crystals, each suspended at a precise height so that, en masse, they create a near-spherical chandelier for the post-minimalist age. In Mirror Ball, he updates the eponymous disco essential, using modern production techniques to create a smoothly mirrored surface of real chrome metal on polycarbonate orb-like lights. Singly or in groups, on the floor or suspended from the ceiling, these lights combine style and simplicity in one glamorous whole.

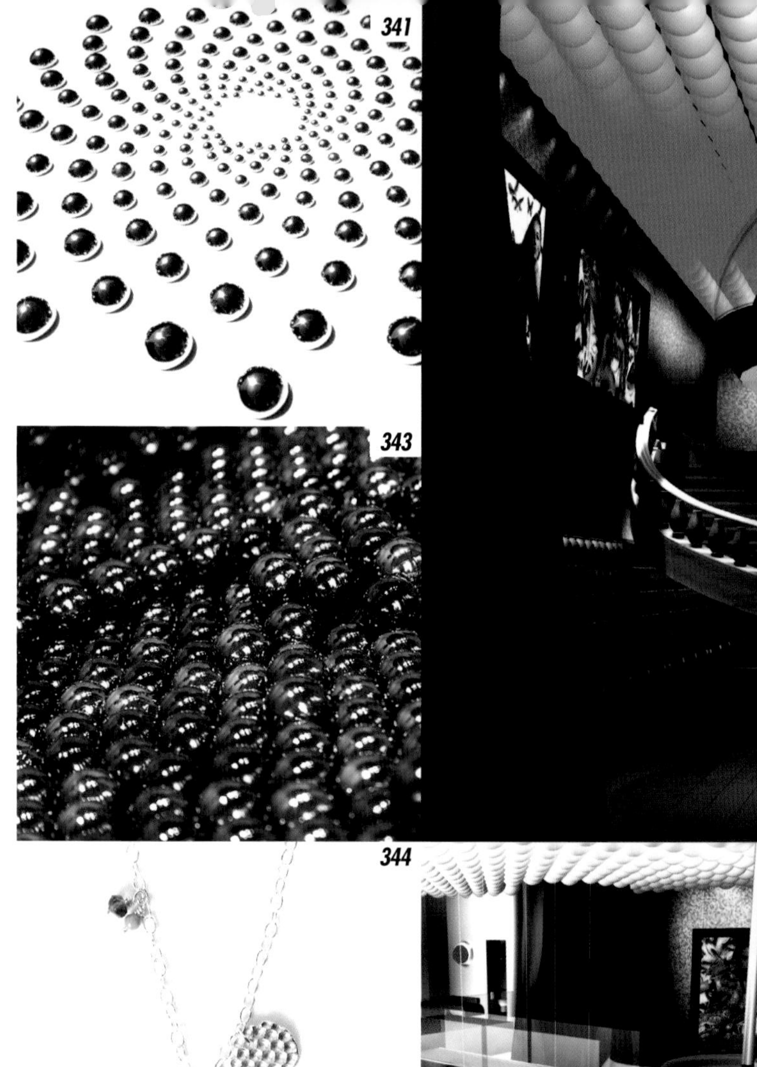

341 *Matthew Harding's Phyllotaxis, a wall sculpture in spun mirror-polished stainless steel, was displayed at the National Gallery of Australia. It explores the beauty of the phyllotactic spiral that occurs in nature.*
342, 345, and 346 *Slick Design, US, designed the interior of dance club, Flutterby's. To shield an unsightly ceiling and avoid the use of typical spotlights in the club, thousands of globes were suspended from the ceiling, containing LED lighting to create an ever-changing glowing hue.*
343 *Clusters of ball bearings have a shiny jewel-like glamor.*
344 *Designer, Renu Tom, US, creates "modern little luxuries to covet and keep or to share with your best friends." Particularly glamorous is this Multi Honeycomb necklace—definitely one to keep.*

342

"Designing a space that reflects the conceptual imagery of a butterfly, the elements introduced into the ultra dance club, Flutterby's, had to embody the unique attributes of the butterfly. The circle offered a direct relation to the natural characteristics of the butterfly's existence. They exist on the wings of a brightly colored species and the color, opacity, and suspension of the pod-like globes mimic the appearance of a cocoon."

Rocco Laudizio,
Slick Design, US

346

"So much in nature is made of round shapes—whether that is the molecules that we are composed of, the shape of the globe we stand on, or the wheels of the vehicles we travel in—that it is surprising that the most pleasing and satisfying of all shapes is not used even more often in design."

Tom Dixon,
Designer, UK

347 *Tom Dixon, UK, reinvents the disco classic with hi[s] Mirror Ball light.*
348 *The original: a disco mirror ball fills the room wit[h] twinkly light as a love song plays.*
349 *Cox and Power's London flagship store was designed by Sybarite, UK. The jewelry is displayed in Perspex spheres, which double up as both showcases and light source for the boutique.*
350 and 351 *Stealth wealth: strings of pearls are th[e] epitome of understated glamor.*

348

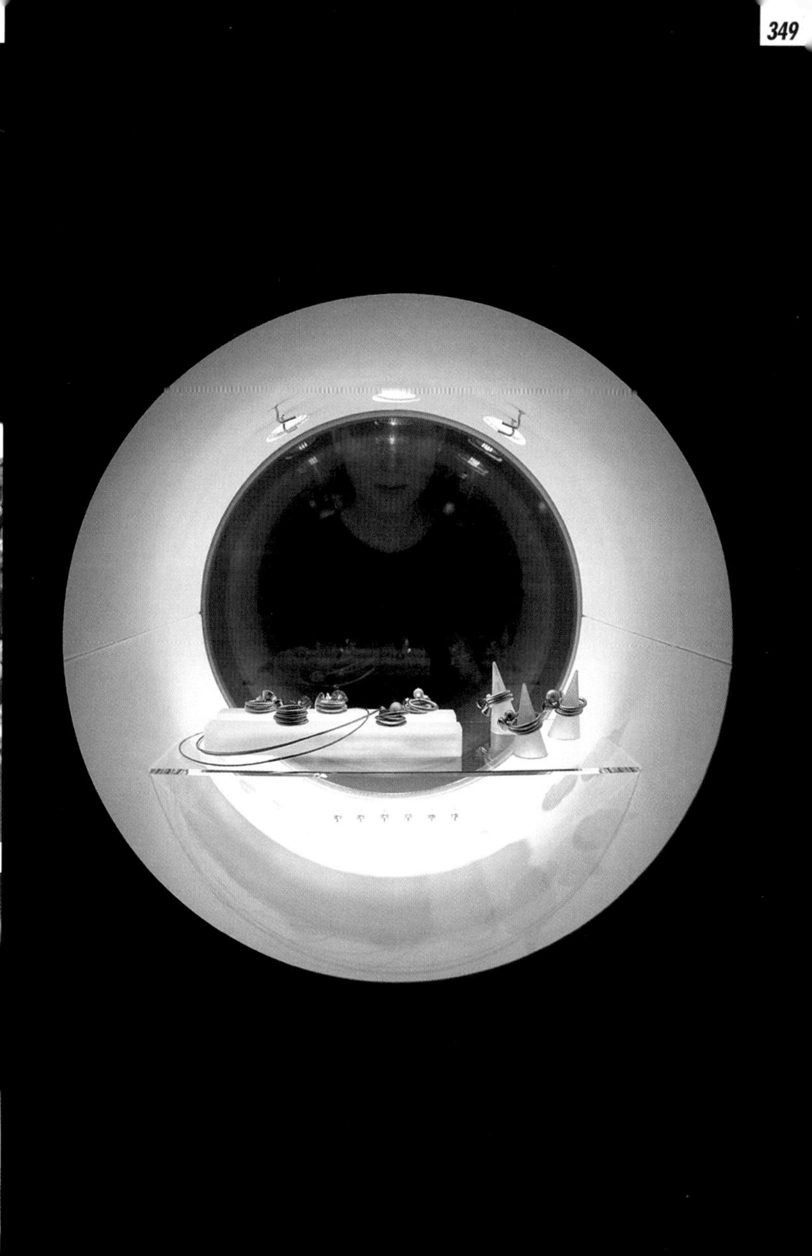

350

351

349

Sport and Leisure

Countless sports are played with round balls, which puts circles at the heart, not only of game play, but also the communication of sporting bodies, clubs, and organizations. The variety of balls is as wide as the variety of sports. Size, texture, and weight all offer different qualities that fit the requirements of the sport. Little, hard, dimpled golf balls; shiny, stitched leather cricket balls; and furry, bouncy tennis balls all move at different speeds and with different characteristics, governing each sport's dynamics of play. The balls themselves display a range of colors and surface graphics that stimulate the designer—from boldly numbered pool balls to the candy appeal of colored bowling balls and the black and white geometry of the soccer ball: the colors and shapes instantly convey a sporting mood.

Circles aid the rules of play. There are the dots that mark positions, from the penalty spot to the placing of snooker balls. And circles define the field of play and the scoring of points: the baseball is pitched from a circular mound, basketballs are shot through round hoops, and golf balls are putted into impossibly small round holes. These circles are marked in paint on tarmac and grass and contribute to the colorful graphic language of sport. →

352 and 357 *Balls await gym class.*
353–355 *Circles on the basketball court: the key, named for its keyhole shape, is the area in front of the basket incorporating the free throw line; the center circle and half court line; the hooped net.*
356 *The International Cricket Council identity by Minale Tattersfield, UK, incorporates the ball and the wickets.*

353

355

356

357

358 *Pool balls.*

359 *Timmy Perez's picture of bowling balls racked up ready for play is a beautiful image and also highlights how the colors of the balls act as a coding device, indicating their weights. Note also the extra circles formed by the finger holes.*

360 *Pool was the inspiration behind the Cue n 8 (salt n pepper) shakers, designed by Alex Turner, UK. The eight ball has particular cultural significance in the US, where the term "behind the eight ball" means "in a difficult position," relating to the rules of certain versions of pool. The balls have to be pocketed in sequence, with the eight ball last—if the eight ball is pocketed out of sequence the game is forfeited—so being behind the eight ball puts the player in imminent danger. In addition, the term "eight ball" is sometimes used as an insulting name.*

361 *An eight ball design makes a goofy spare tyre cover.*

↑ 7lbs Red
9T40298 L

LA

362 *A bird's eye view of the circular pitcher's mound, taken by Paul Duree.*
363 *Baseball.*
364 *Golf ball.*
365 *Ping-Pong ball and bat.*
366 *Soccer ball.*
367 *The Mexico 1970 World Cup identity by Lance Wyman, US. The number 70 is formed by a soccer ball in motion.*
368 *These balls might be bingo or lottery balls—either way, they could be winners.*
369 *Snooker balls—the black carries the highest score.*

→ No less compelling are the circles involved in a host of leisure activities, games, and puzzles. Circles are intrinsic to gambling: we pin our hopes on bouncing lottery balls, a double-six roll of the dice (12 dots), and the spin of the "luck be a lady" roulette wheel. These circles have a lighthearted edge for all but the most hardened gambler—dominos and dice are graphically fun, as are noughts and crosses, evoked by Josh Owen's ingenious no-tools-required, self-assembly, XOX table.

***370** Dominos.*
***371 and 375** Dots carpets by Tai Ping Carpets, China, one of the world's leading custom handtufted carpet manufacturers.*
***372** Roulette wheel.*
***373** Funky Fresh car air freshener in kitsch hanging dice design from Worldwide Co, UK.*
***374** Playing with your food: Solitaire dish by Barnaby Barford & André Klauser, UK.*
***376** Bauerware, US, has a huge collection of knobs and pulls. Its Gamepiece collection includes these domino knobs in white with a choice of dot color.*
***377** Let's hope the owner of this sports car is displaying these furry dice with irony.*
***378** Josh Owen, US, shows how stylish and easy self-assembly furniture can be with his XOX table.*

372

373

Monte Carlo
Scent
ACCOUTREMENTS
FUNKY
FRESH
Air Freshener
Dés odorisant Aromatizante

378

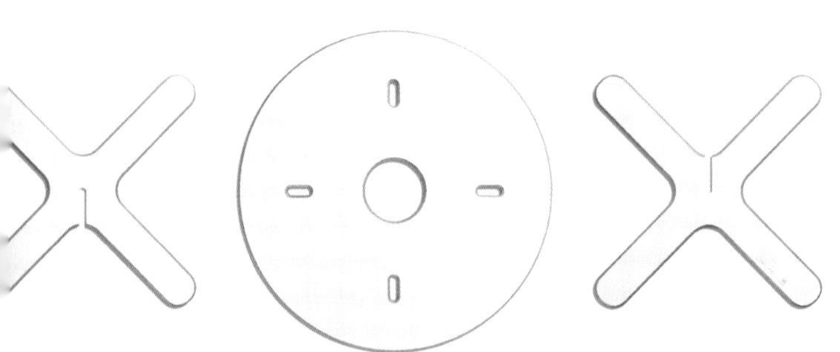

Fantasy and Fun

It's ironic that the red and white spotted toadstool is so commonly depicted as cute and fun in cartoons, because in reality, the Fly Agaric species is both hallucinogenic and poisonous. The popularization of mushrooms and toadstools in modern children's fantasy is often attributed to Lewis Carroll's *Alice In Wonderland* in which Alice shrinks, then grows after eating from a mushroom on the advice of a hookah-smoking caterpillar. The drugs references are not too difficult to decode, though nowhere in the original text or illustrations is the red and white spotted variety referred to.

Spotted toadstools were a big feature of the 1990s video game, *Super Mario*, and appear in many fairy tales, perhaps because they combine a sense of magic and danger at the same time. A similar tension exists in other fantasy circles. Much to do with witchcraft and magic derives from a genuine belief in, and fear of, evil forces. →

379 *Hilde Bakering spotted these Fly Agaric mushrooms.*
380 *The pentangle, or pentagram, is thought to herald from Ancient Mesopotamia, possibly as far back as 3500 BC.*

→ According to which opinion you favor, the pentangle is either a magic symbol or a satanic emblem; even carved pumpkins have a sinister origin. According to Irish myth, Stingy Jack tricked the Devil and was banished from Heaven and Hell, destined to roam the Earth at night with only a burning coal to light his way. Jack put his burning coal in a hollowed-out turnip, earning the name Jack-o'-Lantern. Ever since, people have made similar lanterns to ward off Jack and other evil spirits. →

381–383 *Halloween treats, featuring spider web biscuits and cakes.*
384 *Witches only, thank you.*
385 and 386 *Jack-o'-Lantern design can range from primitive to sophisticated, humorous to frightening.*

→ Circles, spots, and dots are also used to denote pure, innocent fun. Think of a handful of multicolored marbles, bright yellow smiley faces, and the domino-style dots on Lego bricks. Many things associated with childhood are spotted. Spots and dots confuse the eye; they break up a surface in much the same way that stripes do—so they're often considered a bit garish. This gives designers unlimited license to use them on children's clothing and toys.

Since it first made an appearance in 1866, the polka dot (named after the dance craze that was sweeping the US in the mid-19th century) has gone from a statement of high fashion to a fun print. No longer confined to the catwalk, it is used as a lively print on pillows, quilts, accessories, mugs, and even Mobi zipper sandwich bags that make healthy eating fun for kids. →

"The name expresses optimism for the future and symbolizes the company's philosophy of providing customer satisfaction in a fun and enjoyable way. The mark is made of two circles placed closely together with the words 'Joy' and 'Co' making two happy, brightly colored faces that signify the joining together and collaboration of the separate companies."

John McConnell, Partner
Pentagram, UK

387 *This brightly colored, spotty Gymboree ball makes anytime playtime.*
388 *Described by Totem Design, UK, as Multifunctional Interactive Sensory Furniture. They're called Boo! and they're as fun as they sound—lighting up as you sit and dimming as you stand.*
389 *Marbles.*
390 *Abby Chicken's journeys took her to a lantern shop in Hanoi, Vietnam, where she took this colorful shot.*
391 *Bright and bouncy balls.*
392 *The name and design say it all. Pentagram, UK, united the diverse companies of international Spanish confectionery company, GC Group, by creating one memorable name, Joyco. Design by John McConnell and Hazel Macmillan with illustration by Javier Mariscal.*

393 A happy ball.
394 Necco wafers are an American candy classic in eight flavors and colors: lemon (yellow), orange (orange), lime (green), clove (purple), cinammon (white), wintergreen (pink), licorice (black), and chocolate (brown).
395 Spotty zipper bags from Mobi, US, for fun lunches.
396 Balloons at the circus.
397 Kitsch plastic polka dot beakers seen here in vintage furniture store, Rokit, London.
398 Smiley culture: vintage sew-on badge on denim.
399 Up, up, and away!
400 Polka dot mugs with ribbon handle from The Tabletop Company, UK.

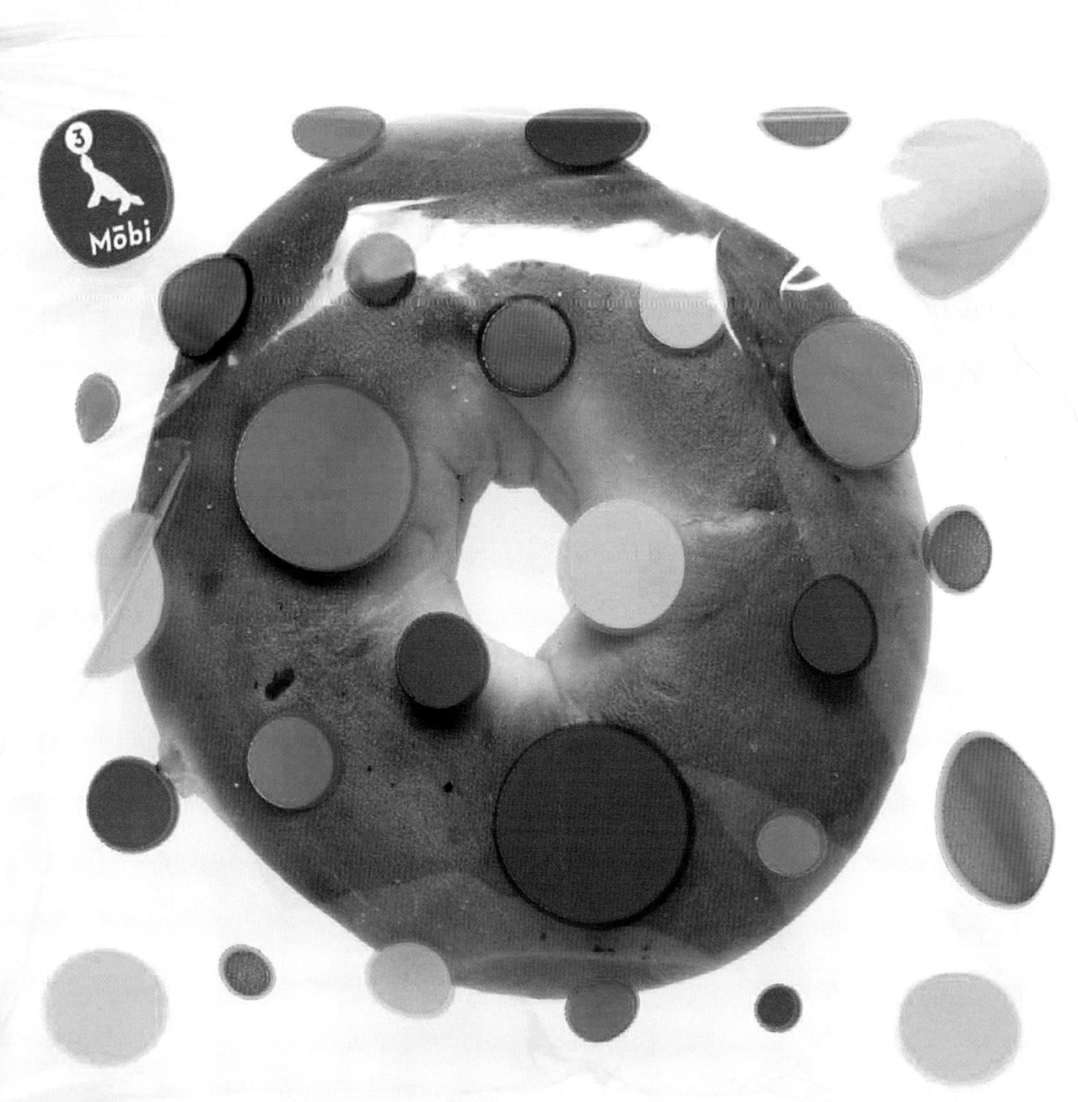
3
Mōbi

→ The three circles that make up Mickey Mouse's head and ears are, perhaps, the best-known fun circles of all—the perfect accompaniment to Ferris wheels, balloons, and big bursts of fireworks—the stuff of magical children's days out.

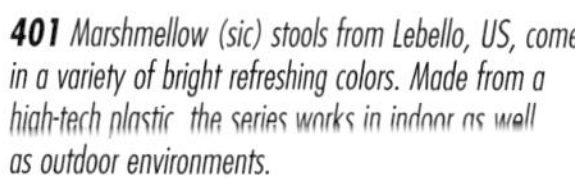

401 *Marshmellow (sic) stools from Lebello, US, come in a variety of bright refreshing colors. Made from a high-tech plastic, the series works in indoor as well as outdoor environments.*
402 *A squashy, bobbly, ball thing.*
403 *Hand-decorated marbles.*
404 and 408 *The funfair is full of circular rides.*
405 *Aerial shot of a children's playground.*
406 *Lego bricks with their trademark construction circles.*
407 *Jemma Lumber, UK, Multi Storage units are bold and fun and the circles slot together to build them up.*
409 *Sybarite, UK, used circles as both architectural and graphic language for this children's clothes shop in London.*
410 *You can't leave Disney World without a pair of Mickey Mouse's signature ears.*
411–420 *Spectacular showers of fireworks help Thom Watson celebrate the Fourth of July in Washington DC.*

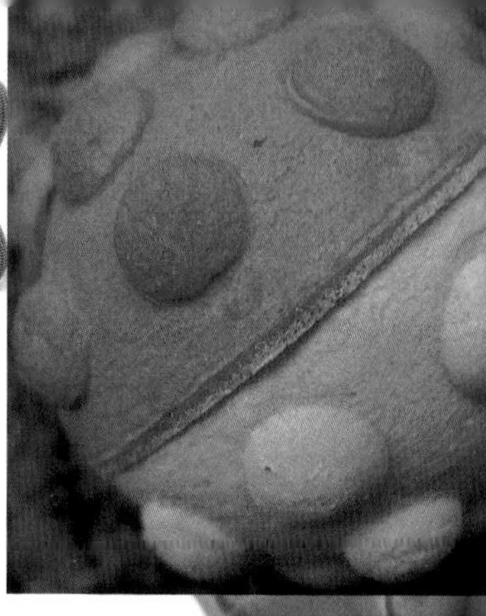

403
404
407
410
Keith

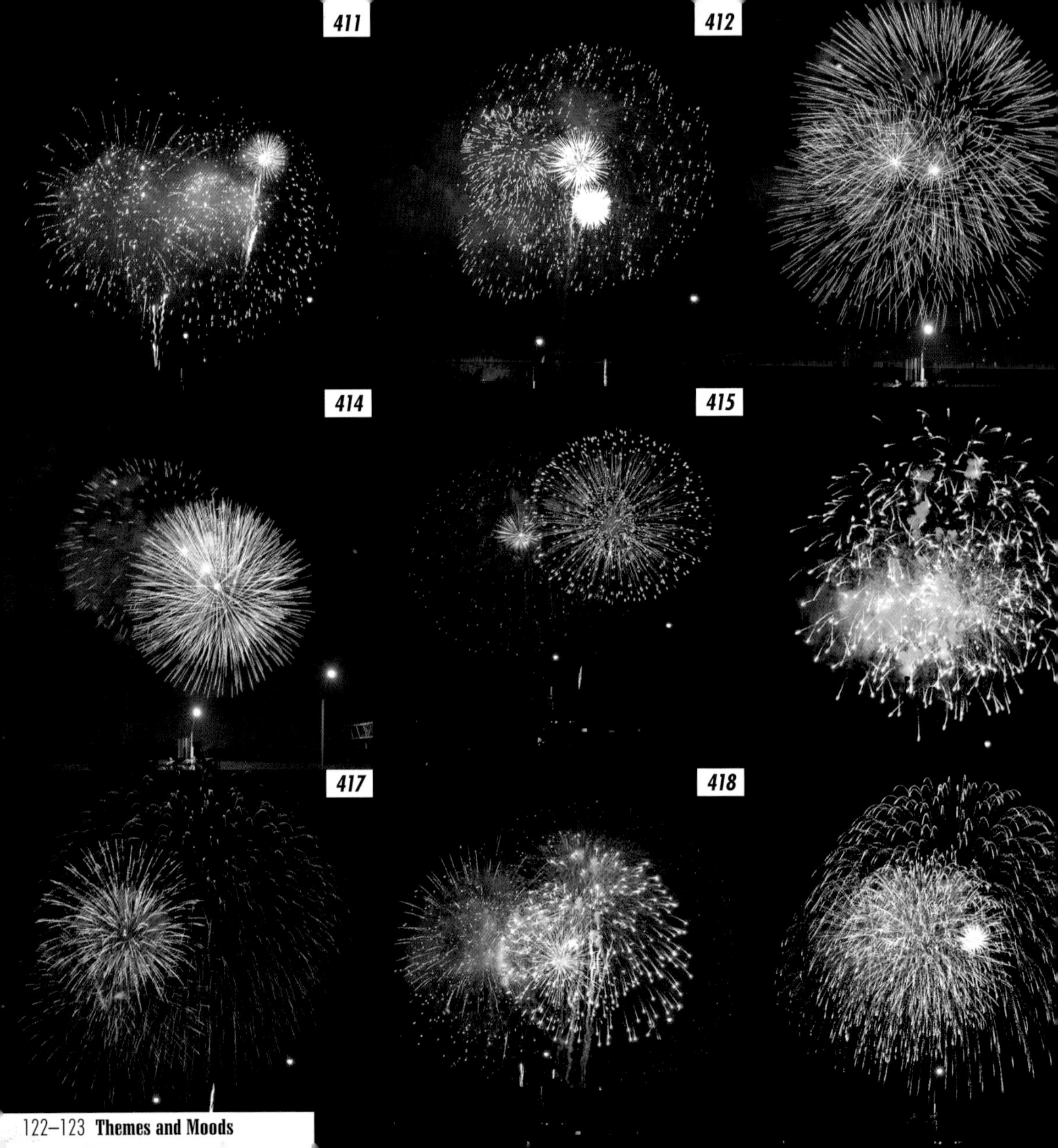
411
412
414
415
417
418

Dynamism

Dynamic spirals and swirls are used as shorthand for the circular motion of wheels, fans, windmills, and roundabouts—anything that spins round fast. Designers use dynamic circles, in blurred motion or spiraling with momentum, as a means of conveying energy and speed. It is a graphic representation of what we often call "centrifugal force." However, this force does not really exist. When your sunglasses slide away on the dashboard as you corner a tight bend, it is actually the lack of a "centripetal force" that makes them move. A centripetal force is the force that maintains objects moving in a circular path. While physics disproves the notion of centrifugal force, it still feels real when you are holding tight on a spinning roundabout, and the dynamic circle offers an effective means of conveying the exhilaration you feel.

The word "dynamic" is derived from the Greek word "dúnamis" meaning "power." As wind energy becomes an increasingly viable alternative to fossil fuel generated power, energy companies embrace dynamic circles, depicting the rotating blades of modern wind turbines, as a means of communicating this sustainable, alternative energy.

421 and 427 *These dynamic, ghostly images were created by Charlie McRae, US.*
422 and 423 *Hold tight! Fast spinning rides at the fair look even more exciting when illuminated at night.*
424 *Vintage Matchbox car collection with dynamic Superfast logo.*
425 *Branding for UK media consultancy, Road Trip, by Absolute Zero Degrees, featuring the director on her vintage Vespa Gran Turismo.*
426 *A child's windmill.*

428–430 *Industrial fans and turbines.*
431 and 432 *Identica, UK, created this icon system for electrical company, GET. The dynamic swirl highlights its wind circulation products.*
433–435 *Wind us u source of energy—past, present, and future.*
436–438 *Final Draft domestic fan by UK designer, Simon Sheeran. The fan uses the graphic language of the dynamic circle instantly to communicate movement. It also helps distinguish the front from the back—the elevation detail depicts rotation while the back grill uses a static circular design.*

436

437

438

"A product's functionality must unconditionally communicate itself to a consumer at first glance. Through semantic detailing the swirling pattern of this domestic fan creates an optical movement for one to interpret whether the fan is in motion or not. The stimulating pattern denotes momentum subconsciously through the user's inherent understanding of visual convection and wind."

Simon Sheeran
Product and Furniture Designer, UK

Water and Air

In design terms, water and air are hard to represent because they are both colorless. But science and physics offer their own solutions. Pass oxygen through water and you get a myriad of air bubbles that create a feeling of lightness. Drop a pebble in the water and you create a series of concentric rings on the surface. Taken in isolation, the bubbles represent air; the rings represent water. Separately, or in conjunction, water and air create a feeling of purity, clarity, and tranquillity.

Tiny circular droplets of water suggest freshness and flavor when used in the context of food merchandising. Any fresh food—from meat and fish to vegetables and beverages—looks more appealing when chilled (try marketing warm beer). A covering of fine drops of condensation shows the product is cool and fresh in photography and film.

In the competitive UK mobile telecoms market, strong brands create customer preference and loyalty. Late entrant into the market was O_2—created by UK brand consultancy, Lambie Nairn. The name, taken from the chemical symbol for oxygen, suggests that the phone has become as essential a part of our lives as the air we breathe. The simple, circular identity, in a palette of blue and white, reflects this positioning and the way that technology has become accessible and usable. And to represent O_2 in advertising and at point of sale, a circular communication language was created, based on air bubbles.

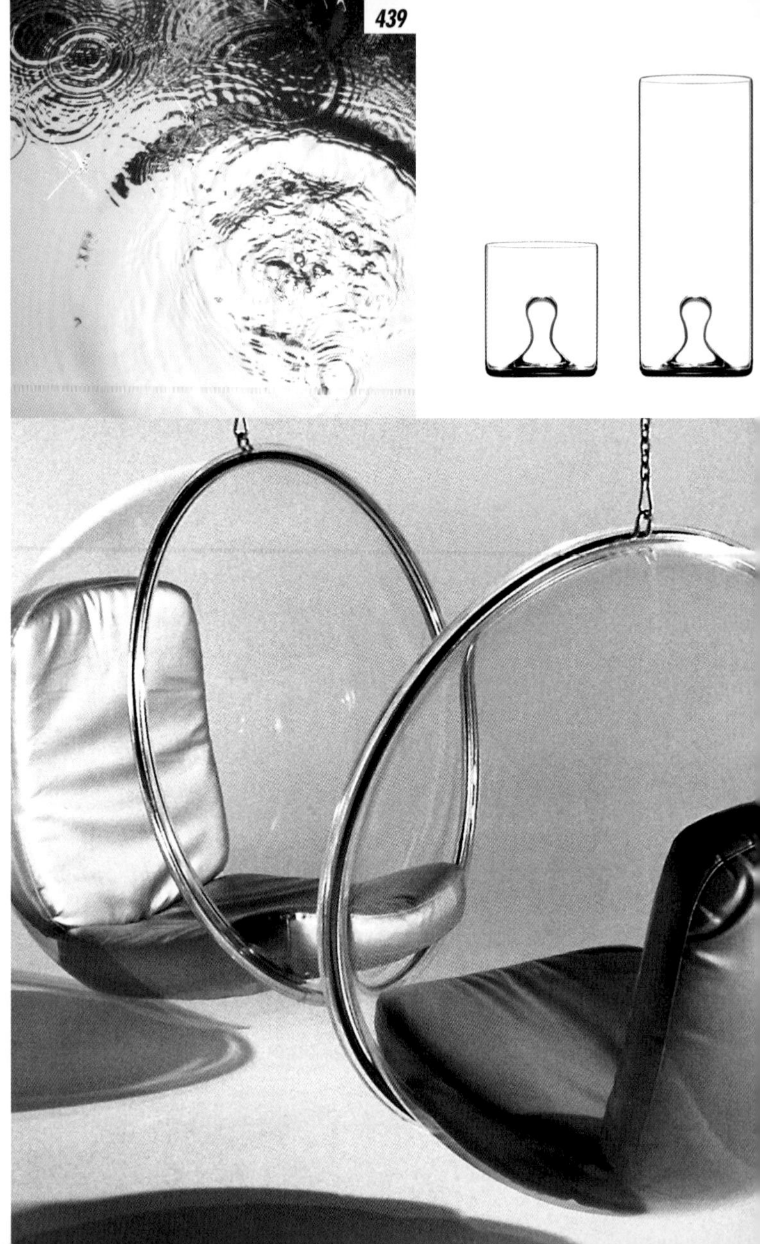

and 445 Rings on the water's surface.
)rop handblown drinking glasses by intoto, US.
Aultidot umbrella by pare*umbrella, US.
Tiny beads of water cling to a leaf.
and 446–449 M Worldwide, UK, created the identity
, interior design, and promotional material for 10-11,
1 of convenience stores in Iceland. The color palette
e of circles to suggest water, frost, and air helps to
nt the store and promote the freshness of produce.
Eero Aarnio, Bubble chair, 1968. The designer said of
ece: "After I had made the Ball Chair I wanted to have
ht inside it and so I had the idea of a transparent ball
light comes from all directions. The only suitable
al is acrylic which is heated and blown into shape like
bubble... I had a steel ring made, the bubble was
and cushions were added and the chair was ready.
gain the name was obvious: Bubble."

450

451

"Circles are very important to Sybarite as we draw our inspiration directly from nature and the circle is recognized as the purest geometric form. The inspiration could be the raindrop 'ripple' effect on the surface of water or even one of Saturn's rings. The beauty of the circle is that its perspective and color can change according to what angle a circular object is viewed from."

Simon Mitchell, Sybarite, UK

0 *Bubble wrap: once you pop, you can't stop.*
1 *The luxurious Bubble Suite at the Pelirocco Hotel, ghton, UK, was inspired by bubbles, circles, and curves. even has an 8ft (2.4m) round bed.*
2 *Bubbly design detail by pare*umbrella, US.*
3, 456, and 457 *Lambie Nairn's point-of-sale design UK telecoms company, O_2 uses air bubbles, bubble- ped display cases, and a giant circular logo.*
4 *Cox and Power's London boutique by Sybarite, UK. etail of the polished interior wall, punctured by bubble- spheres that showcase the jewelry.*
5 *Part of the Very Important Product Collection for bitat, UK, these champagne flutes designed by world mpion freediver, Tanya Streeter, feature tiny air bubbles pended in the glass.*

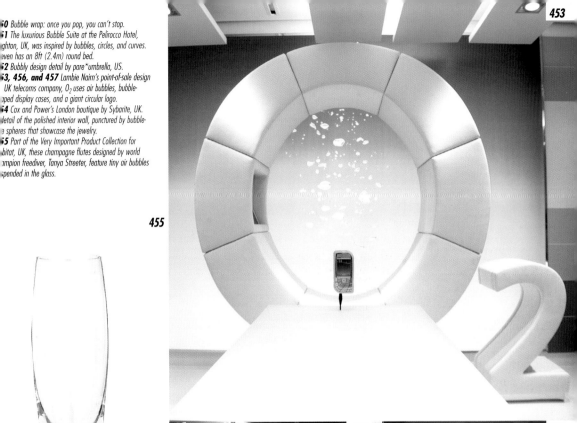

453

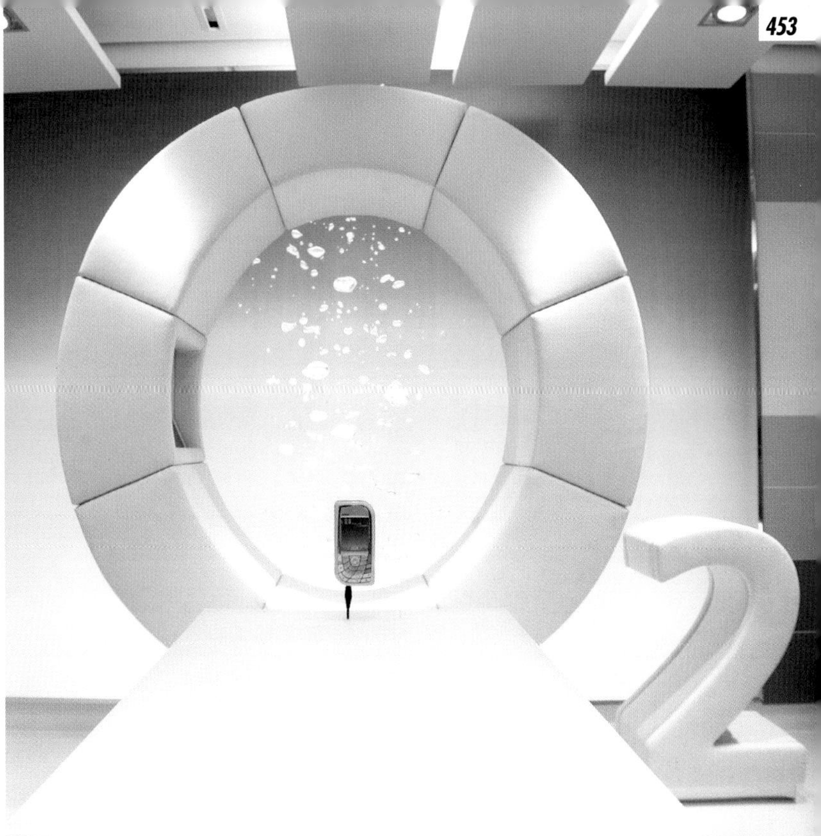

455

456

457

Light and Heat

Given that the sun is our essential source of heat and light, it's hardly surprising that circular motifs appear in creative representations of these themes. Light projected from any source illuminates objects within a circular halo; the precision of the sApotlight offers a sharp circle of light with the ability to follow its subject. The spotlight is an emotive circle—when those super trouper beams find you, you know your big moment has arrived—and design work that features spotlight motifs, like the logo for the UK's Big Lottery Fund, capture a sense of drama and excitement.

When it comes to lighting design, the circle is both the most common and the most effective shape. A circular skylight holds more allure than its square equivalent. Chandeliers, traditional and modern, are most often configured as a series of rings. But it is the sphere that proves the most enduring shape. Based on Isamu Noguchi's 1950s Akari light sculptures in bamboo and paper, the oversized globe paper lantern became de rigeur in every 1970s student residence. Modern variations abound in plastic, paper, and woven cane—all try to achieve the same purity of form as Noguchi's classic.

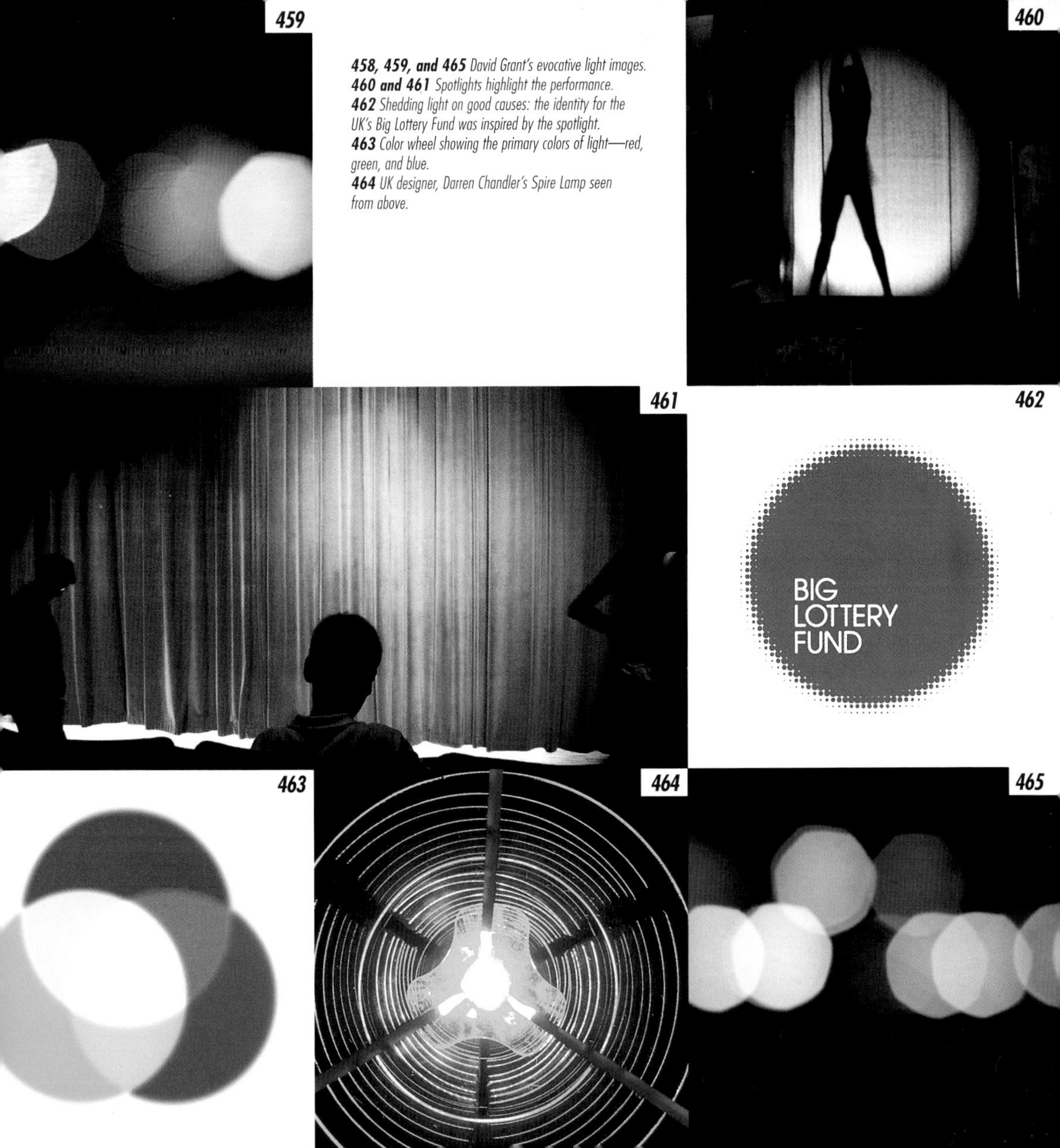

458, 459, and 465 *David Grant's evocative light images.*
460 and 461 *Spotlights highlight the performance.*
462 *Shedding light on good causes: the identity for the UK's Big Lottery Fund was inspired by the spotlight.*
463 *Color wheel showing the primary colors of light—red, green, and blue.*
464 *UK designer, Darren Chandler's Spire Lamp seen from above.*

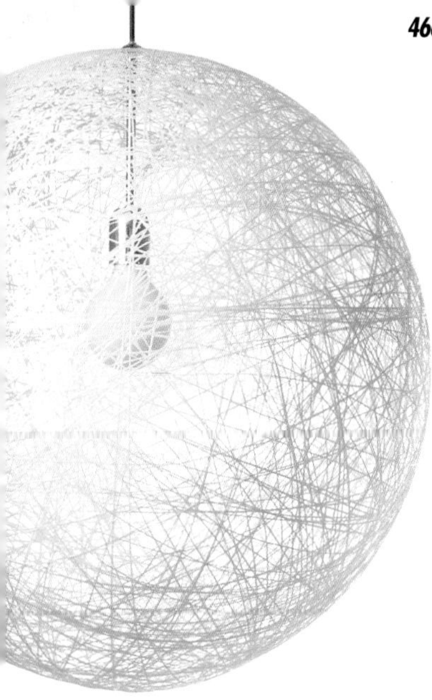

466

467

470

473

466 Moooi Random Light by Monkey Boys, the Netherl
2002 Photographer: Maarten van Houten.
467 1960s inflatable cushion with lantern print.
468 A light installation enlivens a public space in Melbo
Australia.
469 Dearingo, from Moooi, the Netherlands, creates a flexible modern chandelier from anglepoise lamps.
470 Classic paper lanterns.
471 Natural light floods into this shop via these circular portals, designed by Sybarite, UK.
472 Dandelion by Richard Hutton 2005, for Moooi, the Netherlands. Photographer: Maarten van Houten.
473 Cocoon light by Lebello, US.

→ In domestic situations, your means of cooking comes down to a choice between gas and electricity. Ella Doran's photographic tablemats bring the heat of the cooker onto the dinner table, offering trompe l'oeil place settings of blue gas flames or orange glowing spirals. The efficiency of the circle in conducting heat evenly means that the round pan has never been surpassed. Pan design is not generally known for its progressiveness, but UK design studio, Doshi Levien, has opened up the creative possibilities in its work for Tefal. Dropping standard shapes in favor of exotic cooking pots such as the wok and the tagine, the pans escape the mundanity of the everyday. But the real surprise comes when you turn the pans over and discover the bases, embellished with beautifully delicate circular patterns.

468
469
472

474 475 478 479

474–476 and 478 Doshi Levien, UK, designed these delicate circular motifs for the bases of its Mosaic range of pans for Tefal, France.
477, 482, and 484 Out of the frying pan: the OUCH! range by Ella Doran, UK, designed and produced in 2000 in collaboration with James Rouse of SOUP Ltd.
479 The profiles of Doshi Levien's Mosaic pan range are anything but ordinary.
480 At the top of the mountain, above Nariaiji, Japan, you will come across this fiery hoop. Buy two small ceramic discs for 100 yen, make a wish, and then attempt to throw the discs through the ring of fire. If you do so, your wish will come true.
481 A selection of classic pots and pans from Habitat, UK.
483 Electric rings on a stove.

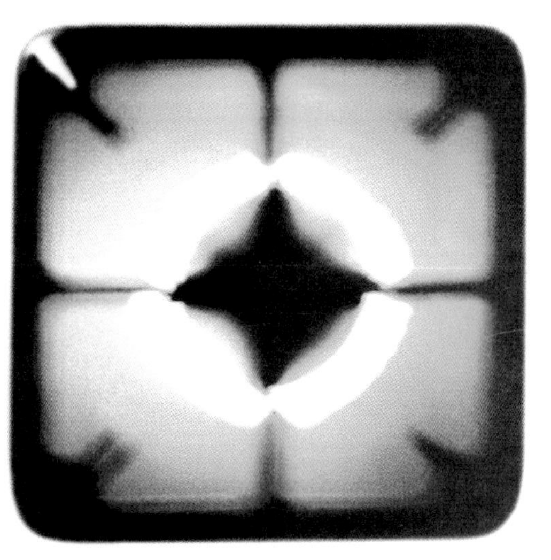

482

483

484

Signals and Information

Signals and Information

Look closely at printed material and you'll discover it's made up of thousands of tiny dots. From the Benday dots of a halftone screen to the scrolling information on a dot matrix LED display, dots and spots help us to convey information and detail. The dot can confuse, too, playing its part in visually distorting optical effects. Larger circles are used as signs. They direct us on roads and public transport, provide commemorative information about buildings and monuments, and intrigue us in the form of crop circles. Are they a sign from another planet? Medals and coins provide us with symbols of merit and financial tokens. Circular dials and measures have enabled man to navigate seas and accurately tell the time while we use segments of circles to demonstrate mathematical problems. From target to thermostat, here we celebrate the informative circle.

485 *Target based artwork can give a room a "pop" edge.*
486 *Christmas wreaths probably hail from the Pagan festival of Brumalia, celebrating the return of the sun after the Winter Solstice.*
487 *This sign does not mean that French dogs must not walk themselves—it means keep them on a lead.*
488 *Scrolling dot matrix sign.*
489 *"NO" in signage is indicated by a circle with a 45º line through it.*
490 *Sun and Doves gallery, UK, uses a pastiche of a commemorative plaque to promote its show.*
491 *Sidewalk signage in circular plates to give directions and information about local heritage.*
492 *The earliest form of timekeeping—a sundial.*
493 *Traffic lights.*
494 *A twist on a roundabout road sign, spotted by Abby Chicken.*
495 *Caution, wheel clamping in operation.*
496 *Dots make up pedestrian signage icons.*
497 *Promotional fly-post material, reminiscent of an old 45 record bag with an optical "pop" influence.*
498 *Coins date back to the 7th century BC.*
499 *Dartboard—the bullseye is worth 50 points.*

487
TENUS EN LAISSE
488
489
492
493
VAULT
494
DIZZY
497
2036
myglass
498
499
20 1 18 4 13 6 10 15 2 17 3 19 7 16 8 11 14 9 12 5

Information and Communication

Dots are used in several nonverbal communication systems, two of the most obvious being Morse code and Braille. Samuel Morse was an American painter, sculptor, and something of a renaissance man. He invented the electric telegraph and a means of communicating across it—a series of dots and dashes representing individual letters. Since 1837 this has been used as an internationally recognized code. Braille uses cells of raised dots in a rectangular 2×3 formation that are "read" by fingertip. The formation offers 64 combinations—enough for letters, numbers, punctuation, and some key words like "and," "of," and "for." This is simple Grade 1 Braille, used only for beginners. Most books are transcribed in Grade 2 Braille, which contracts many words into single characters to fit more on the page and make for a speedier read. Braille appears in public spaces on elevator buttons, public transport, and signage, embossed in metal or plastic. →

500 *Dual signage in text and Braille.*
501 *Anton Parsons' Invisible City 2003, incorporates a poem by blind poet, Peter Beatson in Braille. It is part of the Lambton Quay Sculpture walk in Wellington, New Zealand, captured here by Patrick Quinn-Graham.*
502 and 509 *Morse code transmits information using short and long pulses. Originally created for Samuel Morse's electric telegraph in the mid-1830s, it was also extensively used for early radio communication beginning in the 1890s.*
503 *Named after Louis Braille, its inventor, Braille is the standard form of writing and reading used by blind people.*
504 and 505 *Fashion designer, Shelley Fox, UK, creates stunning clothing from innovative circular structured tailoring. Collection No.7, Autumn/Winter 1999 Morse Code, uses the code as a textile print.*
506 *Morse code inspired this rug by Habitat, UK.*
507 *Raised dots underfoot indicate a pedestrian crossing.*
508 *Detail from Shelley Fox's Autumn/Winter 1998 show invitation.*

502

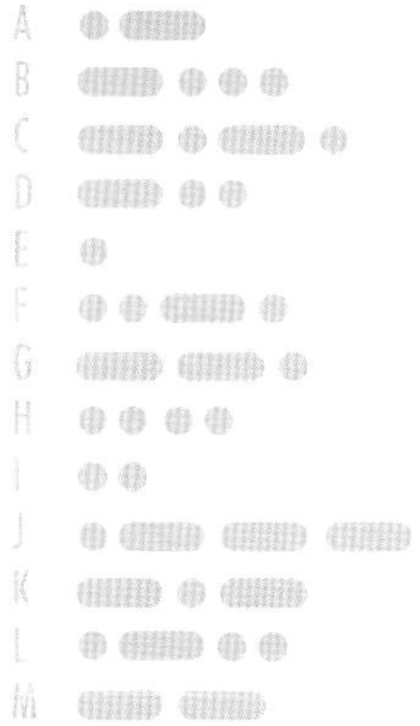

A
B
C
D
E
F
G
H
I
J
K
L
M

506

509

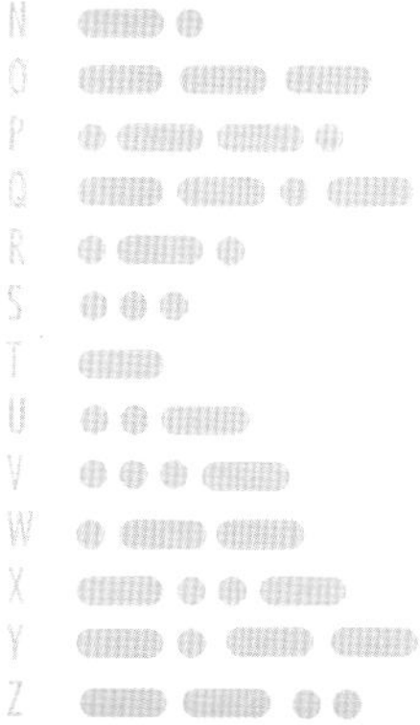

N
O
P
Q
R
S
T
U
V
W
X
Y
Z

503

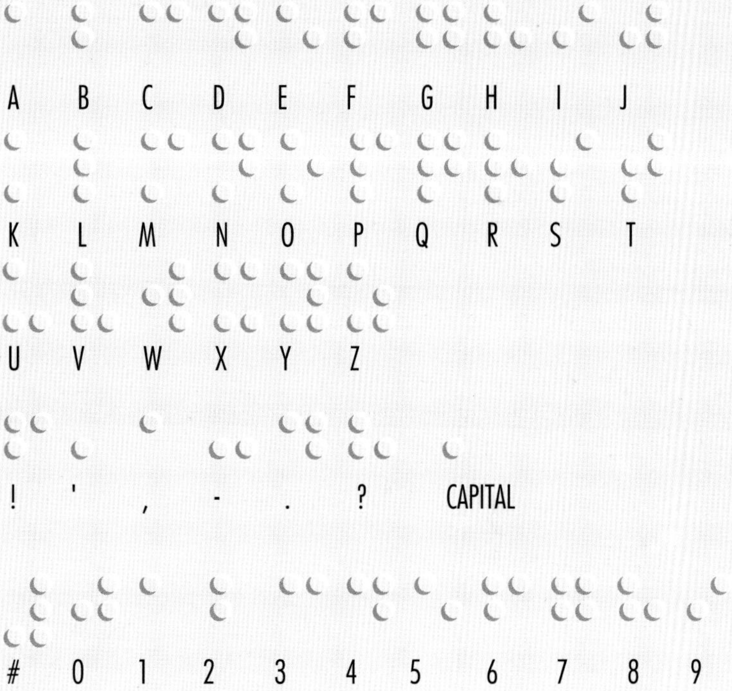

A B C D E F G H I J

K L M N O P Q R S T

U V W X Y Z

! ' , - . ? CAPITAL

0 1 2 3 4 5 6 7 8 9

→ Dots are fundamental to visual communication as well. One of the most popular display configurations for LEDs (light emitting diodes) is the dot matrix—a block of tiny circular lights that are lit to display letters, numbers, or icons. In 5×7 formation, it takes 35 individual LEDs to form one letter. The scrolling dot matrix has been used to convey information from trading floors to Times Square, but the technology is now considered outdated as plasma and LCD (liquid crystal display) monitors can offer much richer information. The graphic language of the dot matrix is consigned to the old school, but remains a source of creative inspiration for low-tech graphics, art, and products.

To be reproducible on press, an original color image, such as a photograph, must first be converted into a pattern of small dots for each of the four colors (CMYK). We don't register these dots, but if you look closely at an advertising hoarding, they are apparent. It's not a new idea. French artists, Seurat and Signac developed pointillism in the late 19th century. In the technique, primary colors of red, yellow, and blue paint are applied in tiny dots or "points." The colors in the painting are mixed in the viewer's mind rather than on the canvas. →

510 and 511 *Pixel tape by Random, UK.*
512 *Pop-out dots allow recipients to design their own snowflake on this Christmas card by design consultancy, Nextbigthing, UK.*
513 *Icons for the Rockerfeller Family Fund, US, designed by Lance Wyman, US.*
514 *Directional signage using LED dots.*
515 *A modern twist on the bedside lamp, by Nic Fraser, UK. Section Lamp reinvents the archetypal lamp profile through a simple manufacturing technique using light gathering acrylic rods and a variety of hardwoods.*

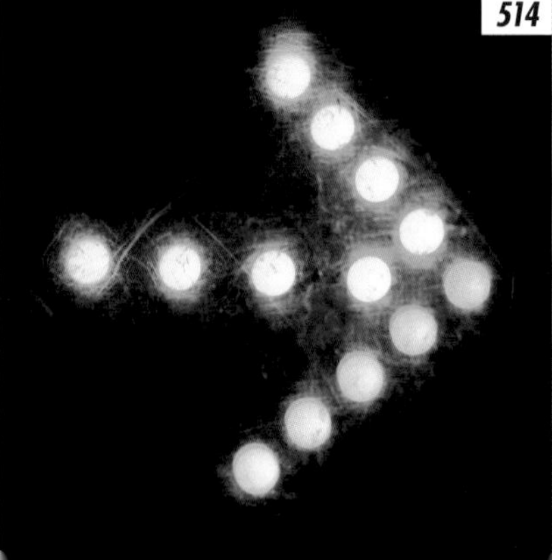

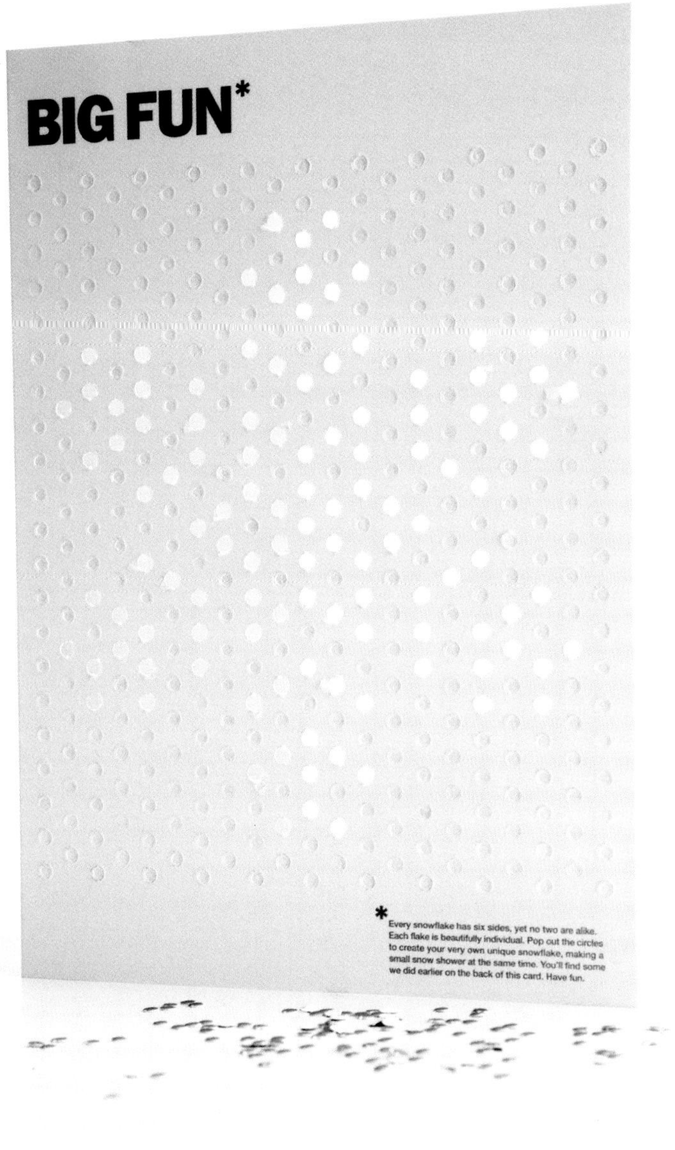

512

BIG FUN*

*Every snowflake has six sides, yet no two are alike. Each flake is beautifully individual. Pop out the circles to create your very own unique snowflake, making a small snow shower at the same time. You'll find some we did earlier on the back of this card. Have fun.

513

→ When viewed under magnification, a print that has been produced using a halftone screen shows a dot pattern, sometimes referred to as Benday dots. One of the key figures of the pop art movement, Roy Lichtenstein, adopted the use of Benday dots in his comic book influenced works. Lichtenstein reproduced these dots by hand with a brush or stencil, conveying shading, tone, and form. They became his signature and continue to be emulated in modern graphics and advertising.

516 *Random, UK's promotional material uses a dot screen.*
517 and 518 *Before and after use of the Schafline process. Jim Sharp, UK, developed Schafline in the 1970s, due to the poor quality of letterpress print on newspaper. It is a dot-enhancing process that creates the illusion of a greater tonal contrast range. News printed inks were not 100% black but only about a 60% tint of black. Halftones in newspapers, Sharp realised, only used a limited amount of tones—he estimated about 10 different tones, where the shadow end of the scale was 85% dot and the highlight end was about 10% dot. Using what is known as "instantaneous contrast," Sharp added an almost invisible, artificial line to the low contrast halftone image, tricking the brain into seeing a greater contrast range.*

519–521 *To accompany "Creative Review" and AGFA Monotypes' series of typographic talks at Pentagram, "V Without Feet," Pentagram, UK, designed this striking set posters, each one bearing the portrait and biography of a pioneer of modernist typography. Herbert Bayer, Max Bil El Lissitzky are all represented, with ASCII-art based port generated by a custom-made 10-dot typeface. From a sh distance, the features of each pioneering typographer be clear. The serif type reflects the subtlety of the portraits, key information about the title, date, and venue of each printed in black, and a short biography of each pioneer p in silver. It is a visual language that conveys a sense of ele and modernism appropriate to each poster's featured pio Designed by Pentagram partner Angus Hyland and Sharon H*

517

518

519

With or without font: a series of talks about type
presented by Creative Review and sponsored by Agfa Monotype

Type on screen

Pentagram 11 Needham Road London W11 2RP Wednesday 14 May 2003 6.30 PM
tickets £10 students £7.50 email aminah.marshall@centaur.co.uk telephone Gavin Lucas 020 7970 6256
in association with Pentagram Design and Gavin Martin Associates

With or without font: a series of talks about type
presented by Creative Review and sponsored by Agfa Monotype

Typography by hand

Pentagram 11 Needham Road London W11 2RP Wednesday 16 July 2003 6.30 PM
tickets £10 students £7.50 email aminah.marshall@centaur.co.uk telephone Gavin Lucas 020 7970 6256
in association with Pentagram Design and Gavin Martin Associates

With or without feet: a series of talks about type
presented by Creative Review and sponsored by Agfa Monotype

New type design

Pentagram 11 Needham Road London W11 2RP Wednesday 19 February 2003 6.30 PM
tickets £10 students £7.50 email aminah.marshall@centaur.co.uk telephone Gavin Lucas 020 7970 6256
in association with Pentagram Design and Gavin Martin Associates

522

523

525

522 Art on the underground. Lichtenstein-influenced mural at 42nd Street subway station, Times Square, New York.
523, 524, and 526 These two promotional windows for the Harvey Nichols department store, London, were designed by Zip Design, UK, and inspired by the large piece of illustrative work, previously created in-house at Zip Design and inspired by elements of classic pop art and the Japanese artist, Keiichi Tanaami.
525 Peacock print displaying CMYK halftone screen effect.

526

“STOP! Look at this:

Lichtenstein introduced speech and thought bubbles into high art—graphic shorthand for communication and ideas. Dots and circles are fundamental to written communication in the form of punctuation too. It's not just about commas and semicolons; we dot above i's and below exclamation marks! The German umlaut indicates a change in vowel sound—schön. Circles are used in copyright © and registered ® signs.

Highlighting elements of punctuation can create standout or add greater depth to identity design—like the full stop that represents the stated mission of UK children's charity, NSPCC.

527 *Punctuation uses dots that help make sense of a sentence.*
528 *Circles and dots are used in all kinds of written communication.*

Interested? Read on, there's more.” to be continued..

ACID

ANTI COPYING IN DESIGN

"Staying ahead of the design game in today's competitive world is a major challenge made increasingly difficult by the threat of design theft, globally. The rise in indiscriminate copying means all designers need to be vigilant and aware of their rights. ACID is a hard-hitting organization set up by designers for designers to help combat intellectual property infringement. The ACID logo incorporates the circular symbol of the copyright C, at a scale not normally used to reinforce ACID's powerful brand of deterrence and prevention against copying."

Dids Macdonald, Chief Executive, ACID (Anti Copying In Design), UK

530

529 ACID (Anti Copying In Design) identity uses an enlarged copyright icon to stress its intentions and purpose.
530 Captain Memo notes from Worldwide Co, UK.
531 Exclamation mark on building site warning signage.
532 The UK charity, NSPCC identity uses a period, or full stop, symbolizing an end to child cruelty.
533 Minale Tattersfield, UK, created the branding for a free commuter newspaper to be piloted in Milan. The name "City" refers to its urban location. The dots on top of the masthead seem to be revolving—passing by in a hurry like its readership.
534 Identity for Tamarind, an Indian cuisine condiments range. By highlighting the dot of the i in the logo, Lewis Moberly created a strong visual identity that is understated yet striking, with a little bit of heat.
535 Peacocks is a leading UK value-for-money retailer of clothing, footwear, and homewares. Using the thought bubble in its identity indicates the great range of ideas in store.

531

NSPCC
TM
Cruelty to children must stop. FULL STOP.

533

535

534

tamarind

Public Signs

The simplicity of the circle makes it the ideal shape to communicate information in the public domain. The circle has a no-nonsense profile, less noisy than the warning triangle, yet more arresting than the neutral square. Orders and instructions are printed in circles and the color-coding helps clarify the nature of the communication. Red circles are usually prohibitive: no entry, no smoking, no motor vehicles. Blue circles offer more positive instruction: wear safety gear, turn right, cycles only.

Perhaps because they contrast effectively with the right angles of the urban landscape, circles make effective public signage. London Underground's distinctive roundel has acted as a beacon for tired London pedestrians for nearly a century, while the letters and numbers that identify the lines on the New York Subway are all the more effective, contained as they are in color-coded circles. →

536–539, 541, and 542 *Public signage.*
540 *Dots on windows prevent accidents.*
543 *Danger, low flying dogs! Photo by Mark Strozier.*

DANGER!

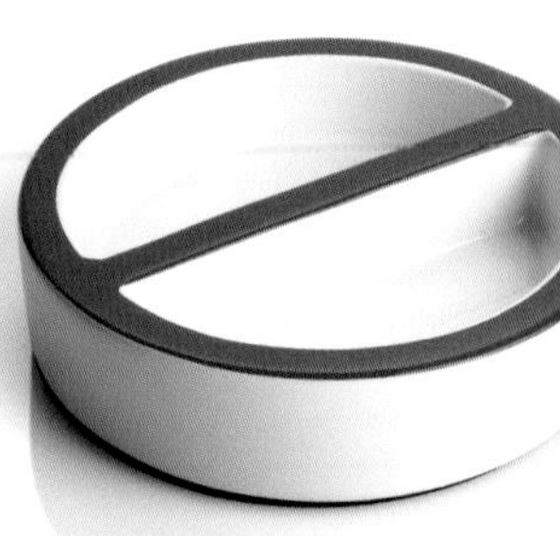

544, 546, 547, 549, 550, 552, and 553
Public signs.
545 *All Zones clock design based on the original Gants Hill Station clock. © Transport for London.*
548 *The London Underground roundel was first introduced on station platforms in 1908. Edward Johnston applied his sans serif typeface to the bar and circle in 1916. © Transport for London.*
551 *The Don't Ashtray by Josh Owen for Kikkerland, US, employs graphic iconography negatively to influence the smoker against his or her habit, while at the same time providing a receptacle for it.*
555 *London Underground logo luggage tag by Authentics, UK, for All Zones. © Transport for London.*
556 *New York subway signage indicates lines in circles.*

547
548
UNDERGROUND
552
554
555
UNDERGROUND
556
14 Street Statior
F
L
1
2
3
9

→ So universally recognized are the red, amber, and green of the traffic light sequence that their colored circles are used for more than just regulating traffic flow. The red light is bold and stands for danger, amber alerts us to be cautious, and green offers permission and encouragement.

The traffic light system of signage offers many graphic possibilities and has been recommended by the UK Food Standards Agency to help consumers understand the levels of potentially unhealthy additives in food: green, meaning eat plenty; amber, in moderation; and red, eat sparingly.

557

__557__ Pedestrian traffic lights.
__558__ A version of the traffic light system used on railwa
__559__ Signage indicating end of temporary traffic lights.
__560__ Standard UK traffic lights.
__561__ The Australian sign for "traffic lights ahead."
__562–564__ Leo Reynolds spotted this signage in a restaurant in the US—it clearly gives its customers the green light to indulge.
__565__ Detail of Traffic Light Tree, a sculpture by artist Pier Vivant, erected in London's Docklands in 1998. Photo ta by Hector Loudon.
__566__ Traffic lights for cyclists and pedestrians.

559
560
561
563
EAT-H
564
EAT
565
566

567
Nathan Walker
Walked past here 47
times during 1968
on the 21st May 1968
he looked up
568
David Williams
Watched the rain
from here
7th September 1979
Anne Huxtable
Waited for a Friend
Who did not arrive
8th December 1952

Commemoration and Awards

Our cities are full of commemorative circles: on sidewalks, designating the routes of memorial walkways; on buildings and edifices, indicating the date erected or identifying famous past residents. Their circular form in brass or enamel sits in contrast to rectangular bricks and stone, making them a prominent feature.

Since the 1850s, London's blue plaques have celebrated actors, authors, politicians, painters, scientists, sportsmen, campaigners, and reformers by indicating where they lived, died, or achieved success. The Society of Arts erected its first plaque—to poet, Lord Byron—in 1867 and there are now around 760 in London. English Heritage has extended the scheme countrywide with plaques in Merseyside, Birmingham, and Portsmouth. Their distinctive white type on blue has, arguably, become the generic style for commemorative plaques. Using these colors in a circular form immediately contextualizes any art or cultural piece based on them. →

567–570 *Celebrating the mundane: these commemora street plaques in Newcastle upon Tyne, UK, by locally base artist, Rupert Clamp, formed part of the "Art for the Stree project, originated by the Grainger Town Partnership. Imag by Sam Judson.*
571 *Plaques can commemorate a variety of events and occurrences—like this Muhammad Ali plaque in Norwich,*
572–577 *Photographer, Leo Reynolds, collected these different commemorative plaques, which range from datin display at the Chelsea Flower Show, UK, to the stones set facades of buildings, commemorating the date they were*

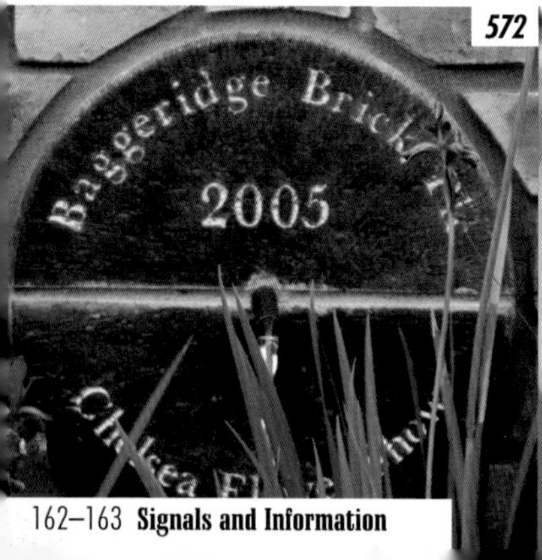

570
Mrs Mary Howard
Adjusted her hat
In the reflection in
this window
3rd June 1921
571
MUHAMMAD ALI
World Heavyweight boxing champion
visited a supermarket on this site
on 19 October 1971 as part of a
promotional tour for Ovaltine.
The Eastern Daily Press
Norwich School of Art & Design
575
VR
576
1907
577
2001

578

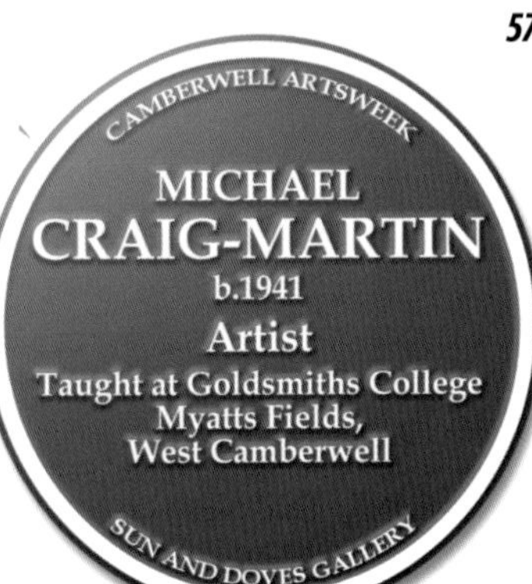

CAMBERWELL ARTSWEEK
MICHAEL
CRAIG-MARTIN
b.1941
Artist
Taught at Goldsmiths College
Myatts Fields,
West Camberwell
SUN AND DOVES GALLERY

579

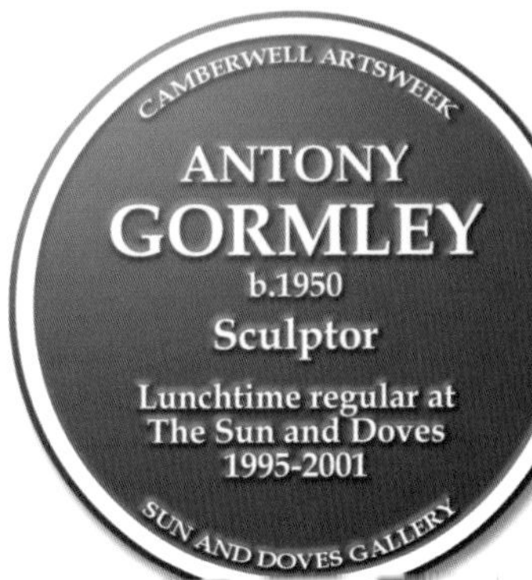

CAMBERWELL ARTSWEEK
ANTONY
GORMLEY
b.1950
Sculptor
Lunchtime regular at
The Sun and Doves
1995-2001
SUN AND DOVES GALLERY

CAMBERWELL ARTSWEEK
CHRIS
OFILI
b.1968
Painter
Was showing at
the Sun and Doves Gallery
when he won the
Turner Prize in
1998

581

CAMBERWELL ARTSWEEK
BRYAN
FERRY
b.1945
Newcastle Upon Tyne
Jealous guy
Had sausage and mash at the
Sun and Doves 2004
SUN AND DOVES GALLERY

582

584

578–585 *Celebrating the Camberwell area of London where it is based, the Sun and Doves Gallery produced these faux commemorative plaques to highlight some events in its 10-year life span and promote its exhibition of local artists' work.*
586 *An example of one of London's blue plaques, celebrating the city's great and good, which influenced the Sun and Doves Gallery pastiche.*

CAMBERWELL ARTSWEEK
LORRAINE
CHASE
b.1952
Eighties actress,
model and singer
Lives in Camberwell
SUN AND DOVES GALLERY

1879 - 1905

SIR
GEORGE
WILLIAMS
1821-1905
Founder of the
Young Men's
Christian
Association

LIVED AT NO. 13 RUSSELL SQUARE

→ The wreath signifies both commemoration and award. Wreaths of laurel leaves were awarded to victorious athletes in the Ancient Greek Olympic games. The Romans used them to crown military heroes and instigated the practice of hanging wreaths on walls as a sign of victory. Used by brands like Fred Perry, Cadillac, and Sheraton Hotels, the laurel wreath still signifies a winning spirit and quality standard.

The more solemn association of wreaths is with death and remembrance, dating back to the Romans' use of them, carved on sarcophagi and subsequently on gravestones. Every year, on Remembrance Sunday, the Queen lays a wreath on the cenotaph in London in honor of those who died in service. The poppy is the symbol of the Royal British Legion, poignantly chosen because it was the only thing that grew on the fields of Flanders and Picardy, Northern France, in the aftermath of WWI battles. →

587 and 592 *Remembrance Day at the Cenotaph in London, UK.*
588 and 589 *Commemorative wreaths carved in gravestor*
590 *War memorial at Our Lady of Peace Church (RC), Ca Gardens, Brooklyn, US.*
591 *Banner celebrating the 60th anniversary of Victory ir Europe Day, seen here in Red Square, Moscow, Russia.*
593 *A reminder of Flanders Fields: paper poppy wreath tc remember the fallen in WWI and WWII.*

594 *Kings Park War Memorial, Perth, Western Australia.*
595 *Russian V-E Day commemorative banner.*
596 *These silver plaques indicate the route of the Silver Jubilee Walkway—laid to commemorate the Queen's Silver Jubilee in 1977. They guide London visitors along a walk which begins in Leicester Square and includes the City and the South Bank, before ending at Westminster.*
597 *As part of the Cabin project, Jules Goss and Graham Hufton, Canada, created the HWY 400 series of plates, evoking the nostalgia of camping vacations through the combination of the highway that takes you there and the campfire icon.*
598 *Reinventing the collectible plate—the 1930s Modernist London Homes series by UK designers, People Will Always Need Plates.*

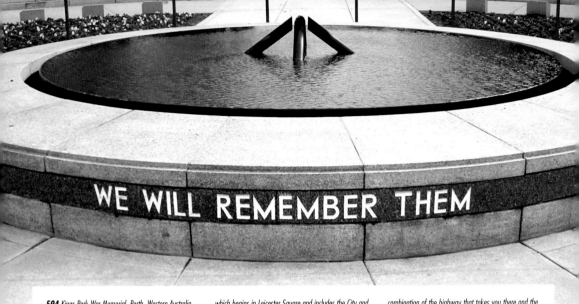

"People Will Always Need Plates aim to use high quality, low volume batch production to create witty, thoughtful, and stylish products as a direct antithesis to the current proliferation of cheap, throwaway design. In keeping with our credo that good design should be used and enjoyed, treasured and shared, we develop products that, while diverse in style and application, always retain the fundamental values of functionality and beauty. 1930s Modernist London Homes is a set of six English bone china plates illustrating the minimal beauty of white-rendered pre-war modern masterpieces across London. There are six images in six colors and, in keeping with the tradition of collectible plates, each image is a limited edition."

Hannah and Robin, People Will Always Need Plates, UK

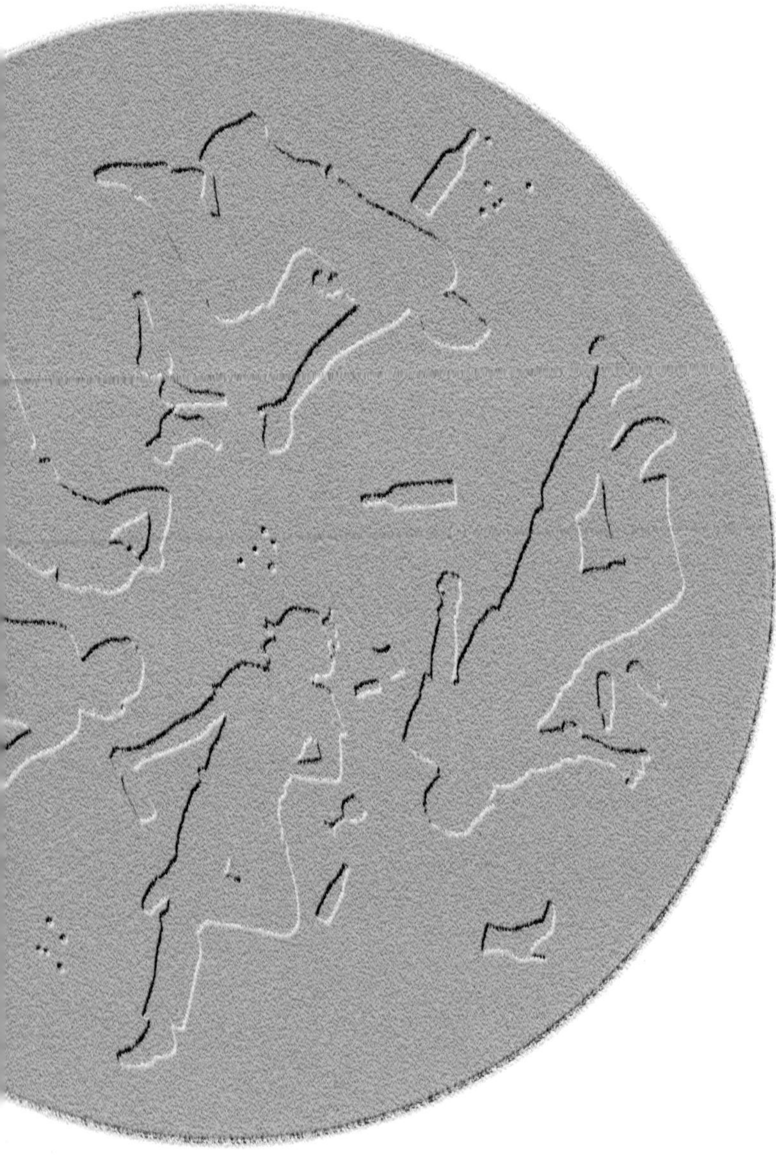

→ The symbolism of the circle is perhaps most overt in the ring. As a symbol of eternity, it represents the lasting devotion between two people. The cultural significance of rings is changing from the notion of ownership (Samuel Johnson described the ring as "a circular instrument placed upon the noses of hogs and the fingers of women to restrain them and bring them into subjection") to a symbol of equality. Imagine the most intimate ring you could share with your partner—one that is crafted from your bone cells. That's the basis of the Biojewellery project—a collaboration between the Royal College of Art and King's College, London, UK. →

599 *Josh Owen's All-American Party Carpet humorously commemorates decadent lifestyles by graphically depicting debris from the aftermath of an indulgent party.*
600, 602, and 605 *Biojewellery, UK, is a collaborative project involving Tobie Kerridge and Nikki Stott, design researchers at the Royal College of Art, and Ian Thompson, a bioengineer at King's College, London. A couple's cells will be prepared and seeded onto a bioactive scaffold. This pioneering material encourages the cells to divide and grow rapidly in a laboratory environment, so that the scaffold disappears and is replaced by living bone tissue. Following consultation with the couple, the bone will be combined with traditional precious metals so that each has a ring made with the tissue of his or her partner.*
601 *Christmas card for jeweller, Temple St Clair, US, by design consultancy, Nextbigthing, UK.*
603 *A model of a Biojewellery ring, using a combination of cow marrowbone and etched silver. The inscription reads ab intra (from within).*
604 *Karl Fritsch's rings are made from damaged or melted mass-manufactured jewelry, often free modeled to create pieces that are intensely intimate (for instance, marked with his fingerprints) and responsive to the life of the owner.*
606 *The simple beauty of the Swell ring by intoto, US, dispenses with the need for a precious stone.*

600

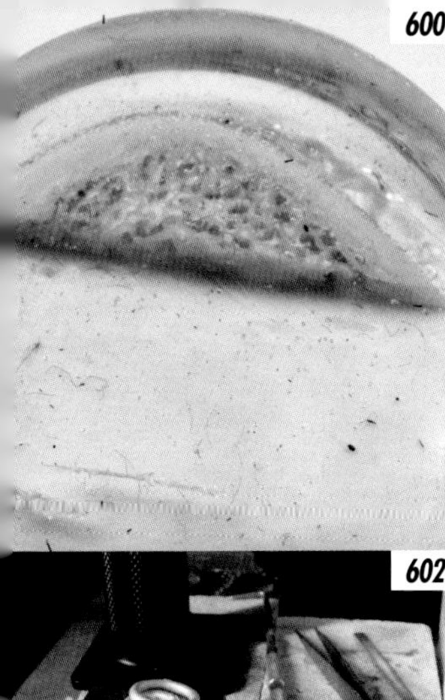

601

FIVE GOLD RINGS

602

603

604

605

606

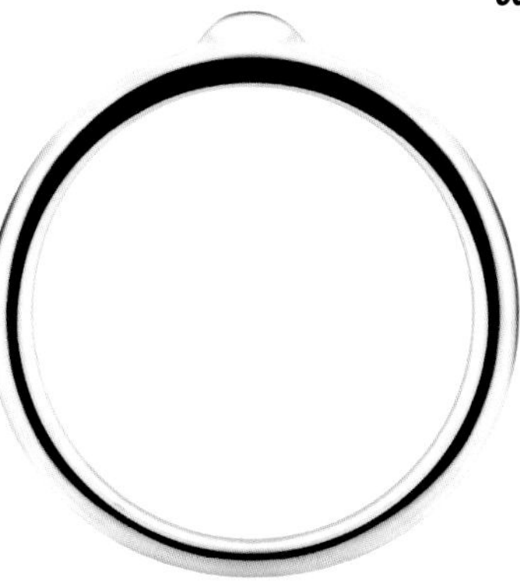

→ The circle is often used to signify the bestowing of an award or as a stamp of authority—in medals, quality seals, rosettes, and guarantees. Medals are a recognized symbol of merit, having moved beyond their military and sporting origins into the consumer domain. The alcohol sector stages regular world championships, with gold, silver, and bronze medals handed out to wines and spirits of distinction. →

607

609

607 *British Red Cross WWI Service medal.*
608 and 613 *Both sides of a Victorian Jubilee commemorative medal.*
609 *The identity to accompany the British Manchester Olympic Bid by Minale Tattersfield, UK, uses the iconography of the familiar sporting medal award.*
610 *Buildings of distinction in Miami Beach are eligible for a facade award.*
611 *A simple award sign from the UK city of Norwich.*
612 *Funrun medal, 2004.*
614 *The medals of Mark Laforet L-R): medal from service in the United Nations Emergency Force in the Sinai (UNEF), the 1988 Nobel Peace Prize, and peacekeeping service medal bestowed by the government of Canada.*

611

612

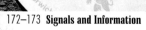

THE NOBEL PEACE PRIZE
1988
UN
PEACEKEEPING
SERVICE DE LA PAIX

→ When brands want to signify quality they often use a series of medal-style icons that are not based on real authority, but offer a subliminal sense of reassurance to the customer. Seals, embossing, ribbons, and circular stamps all act as a mark of authority that the contemporary designer can manipulate to create brand standout and consumer confidence.

615 *Rosettes won by photographer Lisa Brockmeier's dog.*
616 *A rosette design added gravitas to the (now defunct) British Motor Corporation identity.*
617 *A gold seal.*
618 and 620 *Russian Standard vodka's brand identity and packaging by Identica, UK, uses a seal depicting a bear and eagle, created as an emblem of Russian heritage.*
619 *Artist, Emily Clay, UK, mixes medals, branding, and heraldry in her work to create a sense of uneasiness.*
621 *The Chrysler seal suggests quality engineering.*
622 *A symbol of success, the classic laurel wreath communicates quality and high standards.*
623 *Wrestling Palace entrance, Ulaanbaatar, Mongolia, showing the various levels of awards attainable.*

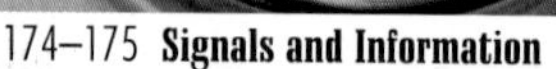

617
CIRCUIT COURT
620
623
Русский
Стандарт
Original
RUSSIAN STANDARD
Original
EXPORT

624

625

Dials and Measures

Clocks in their current form have been in use since the 14th century. The classic round "face" of the analog clock is particularly satisfying because it displays the increments of time in a circle. The second hand makes a 360º sweep in 60 seconds; the minute hand completes the circle in 60 minutes. We're so familiar with the positions of the hands that many clocks dispense with numbers. Predecessor of the clock is the sundial—circular, perhaps, in homage to the sun. The gnomon is the arm that casts the shadow, and on many sundials it visually replicates the hands of a clock, though it is the shadow it casts that indicates the time.

Clocks can evoke civic pride—the Victorians were keen on erecting clocks in public squares and railway stations, on town halls and libraries. In retail design, clocks are frequently used to communicate convenience, making a virtue of a shop's long opening hours. →

630

631

624 The 24 hour clock at the Royal Observatory, Greenwich, UK.
625, 627, 628, 630, and 631 Clocks and timepieces come in many designs, from traditional clock faces to sundials.
626 It's not only the time of day that can be measured on circular dials—as this circular calendar shows.
629 M Worldwide, UK, created the logo for 10-11, a chain of Icelandic convenience stores, incorporating the clock face to stress the benefits of its long opening hours
632 A simple watch face is evoked in the identity for watch brand, Sekonda, by Pentagram, UK.
633 Holes punched in a circular calendar disc indicate either a commencement or expiry date.
634 The Image projection clock by Habitat, UK, creates a sense of drama in a room by projecting the image of a traditional clock on to the wall.

→ The circle is uniquely equipped to perform the task of a dial because of its perfect symmetry, allowing it to turn on its own central point. This function is key to any measuring device that uses hands and circular calibrations—scales, barometers, speedometers, compasses, pressure gauges, tuning devices, and thermostats are all frequently circular. They have a low-tech clunkiness that is often more comforting than digital updates. Design solutions that stray from the classic circle are often controversial—one example was the Cyclops Eye speedometer, introduced to the 1970 Citroën GS, which swapped conventional dials for a revolving cylinder with road speeds and braking distances indicated simultaneously through a magnifying viewer. Innovation, or design for design's sake?

The compass, invented in Ancient China, was key to man's navigation of the seas. Before the invention of the magnetic compass, sailors used celestial navigation, employing the sun, moon, planets, and stars to plot a fixed point. This often meant no sailing during winter when clear skies were unlikely. The design language of compasses still evokes both maritime and astronomical themes—often surrounded by nautical icons or representations of the constellations, linking the compass back to its original use.

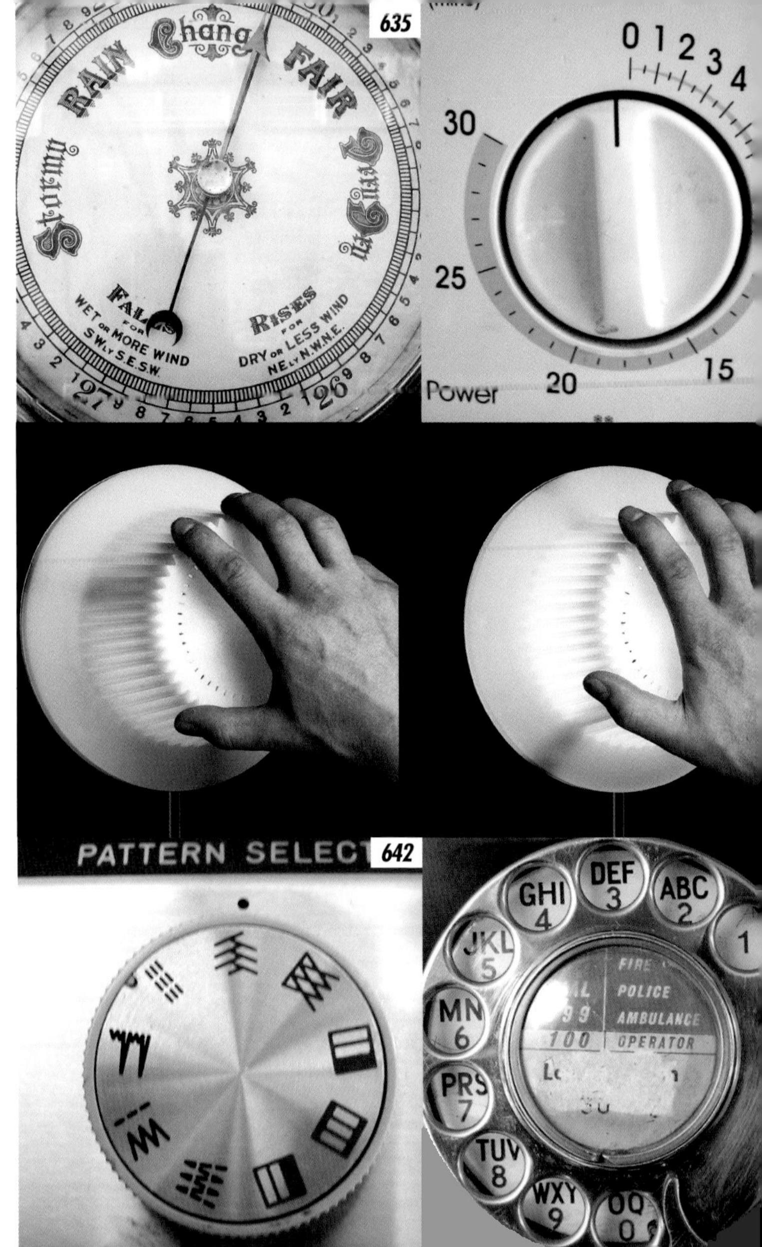

635 *A traditional barometer indicates rain or shine.*
636 and 637 *Dials are commonplace around the home, used to count down the minutes on a tumble dryer, or regulate the central heating thermostat.*
638 *Apple's iPod click wheel.*
639 *Circular meters measure energy consumption.*
640 *The Tone Knob, by Josh Owen, US, for Umbra, is a mutable lighting object, referencing the old analog knobs on musical equipment. When rotated, the giant knob can glow brighter or dimmer and can be configured to shed more or less light on its surroundings.*

637

638

639

640

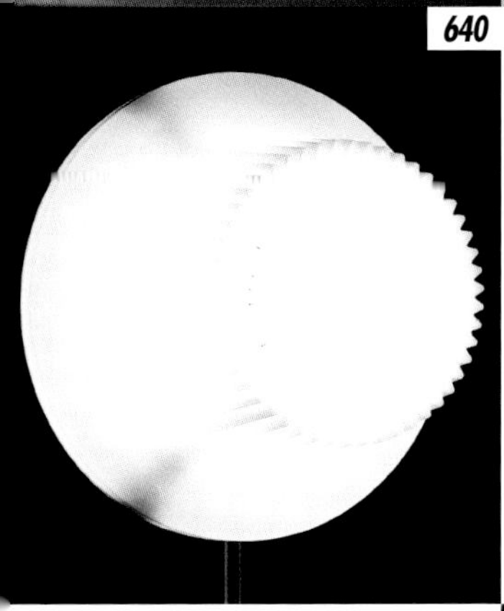

641

641 *Before the invention of the magnetic compass, sailors used the constellations to navigate at sea. Star charts and compass graphics are a fitting combination in this elegant piece by glassware designers Rimmington Vian, UK.*
642 *This dial on a home sewing machine allows for the selection of different kinds of stitch.*
643 *Before Touch-Tone, telephones had dials, not buttons. This worked perfectly well when there were fewer people connected, but the introduction of direct dialling and more connections meant longer numbers—a laborious process when waiting for the dial to return to its original position after dialing each number.*
644 *Designed by Scott Wilson, US, for Nike, the Alti-Compass watch combines a timepiece, compass, altimeter, and barometer. The real time digital compass needle always points north.*
645 and 646 *Two different types of compass.*

644

645

646

647 A vintage Avery coin operated public weighing machine.
648 Kitchen scales.
649–651 The Cook's Measure, designed by Mary Rose Cook, UK, combines a measuring device, recipe, and the means to line a cake tin. Weights of ingredients are measured by creating a cone from the circle of paper and filling with a volume of the dry ingredient.
652 Pressure is measured in bars.
653 Battery tester.
654 Measuring seconds.
655 A tuning dial on a vintage style radio indicates frequencies and global broadcasting locations.
656 Developed by the Egyptians, the abacus divides numbers into units, tens, hundreds, and so on. This installation, by Lost Found Art, US, is a unique design using primitive folk art and vintage abacuses, which they recommend for the walls of any future accountant or investment banker.

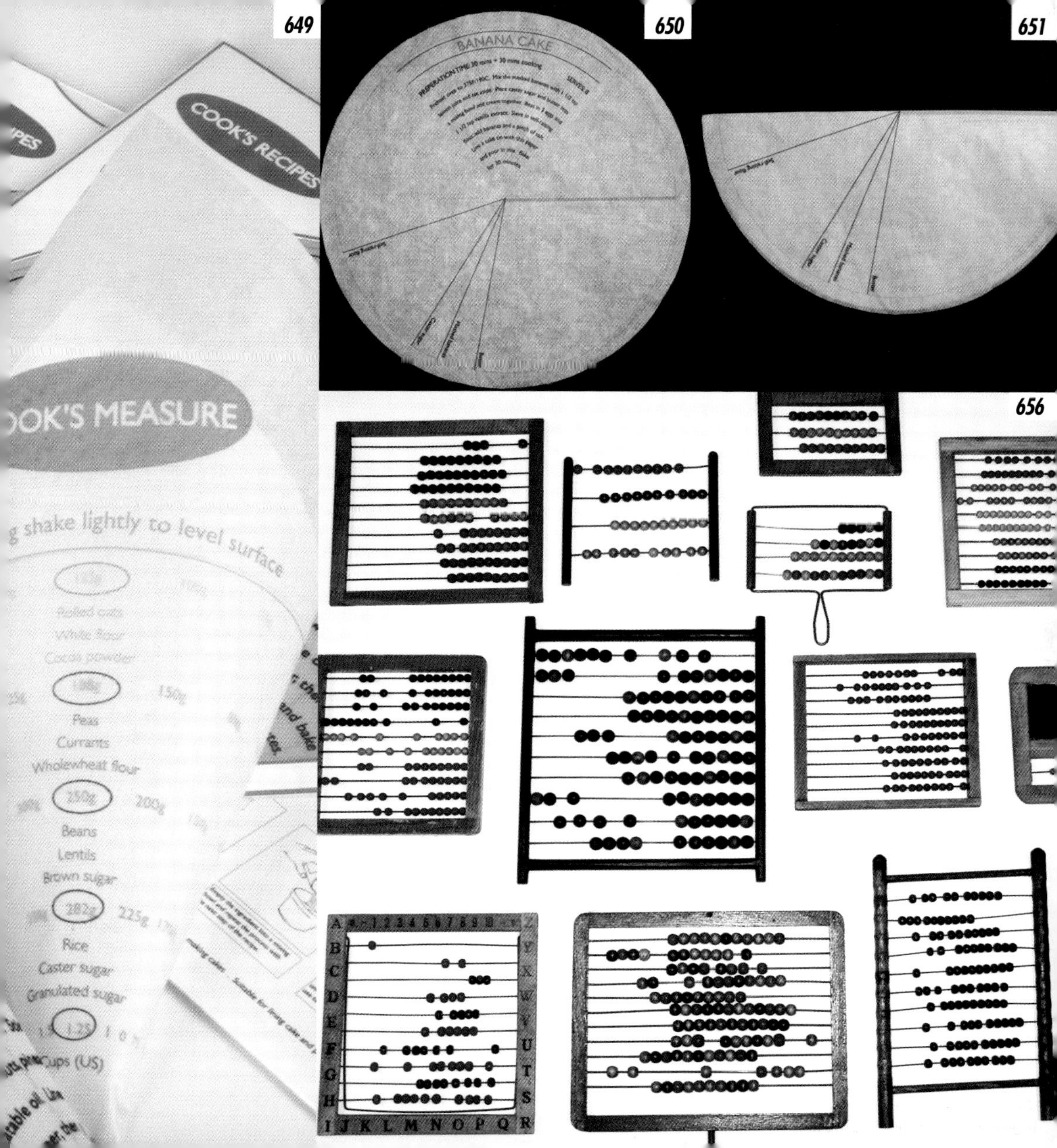
649
650
651
656
COOK'S RECIPES
OK'S MEASURE
g shake lightly to level surface
Rolled oats
White flour
Cocoa powder
150g
Peas
Currants
Wholewheat flour
250g
200g
Beans
Lentils
Brown sugar
282g
225g
Rice
Caster sugar
Granulated sugar
Cups (US)
BANANA CAKE
A B C D E F G H I J K L M N O P Q R S T U V W X Y Z

657

662

Coins

It's sad to think that when society becomes cashless, as social commentators predict, we will lose coins. Since they were invented in Asia Minor during the 7th century BC, coins have been used both as a medium for exchange and for artistic expression, offering historians cultural information about previous civilizations. The first coins were struck from electrum (an alloy of gold and silver) in what is now Turkey, and stamped with a mark to signal their weight and purity. The Greeks and Romans heightened the art of the coin, employing master engravers and introducing realistic portraiture. They spread the coinage system throughout the lands they conquered.

Coins continue to perform a multitude of functions. While their primary function as financial tokens might be in jeopardy, coins also act as national identifiers—their symbols and icons all carefully chosen to reflect a country's sovereignty, political, or cultural heritage. Like stamps, they are frequently used to mark anniversaries or events and perhaps their future lies in their role as commemorative keepsakes.

667

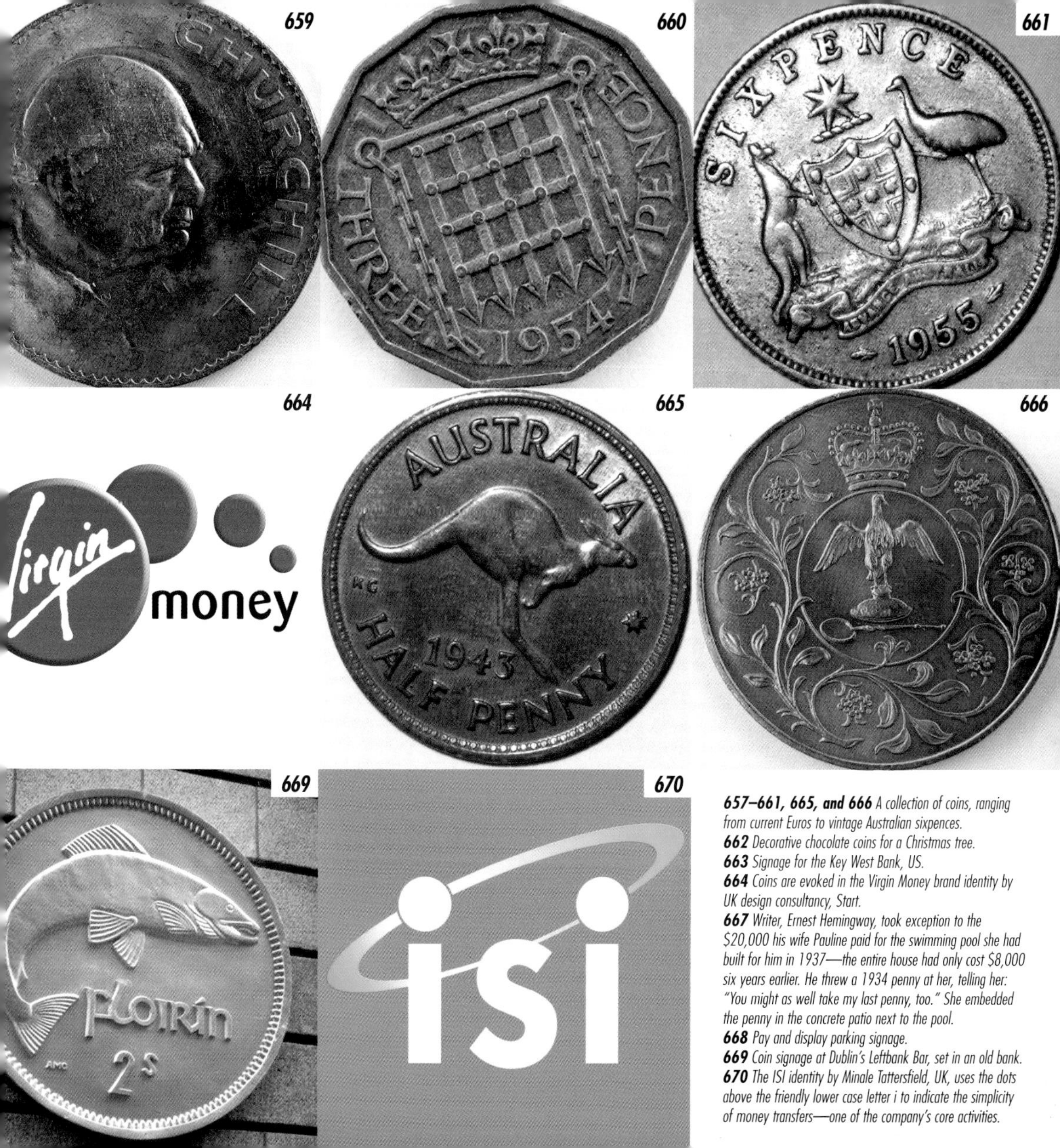

657–661, 665, and 666 *A collection of coins, ranging from current Euros to vintage Australian sixpences.*
662 *Decorative chocolate coins for a Christmas tree.*
663 *Signage for the Key West Bank, US.*
664 *Coins are evoked in the Virgin Money brand identity by UK design consultancy, Start.*
667 *Writer, Ernest Hemingway, took exception to the $20,000 his wife Pauline paid for the swimming pool she had built for him in 1937—the entire house had only cost $8,000 six years earlier. He threw a 1934 penny at her, telling her: "You might as well take my last penny, too." She embedded the penny in the concrete patio next to the pool.*
668 *Pay and display parking signage.*
669 *Coin signage at Dublin's Leftbank Bar, set in an old bank.*
670 *The ISI identity by Minale Tattersfield, UK, uses the dots above the friendly lower case letter i to indicate the simplicity of money transfers—one of the company's core activities.*

Optical effects

When 1950s movie theater audiences first saw the spinning spiral effects in the opening title sequence of Hitchcock's *Vertigo*, they were witnessing some of the earliest optical effects to be used in mainstream movies. Created by avant-garde animator, John Whitney, Saul Bass incorporated them into his title sequence to mirror the spiral visual motifs in the movie. We associate spirals with trance-like states induced by hypnotists—with disorientation and uneasiness—but there's an esthetic side to the spiral too. In the hands of artists and designers, the spiral can be manipulated to create results that are optically playful, beautiful, and even magical.

The phenomenon of the optical illusion can be explained as the brain misinterpreting the information it receives from the eye. The more disruptive the pattern being viewed, the more likely it is to confound the brain. An abundance of dots creates a disruptive pattern and when their size, shape, and scale are further distorted, the results can defy logic. Large circles can be deceptive too. Concentric circles can create false perspective, or, overlayered on a different pattern, can create perplexing moiré effects.

672

673

674

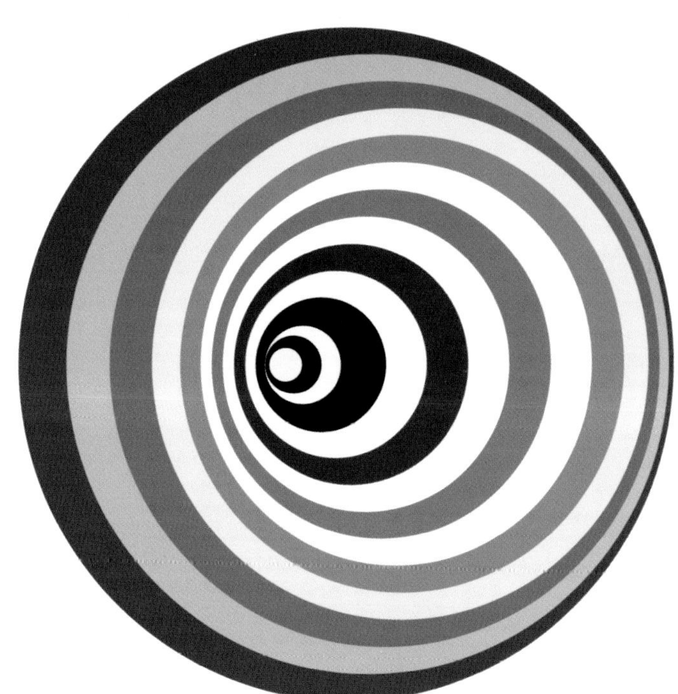

675

671 *This illusion starts to turn slowly the longer you look at it. It helps if you focus on a point to one side of the image.*
672 *Donating to charity can be a visually exciting experience—watch your coins swirl around this op art collecting box.*

673 and 676 *Moxbox, US, creates contemporary furniture with a retro feel by using a modern twist on marquetry to create their design pieces.*
674 *Using op art circles can add a groovy touch to interiors.*
675 *Concentric circles in tones create an illusion of depth.*

676

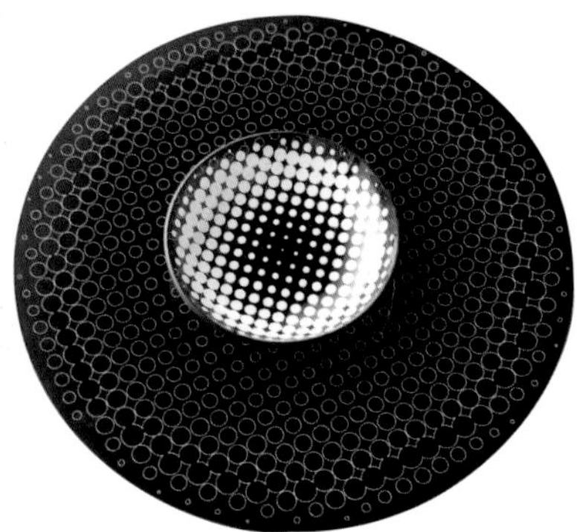

"We are not symmetrical, symmetry does not really exist in nature, a straight line does not even exist in human nature but the biomorphic, the curve, the undulation, the irregular, the skewed, the ovaloid—they exist in nature. So I squash circles, I need to squeeze them a bit, put some tension in them, make a circle more seductive, more characteristic, create consternation, give a circle some personality and individualism. I like the imperfection of the perfect. But circles and perfection are beautiful too and will always be the epitome of our esthetic culture ad infinitum. So sacred, the circle."

Karim Rashid, US

677 *The Bubble platter and dip, by Joseph Joseph, UK.*
678 *2D becomes 3D when circles are uniformly distorted to create a circular fish eye bulge.*
679 *Karim Rashid, US, plays with the perspective of these dots on his Infinity Vase designs.*
680 *Splitting the circle in four quarters produces a myriad of patterns and configurations—as seen in the Thumb Puzzle Table, by Douglas Homer, US, which uses movable tiles for concealed storage.*

681
685
686
516 398-2

683

689

688

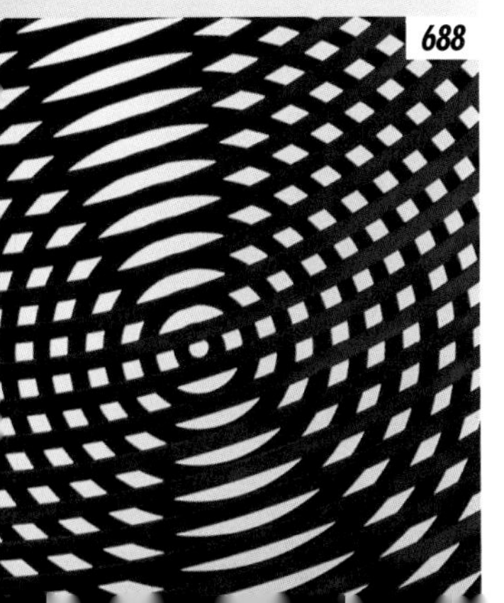

690

681 *"Photo Souvenir: Les Visages Colorés" by Daniel Buren, Buchmann Galerie, Cologne, 2005.*
682 and 687 *Squares and circles don't sit well together—they fight for visual dominance. In the first example, the circle appears to bend the square and in the second, the square makes the perfect circles look elliptical.*
683 and 688 *Australian sculptor, Matthew Harding, uses laser-cutting technology to create the 20:20 screen.*
684 *This CD looks like it plays some pretty warped sounds.*
685 *Aitali K3-PL chair, by Karim Rashid, US.*
686 *Aitali K2-DL chair, by Karim Rashid, US.*
689 and 690 *Stereolab's "Dots and Loops" CD covers, designed by Intro, UK, use optically challenging circles that reflect the clean lines of the band's modernist pop.*

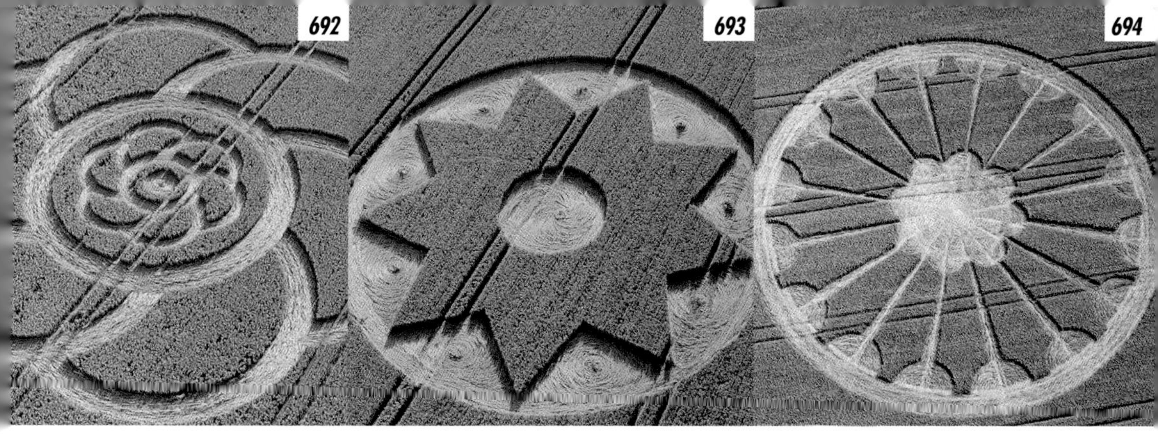

Crop Circles

Signs of extraterrestrial life or skilfully executed feats of the human imagination? Whatever your opinion, there's no denying the crop circle's allure, both as extraordinary design and newsworthy occurrence. The first one was reported in 1972 near Warminster, UK, when two men looking for UFOs witnessed a large circular area of plants collapse within 20 seconds. Since then, debate has raged about their origins. In one camp are the believers in unexplained forces—spaceships, aliens, wind and rain activity, natural energies, and even human telepathic fields have been proposed. In the other camp are those who promote themselves as crop circle makers, creating their art with a surveyor's tape and a plank of wood. The annual UK "Cornference" provides a forum for debate. →

691–702, 704, and 705 *Steve Alexander took all these amazing aerial views of crop circles for his Web site, www.temporarytemples.co.uk, which documents more than a decade of his recording crop circles in the UK.*
691 *This is an image taken in 2002 of Eastfield, Alton Barnes, Wiltshire, UK, which has been home to some of the most elaborate and spectacular crop circles ever seen.*
692 *All Cannings, Wiltshire, UK, 2000.*
693 *All Cannings, Wiltshire, UK, 2000.*
694 *Alton Priors, Wiltshire, UK, 2000.*
695 *Avebury Henge, Wiltshire, UK, 2002.*
696 *Avebury Trusloe, Wiltshire, UK, 2000.*
697 *Etchilhampton, Wiltshire, UK, 2002.*

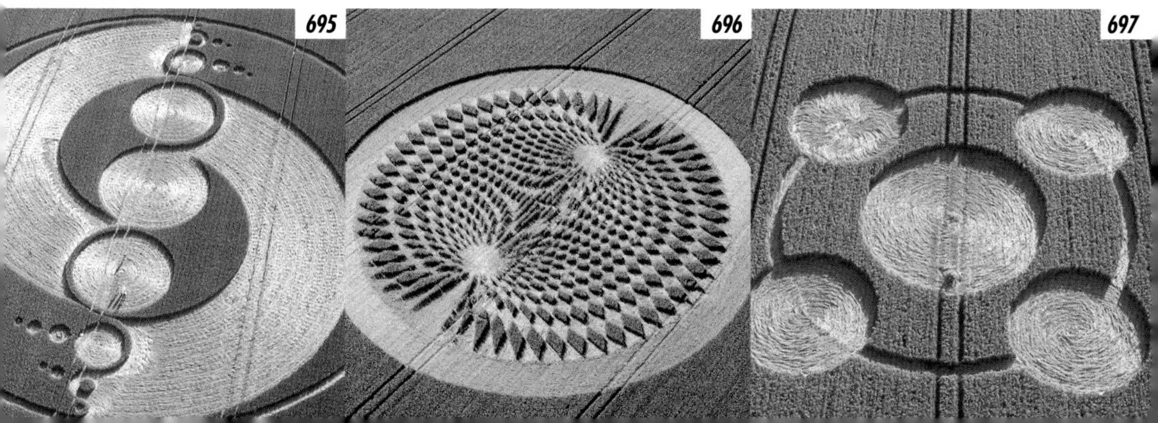

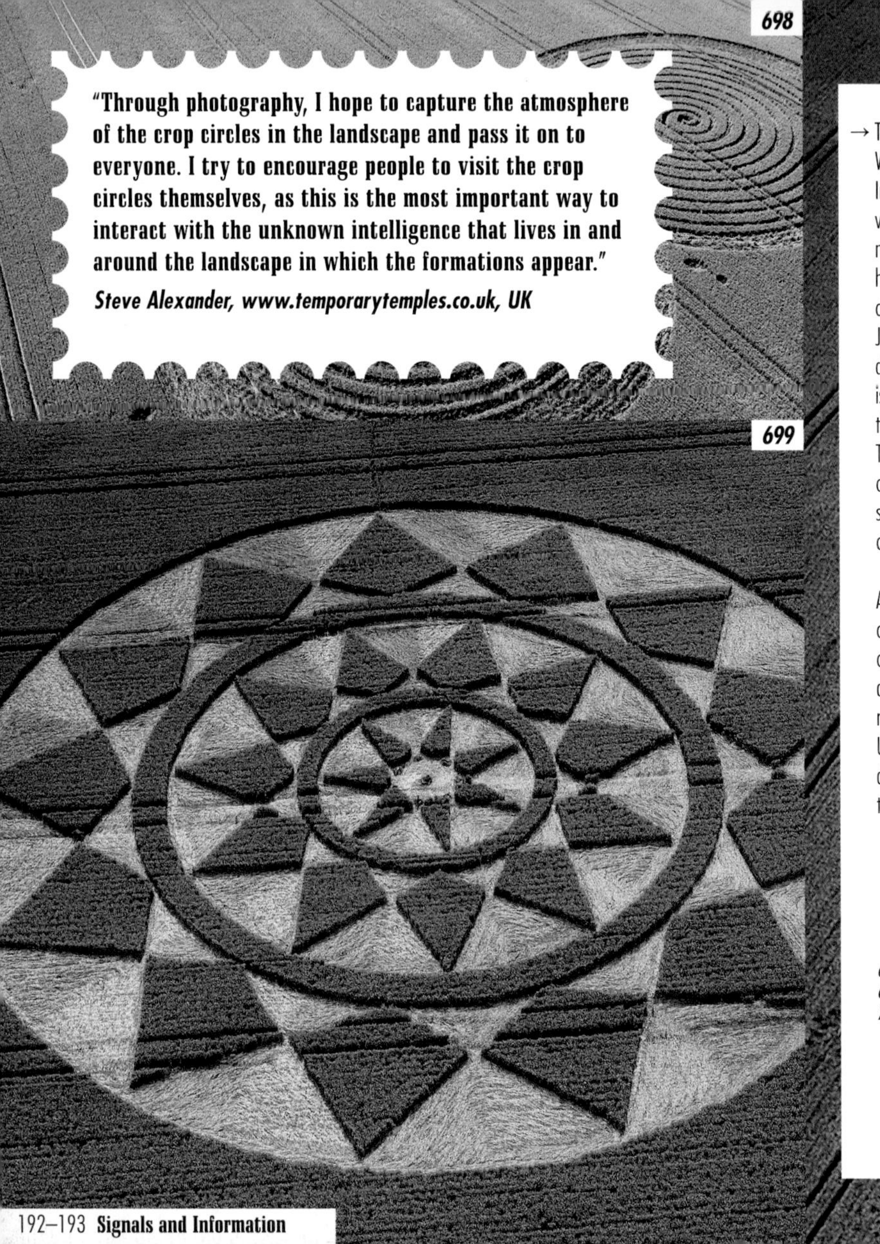

"Through photography, I hope to capture the atmosphere of the crop circles in the landscape and pass it on to everyone. I try to encourage people to visit the crop circles themselves, as this is the most important way to interact with the unknown intelligence that lives in and around the landscape in which the formations appear."

Steve Alexander, www.temporarytemples.co.uk, UK

→ Treated as legitimate tourist attractions Wiltshire, UK, circles can be big busines In 1996, one circle got around 30,00 visitors in a month—more than neighboring Stonehenge. The circle mak have their calendar well planned. April circles are made in fields of oilseed rap June circles are in barley. The best circle don't appear until mid-July when the w is in crop and each stem is upright, givi the designs the highest possible definitic To perpetuate an element of myth, crop circle makers push the designs to extrer so that the public will question how the could possibly be made by humans.

As mediums for signals and information corn circles are often used in PR stunts. circle promoting the UK's 2012 Olympic appeared in a French field, days before result was announced. France lost to th UK. Believer or nonbeliever, there's no denying the beauty and sheer impact of these intriguing designs. →

698 *Porchester, Hampshire, UK, 2004.*
699 *Etchilhampton, Wiltshire, UK, 2004.*
700 *Silbury Hill, Avebury, UK, 2004.*

700

703

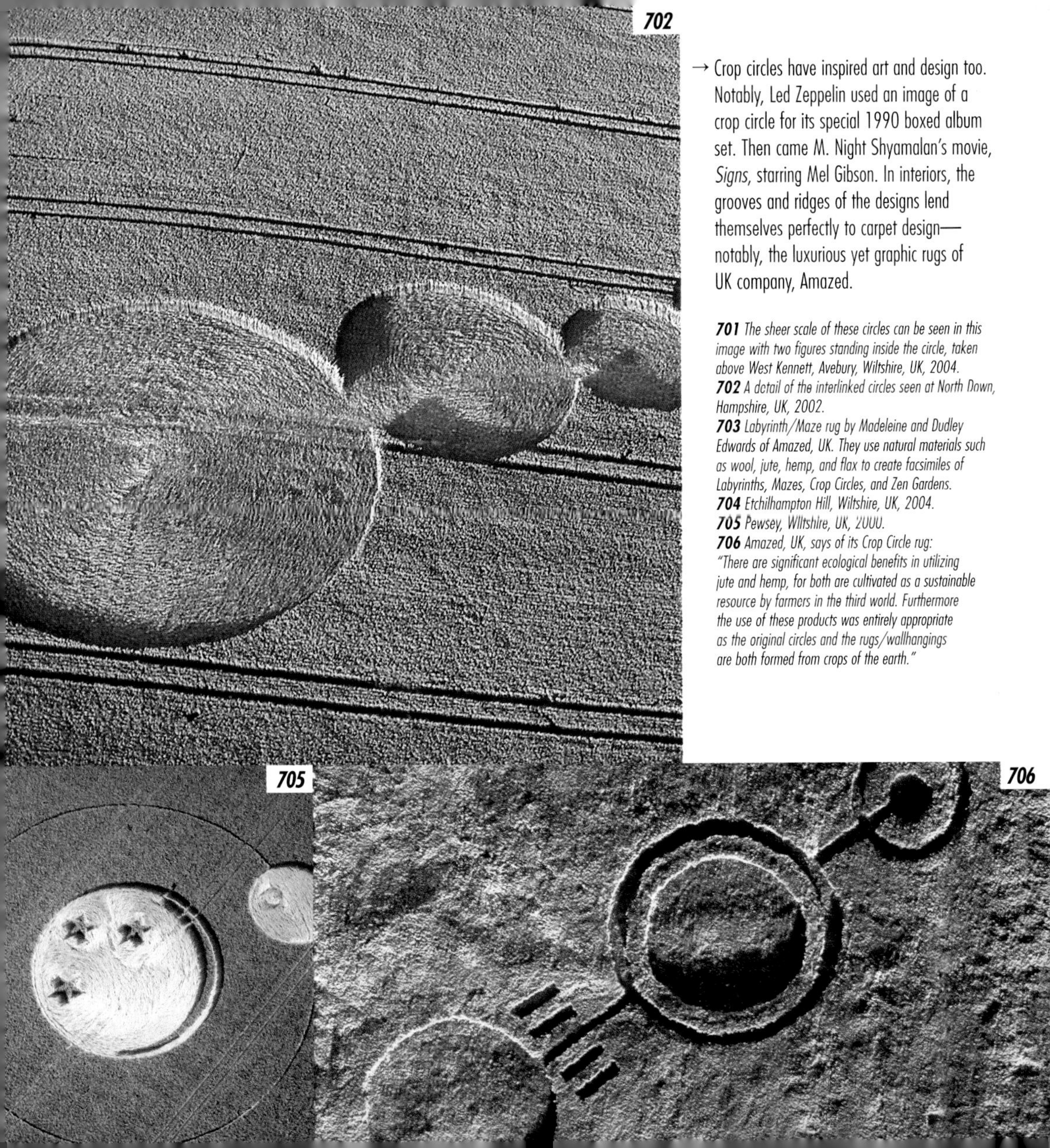

→ Crop circles have inspired art and design too. Notably, Led Zeppelin used an image of a crop circle for its special 1990 boxed album set. Then came M. Night Shyamalan's movie, *Signs*, starring Mel Gibson. In interiors, the grooves and ridges of the designs lend themselves perfectly to carpet design—notably, the luxurious yet graphic rugs of UK company, Amazed.

701 *The sheer scale of these circles can be seen in this image with two figures standing inside the circle, taken above West Kennett, Avebury, Wiltshire, UK, 2004.*
702 *A detail of the interlinked circles seen at North Down, Hampshire, UK, 2002.*
703 *Labyrinth/Maze rug by Madeleine and Dudley Edwards of Amazed, UK. They use natural materials such as wool, jute, hemp, and flax to create facsimiles of Labyrinths, Mazes, Crop Circles, and Zen Gardens.*
704 *Etchilhampton Hill, Wiltshire, UK, 2004.*
705 *Pewsey, Wiltshire, UK, 2000.*
706 *Amazed, UK, says of its Crop Circle rug: "There are significant ecological benefits in utilizing jute and hemp, for both are cultivated as a sustainable resource by farmers in the third world. Furthermore the use of these products was entirely appropriate as the original circles and the rugs/wallhangings are both formed from crops of the earth."*

Targets

"Target'" is the diminutive form of the word "targe" meaning "shield'" in Old English. In the 18th century, a target became known as the object aimed at in archery, and its distinctive concentric circles have appealed to us ever since. The target makes a virtue of the circle's symmetry because it puts the focus on its center—the bullseye. In archery the center carries the highest score and "hitting the bullseye" is a colloquialism for success. The target displays a strange paradox, because its combative origins seem quite at odds with the stylish connotations it carries in contemporary design. The target is frequently associated with the UK's Mod movement of the 1960s (though it features more in Mod revivalist styles than it did at the time). The spiritual home of the Mod is Brighton, UK, and that city's pop subculture inspired Hotel Pelirocco to pay tribute to Mod culture in its Modrophenia room, which is decked out in red, white, and blue targets.

So stylish is the design that US discount retailer, Target, has upgraded its brand image with designer signature lines in clothing and homewares and multimillion dollar advertising campaigns in publications like *Wallpaper**. For some years now, Americans have affectionately dubbed the store "Tar-jay" in honor of its upscale aspirations. Staying with the US, in 1994, the Council of Fashion Designers of America launched its Fashion Targets Breast Cancer campaign, promoted with a target logo designed by Ralph Lauren. The campaign has achieved international recognition—largely due to the target icon, which is used in a variety of colorways in countries all round the world.

707
CHECKPOINT
a novel
NICHOLSON BAKER
A CHATTO & WINDUS PAPERBACK ORIGINAL
711

708

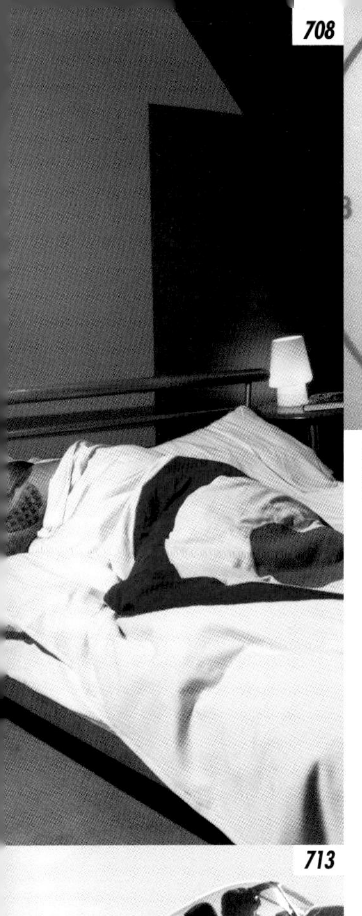

709

710

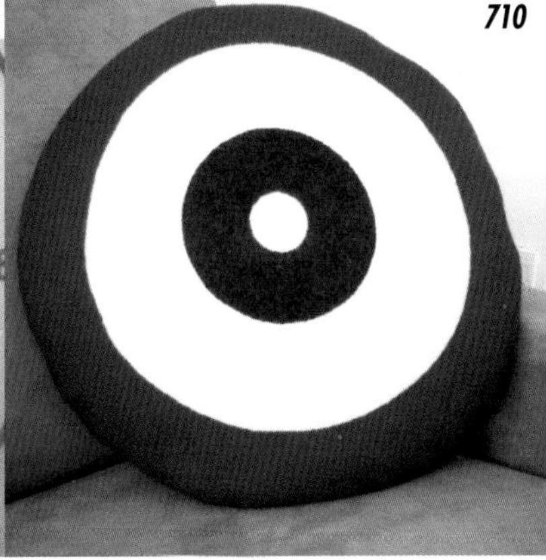

707 *Cover of "Checkpoint" by Nicholson Baker, published by Chatto & Windus, designed by Peter Mendelsund.* **708** *Modrophenia room at the Pelirocco Hotel, Brighton, UK.* **709** *Not a bad score for photographer Andrew Walsh.* **710** *Dot cushion designed by Wendt Design, Denmark.* **711** *Mod parka badge.* **712** *Target.* **713** *RAF roundel.* **714** *Target Internal Communications selling tool by Graphiculture, US.*

714

713

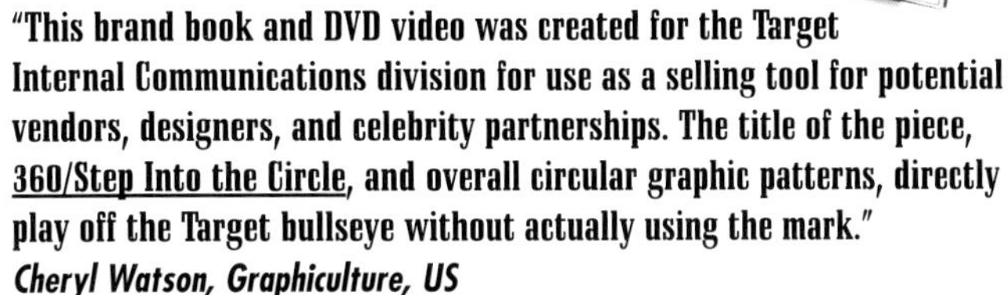

"This brand book and DVD video was created for the Target Internal Communications division for use as a selling tool for potential vendors, designers, and celebrity partnerships. The title of the piece, 360/Step Into the Circle, and overall circular graphic patterns, directly play off the Target bullseye without actually using the mark."
Cheryl Watson, Graphiculture, US

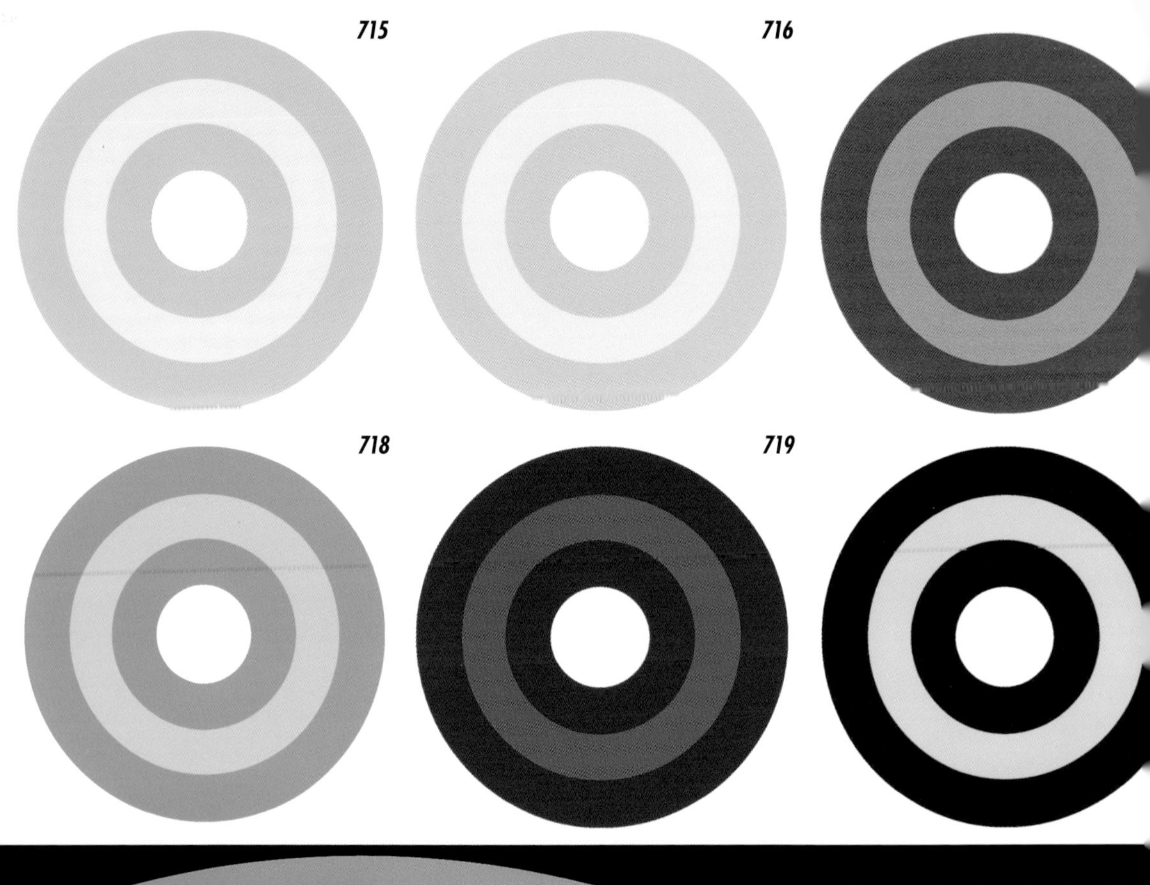

Fashion Targets Breast Cancer (FTBC) is a worldwide charitable initiative of the Council of Fashion Designers of America/CFDA Foundation. FTBC is committed to providing meaningful assistance to women with breast cancer and their families, friends, and other supporters by rallying designers, models, retailers, and other creative energies within the fashion industry. Since its launch in 1994, FTBC has raised over $40 million for distribution to breast cancer charities in 13 countries.

For more information, visit www.fashiontargetsbreastcancer.com.

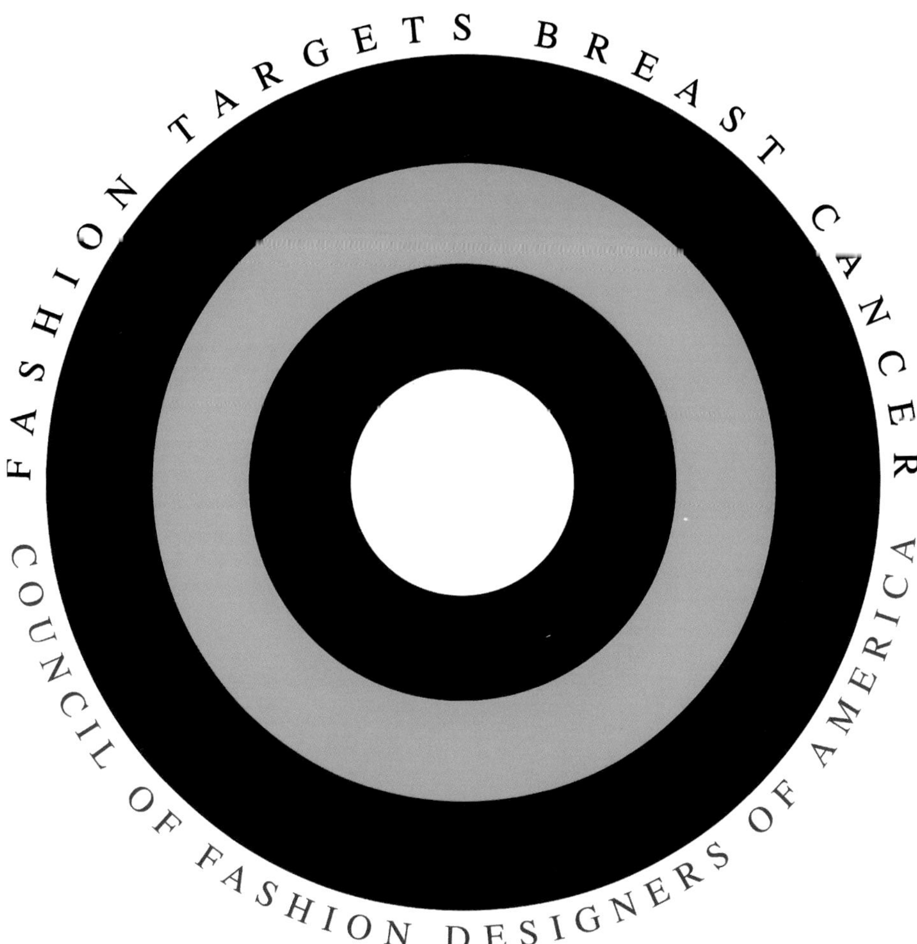

715–720 *Color variants of the Fashion Targets Breast Cancer logo, used in countries around the world.*
721 *The original Fashion Targets Breast Cancer logo, designed by Ralph Lauren, US.*

Segmentation

Circles are perfect for demonstrating simple math, like fractions. It's easier to understand halves, quarters, and eighths when they're represented as portions of cherry pie. The significance of the segment lies in the portion of the whole circle it represents, with the 360º of the circle equivalent to 100%. Circles are frequently used to demonstrate the relationship between diverse sets of data. The Venn diagram is a perfect example of this—it shows the overlap between a number of subgroups, each represented by a circle.

For the designer, segments of circles offer a combination of functionality and esthetics. The semicircle is a practical shape for chair design with the advantage that it retains the generous, enveloping qualities of the circle. A segment-shaped fruit bowl nicely emulates portions of the fruit it is intended to hold. Halved and quartered circles can create graphic interest on packaging, especially when designed in such a way that the circle cleverly mosaics back into a whole when stacked on supermarket shelves.

722–727 *The objective of this game, as photographer Leo Reynolds observes, is to collect as many segments as possible.*
728 *The relationship between colors has been displayed in many ways, including spectrums and triangles, but in the 1960s, Bauhaus colorist, Johannes Itten, created the most enduring way—the color wheel. This wheel shows primaries: red, yellow, and blue; secondaries: orange, green, and violet; and tertiary colors, including tints of these, made by adding white to the original color.*
729 *Segmentation can occur naturally as seen in this orange.*
730 *Portions of pie make elementary math easy.*
731 and 732 *The Cake table by Nicholas Fraser, UK, makes a structural virtue of the segmented circle.*
733 *A pie chart.*

722

724

726

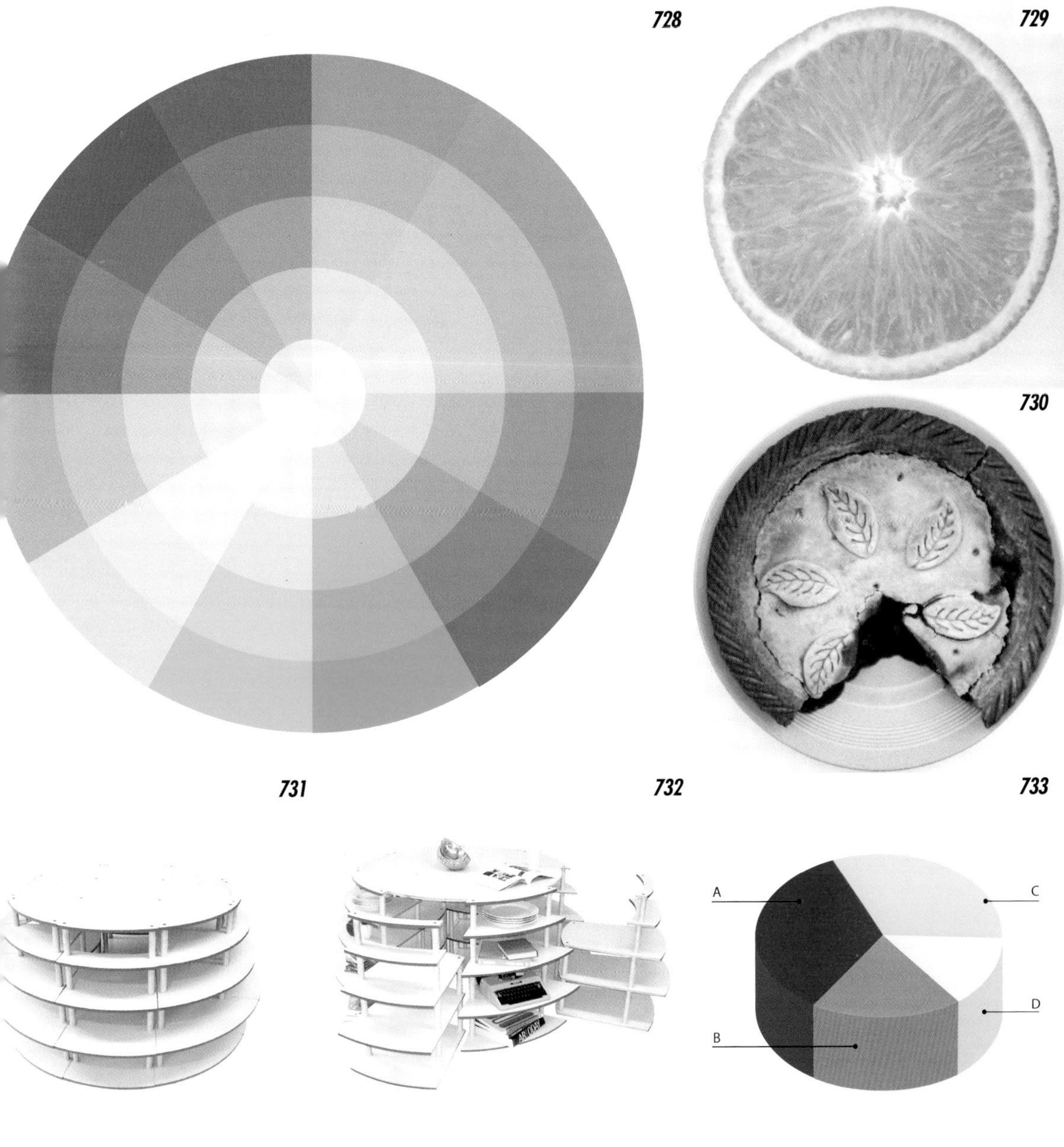
728
729
730
731
732
733
A
B
C
D

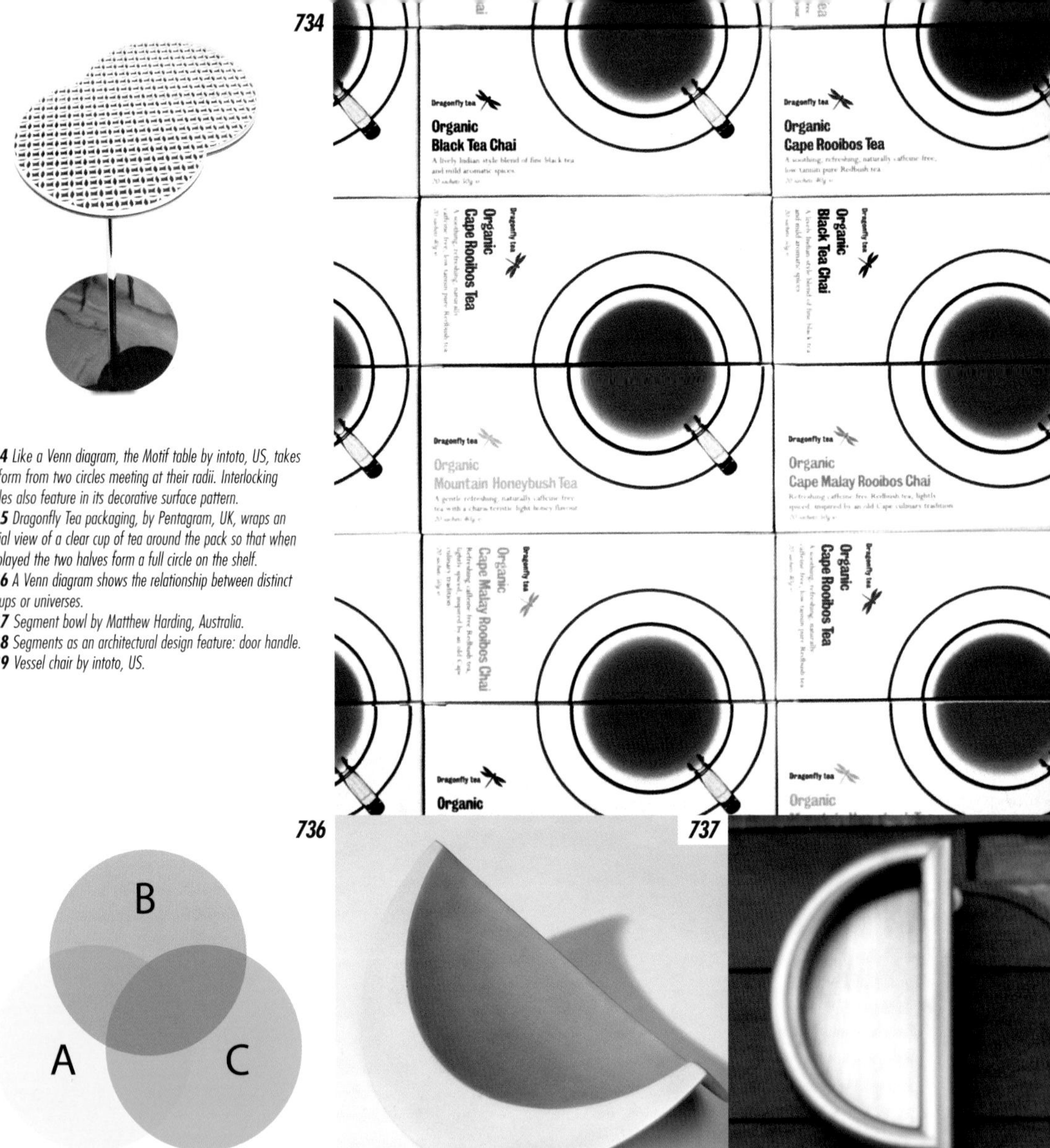

734 *Like a Venn diagram, the Motif table by intoto, US, takes its form from two circles meeting at their radii. Interlocking circles also feature in its decorative surface pattern.*
735 *Dragonfly Tea packaging, by Pentagram, UK, wraps an aerial view of a clear cup of tea around the pack so that when displayed the two halves form a full circle on the shelf.*
736 *A Venn diagram shows the relationship between distinct groups or universes.*
737 *Segment bowl by Matthew Harding, Australia.*
738 *Segments as an architectural design feature: door handle.*
739 *Vessel chair by intoto, US.*

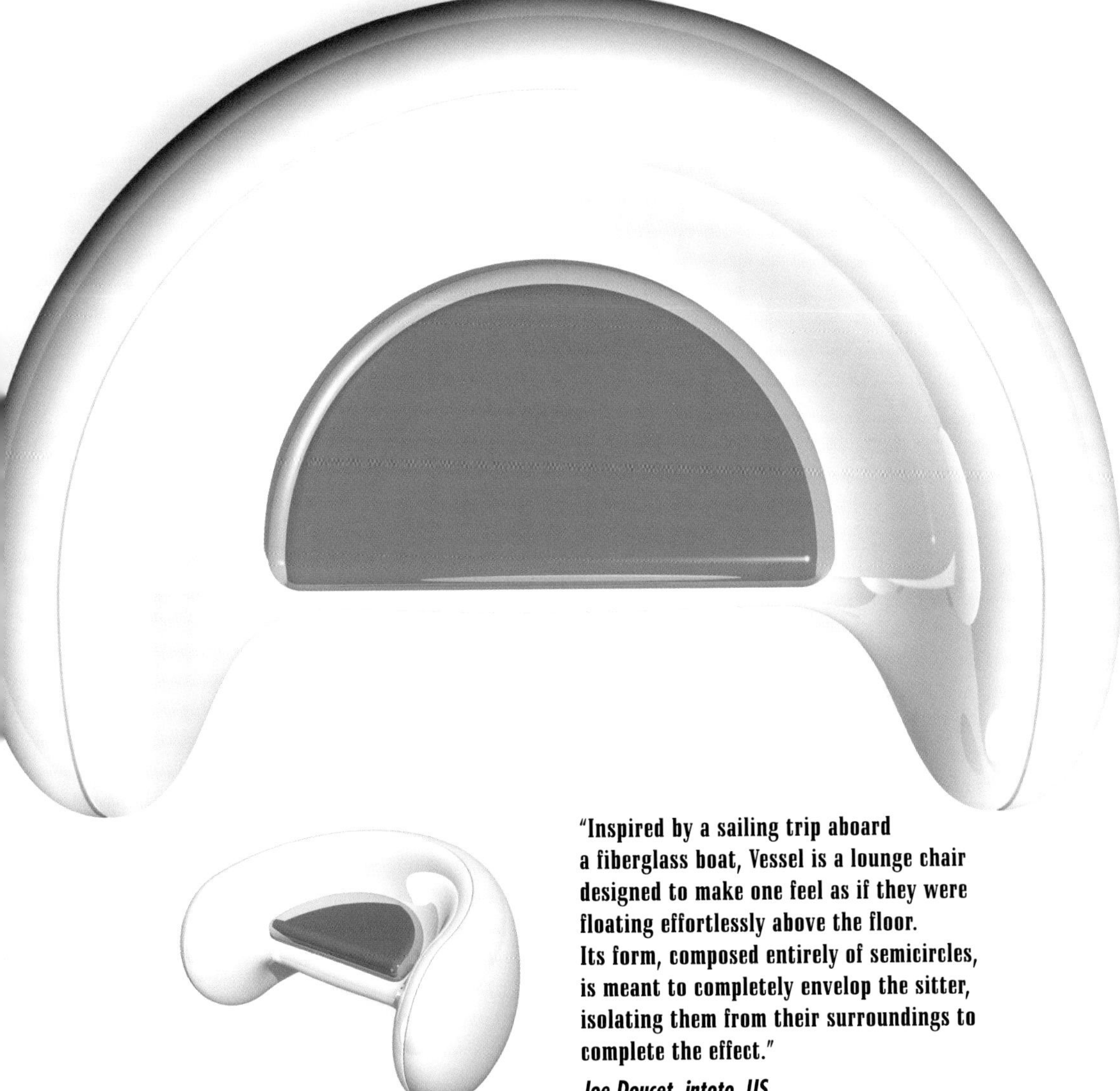

"Inspired by a sailing trip aboard a fiberglass boat, Vessel is a lounge chair designed to make one feel as if they were floating effortlessly above the floor. Its form, composed entirely of semicircles, is meant to completely envelop the sitter, isolating them from their surroundings to complete the effect."

Joe Doucet, intoto, US

Form and Function

Wheels and Gears
Acoustics
Lenses
Covers and Lids
Spirals
Holes and Perforations
Buttons
Architecture
Architectural Details

Form and Function

This chapter pays tribute to man's ingenious use of the circle—like taking the spiral of a snail's shell as inspiration for a spiral staircase, or replicating the way the human eye functions in the camera lens. From the wheels and cogs that propel your car, to the speakers that play the music you drive by, circles are at the heart of engineering and electronics. Circular holes perforate metal and fabric to allow water, light, and air to flow. Circles are present in the simplest and most grand architecture, from round windows to cathedral domes.

Much of the design included here we take for granted—the buttons on our clothes, the manhole covers we walk over. Here we celebrate the circles that surround us in our everyday lives: doing jobs, making chores easier, and facilitating the functioning of machinery.

740 *Manhole cover.*
741 *Circular windows offer a view of your laundry.*
742 *A round air vent.*
743 *Palm trees growing through architectural holes, Miami Beach, US.*
744 *Milk bottle top.*
745 *A speaker in Michael Young's Astro Bar, Reykjavik, Ice*
746 *Look through the lenses for a closer view.*
747 *The spectacular London Eye.*
748 *Convex mirrors help drivers see in blind spots.*
749 *A sculptural gazebo in Chattanooga, Tennessee, US.*
750 *Art deco inspired architecture on Miami Beach, US.*
751 *Circular speakers.*
752 *A cartwheel.*
753 *Denim garments use branded metal buttons.*
754 *A camera lens.*

743
744
SEMI-SKIMMED
PASTEURISED
745
746
QUARTERS ONLY
25¢
1 DROP COIN IN SLOT
2 PULL HANDLE DOWN ALL THE WAY LET GO
747
748
752
753
LEVI STRAUSS & CO
S.F. CAL.
754
Novar-Anastigmat
1:4,5 f=75mm
PRONTO

755

756

Wheels and Gears

Just as a verb is a "doing" word, the wheel is a "doing" circle. Perhaps the hardest working circle of all, the wheel is roundly celebrated as man's most momentous invention. Historians attribute the wheel to the ancient Mesopotamians, dating as far back as 5000–6000 BC and it is believed that its original function was as a potter's wheel. Wheels have enabled so much more than transportation. As part of pulley systems, they facilitate the lifting of heavy loads. Picturesque water wheels and windmills are innovative examples of the wheel used to harness water and wind power. Its mechanical engineering cousin, the gear, is a toothed (or cogged) wheel that is used for maximizing power transmission, involved in the mechanics of anything from a tractor to a delicate Swiss watch.

In design terms, the wheel stands for speed, energy, and progress, and is inextricably linked with the theme of dynamism. Car wheels are sporty; Ferris wheels are fun. As technology progresses, the wheel's connotations move from heavy and industrial to become more high tech and lightweight. The London Eye is perhaps the most graceful wheel you can imagine, elegantly pivoted on one arm, when illuminated at night its circumference appears to float, suspended in space.

755–769 *A selection of wheels on motorbikes, cars, and trucks.*

764

765

758
759
760
761
762
763
767
NISSAN
768
769

770
774
775
776

Gears use interlocking cogged wheels of different sizes
ximize power transmission.
Airside, UK, created this illustration, evocative of a
vork mechanism, for Lemon Jelly's "'64–'95" album.
Truck wheel.
The impressive London Eye illuminated at night,
graphed by Charlie McRae.
and 775 Large-scale mechanical wheels and gears.
and 777 Cartwheels are nostalgic reminders of simpler
or symbols of the Wild West pioneering spirit.
A colorful Ferris wheel looks like fun.

Acoustics

From the sound hole of an acoustic guitar to a set of bass bins, circles are fundamental to the generation and amplification of sound. Even with constant changes in technology, the circle reigns supreme in the creation, reproduction, and enjoyment of music and sound. The simplest instrument, the drum, is crafted from a cylinder. The circular construction of the Whispering Galley in St Paul's Cathedral, London, allows the most quiet utterance to be audible on the opposite side. Headphones, large and small, convey music to the ears via a pair of discs.

Reel-to-reel tape recorders date back to the 1930s and are still in use in some recording studios today. For home use, the Philips compact cassette, launched in 1963, took the place of those bulky pieces of machinery, and later gave rise to mobile music in the form of the Walkman. The cassette tape also became a familiar icon, teamed with crossbones, for the campaign, "Home taping is killing music," which must look quaint and naive to the download generation. Synth-pop bands of the early 1980s provided the last public outing for the reel-to-reel, sitting prominently at the back of the stage, its circular reels turning slowly in place of a human drummer. Its function and esthetic is surely due for a revival. →

779 and 781 *A speaker is the basis of Start, UK's, identity for music download site, Virgin Digital.*
780 *Chris Cain, UK, designed these compressed hay speakers after seeing a barrow load of grass in the park. Their individual looks are a welcome alternative to dull electrical products.*
782 and 785 *The dull version—round speaker bins.*
783 *Earphones come in a variety of sizes—these are big!*
784 *Muji's wall-mounted compact CD player creates a graphic circle within a sound-emitting square.*

781

780
783
784
785
mellow
another mellow summer

→ The circular motif has prevailed from analog to digital reproduction of music. Vinyl records, turntables, and CDs all feature circles. Before the advent of the CD, we played singles at 45rpm and LPs at 33rpm—rpm standing for revolutions per minute—so even the languag by which we categorized music formats was linked to circles and rotation. But things haver changed so much. CDs are smaller and more robust than their vinyl ancestors, but they rem circular because they need to rotate to be play

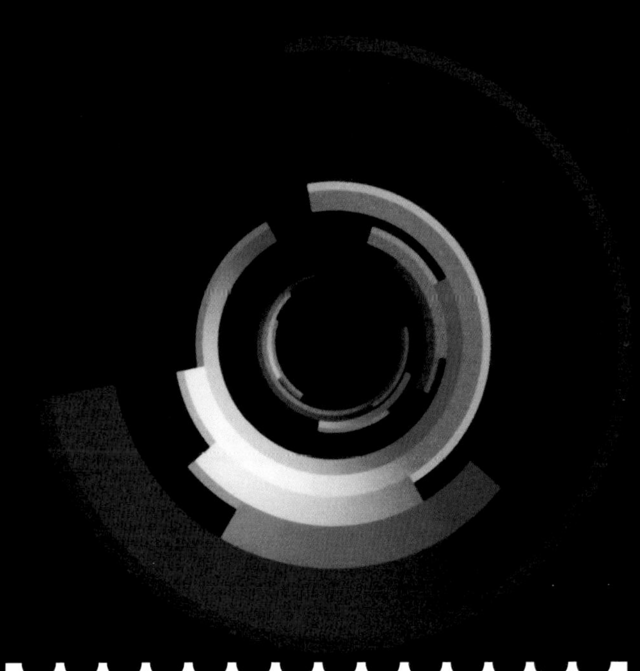

86 Bang the drum.
87 The sound hole is what makes the acoustic
itar acoustic.
88 A cymbal of hope?
89 Chunky is best—a reel-to-reel tape recorder.
90 and 792 Airside's designs for Lemon Jelly's album,
69–'95."
91 Vinyl still holds its appeal for DJs and collectors.
93 Put the needle on the record—a music shop's old-
shioned signage still looks cool.
94 Microphone.
95 The speaker of a Stylophone—an instrument invented
the late1960s, played with a pen, offering all the acoustic
peal of white noise. Very collectible.

"Airside designed circular patterns for Lemon Jelly's recent "'64–'95" album in response to the band's feeling about music being inextricably linked with roundness. CDs are round. LPs are round. The labels in the middle are round. And Lemon Jelly's music is looped. Hence Airside's representation of this concept with a series of circular patterns that were not only illustrated but also animated to melt from one to another."

Airside, UK

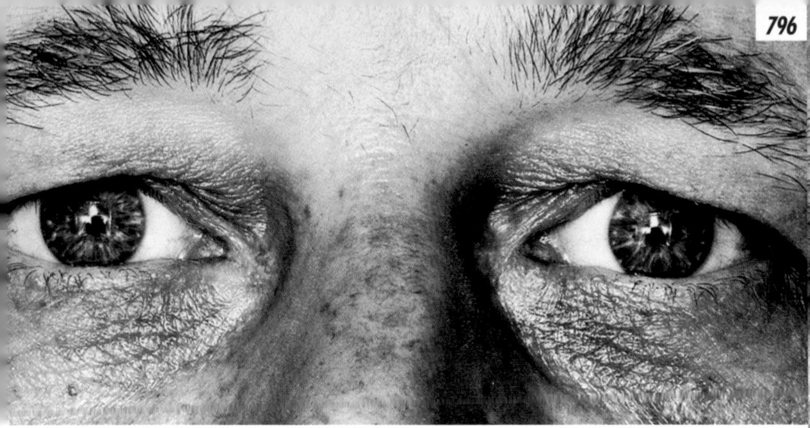

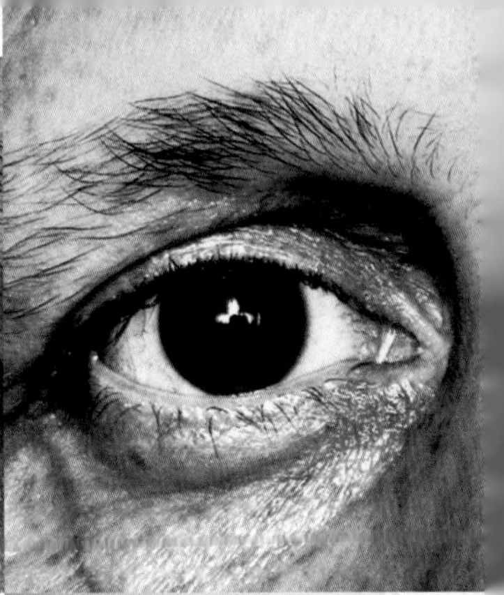

Lenses

Lenses are ground and polished discs of glass with curved surfaces. A convex lens (thickest in the middle) magnifies objects and a concave lens (thinnest in the middle) makes objects appear smaller. These properties make lenses the basis of everyday spectacles and cameras; while in the worlds of science and astronomy, they figure in telescopes and microscopes. Lenses can have decorative appeal, too. Used on the exterior of Klein Dytham's Foret store building in Harajuku, Tokyo, 6,271 cat's-eye lenses act as a reflective skin and give the impression of thousands of crystal studs.

The eye depends on a lens to focus the image on the retina—the area with the concentration of nerves that carry visual information to the brain. A camera imitates this—the lens is the eye and the film its retina. "I am a camera with its shutter open, quite passive, recording, not thinking" wrote Christopher Isherwood in his 1939 novel, *Goodbye to Berlin*. The suggestion is that the camera is an impartial recorder of events. Eyes, on the other hand, are hugely emotive. We talk of eyes being the "windows to the soul" and we judge people to be deceitful if their eyes are too close together. Eye metaphors extend into the design world too. Eyes stand for focus, insight, and curiosity. Spectacle wearers are depicted in fiction as intelligent and bookish. The big circular eyes of the owl are used to suggest wisdom—an odd attribution, as their eyes are big purely to help them see in the dark. Owls are often used as symbols for libraries; especially bookish owls are even depicted wearing glasses.

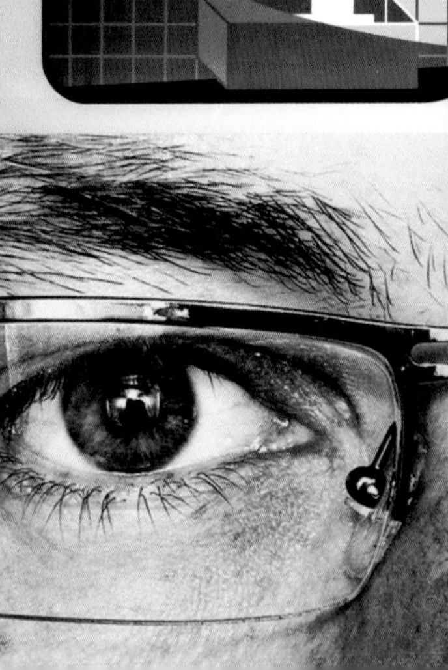

796–798, 800, and 801 *Photographer, Ashley Cameron, UK, uses an innovative technique to capture these extremely detailed shots of his male subjects in which the eyes become the main focus and the key to each portrait's personality.*

799 *Eyes act as a metaphor for curiosity. UK design studio, Doshi Levien, created this window installation at London's Wellcome Trust HQ. The Trust organizes arts and educational programs that help heighten awareness of biomedical issues. The designers created a series of three installations to explore themes of personal health and well-being—this one focuses on the idea of curiosity funding, encouraging people to seek health through questioning and self-reflection.*

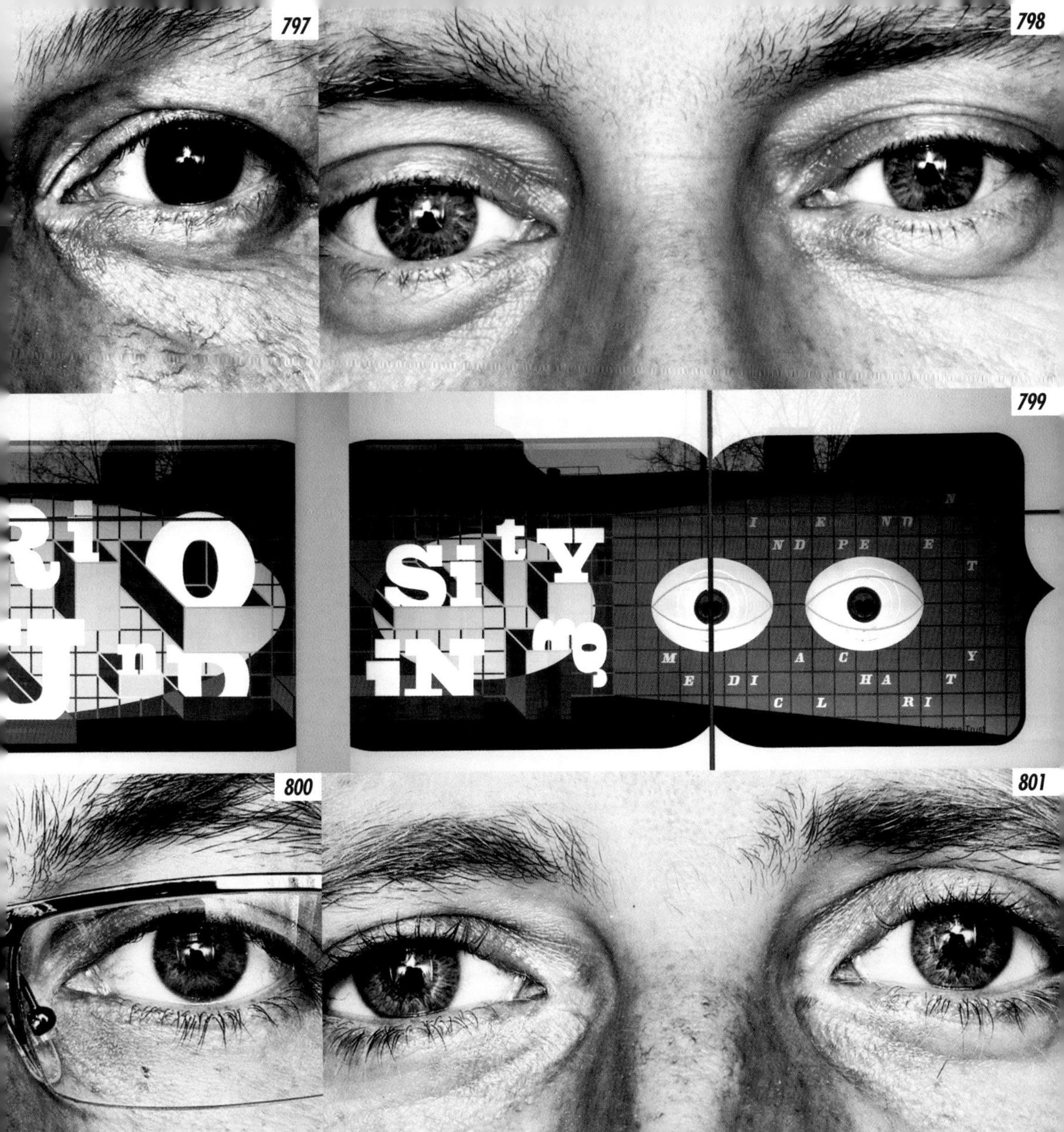
797
798
799
800
801

802 *Identity for Fotonauta, an international photography gallery in Barcelona, Spain, by Lance Wyman, US. The identity arranges rectangular frames in a circle to suggest a camera lens.*
803 *Camera lens.*
804 *Lance Wyman uses the circular form of the camera lens to create this photographer's identity.*
805 *A wise owl—part of the ceramic menagerie by ceramicist, Jonathan Adler, US.*
806 and 811 *Public observation binoculars.*
807 and 808 *Viewmaster offers hours of fun.*
809 *The Aperture pendant light, designed by Claire Norcross for Habitat, UK, allows each box to be closed or opened to shine a star-shaped reflection on the wall.*
810 *City view through a telescope.*

805
806
807
Seattle
Washington
UP FOR VIEWER
A
1 Seattle Skyline and Mt. Rainier
2 Skyline at sunset
3 Night view of Seattle Skyline from south
4 Space Needle and City Skyline
5 Space Needle and Seattle Skyline
6 Monorail links downtown and Space Needle
7 Pioneer Square
808
810
811

"We like circles—they are friendly, convenient, they have round corners, they fit into almost any space or facade, and they always seem to group effortlessly!

Maybe their hidden attraction comes from their origin in nature, whether bubbles, cells, or electrons."

Mark Dytham,
Klein Dytham Architecture, Japan

2 and 813 The Harajuku district of Tokyo is a young trendy area and deserved a landmark store. Klein Dytham itecture's revamp of the Foret store involved covering facade in round delineator road reflectors, which makes building sparkle in sunlight and pulsate in the neon night t. Photography by Katsuhisa Kida.

4 The I Spy chandelier, designed by Ria Hawthorn for itat, UK, uses magnifying glasses for a decorative effect.

5 Inspect Your Face shaving mirror by Alex Turner, UK. mirror magnifies for a closer view, inset in a magnifying s shape for a humorous twist.

6 and 817 Klein Dytham Architecture's design for Mori Arts Museum café uses convex mirrors to reflect panoramic view from the 52nd floor of the Roppongi Hills plex in Tokyo, Japan. Photography by Kozo Takayama.

Covers and Lids

There's a good reason why so many lids and caps are circular—it's because they're designed to screw off. Only a circle has the symmetry required for a true twist cap action. Screw top lids that appear square or oval will usually reveal that they are circles with another form grafted onto them. Many vessels have a cylindrical form and their corresponding covers are necessarily circular. It's hard (though not impossible) to open a noncylindrical can with a can opener. The circle offers the least resistance to the action—as anyone who's tried to open one of those triangular shaped tins of ham will testify. The kitchen is particularly rich with circular utensils and vessels. Pots, pans, tureens, bottles, and bins all have circular lids, covers, caps, corks, and stoppers.

Circular manhole covers offer access to sewers, drains, and gas valves, and in addition provide historians with valuable information. As well as signaling the services that lie beneath them, their cast metal designs can be intricately embossed—some worthy of brass rubbing—and often contain information about the metal works that cast them and the date they were manufactured, making them valuable pieces of social history. Their role thus combines the functional with an element of commemoration—a duality captured by Karim Rashid's Millennium Manhole Covers, installed in Times Square, New York, by Con Edison Inc. to celebrate "energy and ideas for the Millennium."

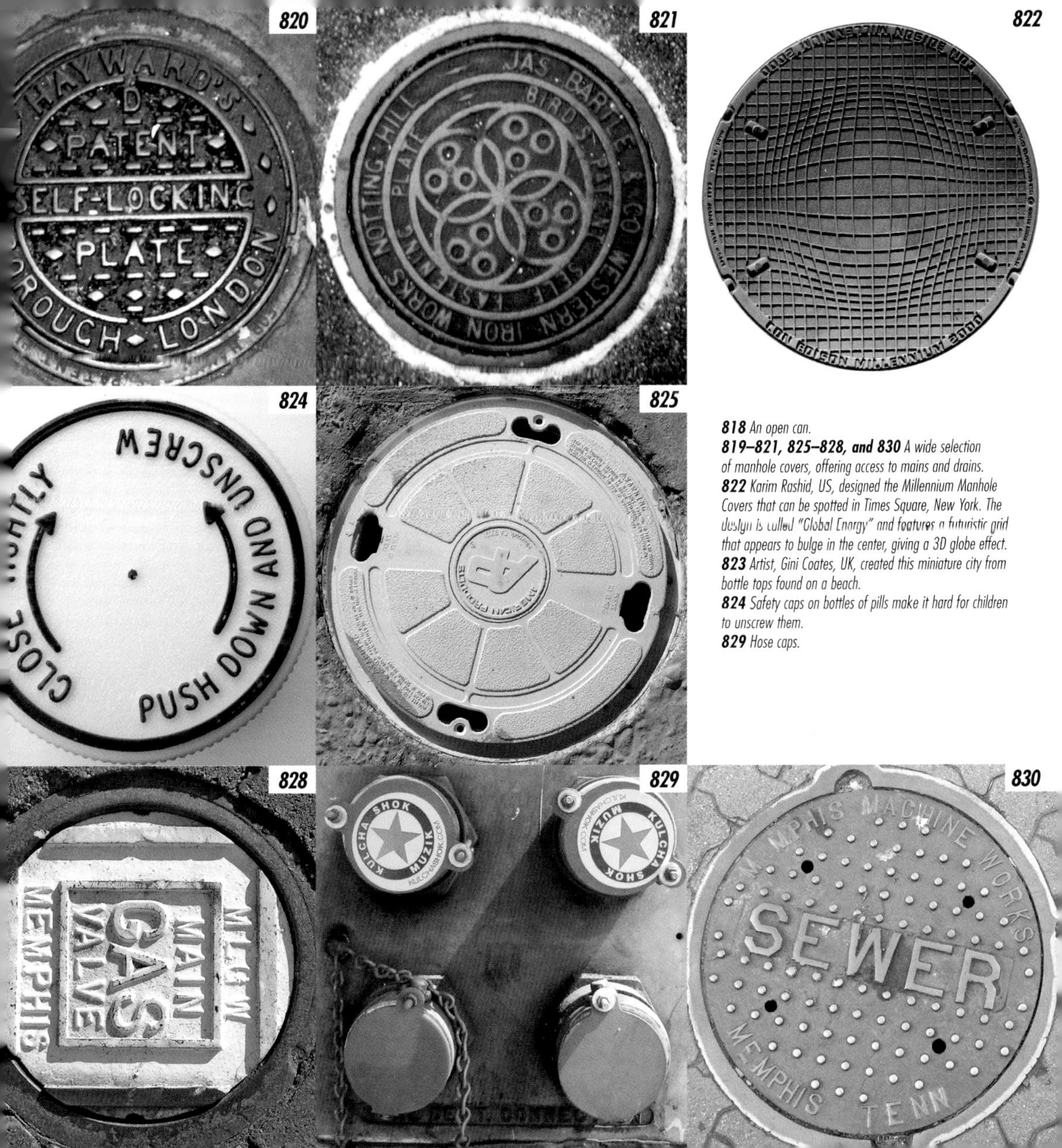

818 *An open can.*
819–821, 825–828, and 830 *A wide selection of manhole covers, offering access to mains and drains.*
822 *Karim Rashid, US, designed the Millennium Manhole Covers that can be spotted in Times Square, New York. The design is called "Global Energy" and features a futuristic grid that appears to bulge in the center, giving a 3D globe effect.*
823 *Artist, Gini Coates, UK, created this miniature city from bottle tops found on a beach.*
824 *Safety caps on bottles of pills make it hard for children to unscrew them.*
829 *Hose caps.*

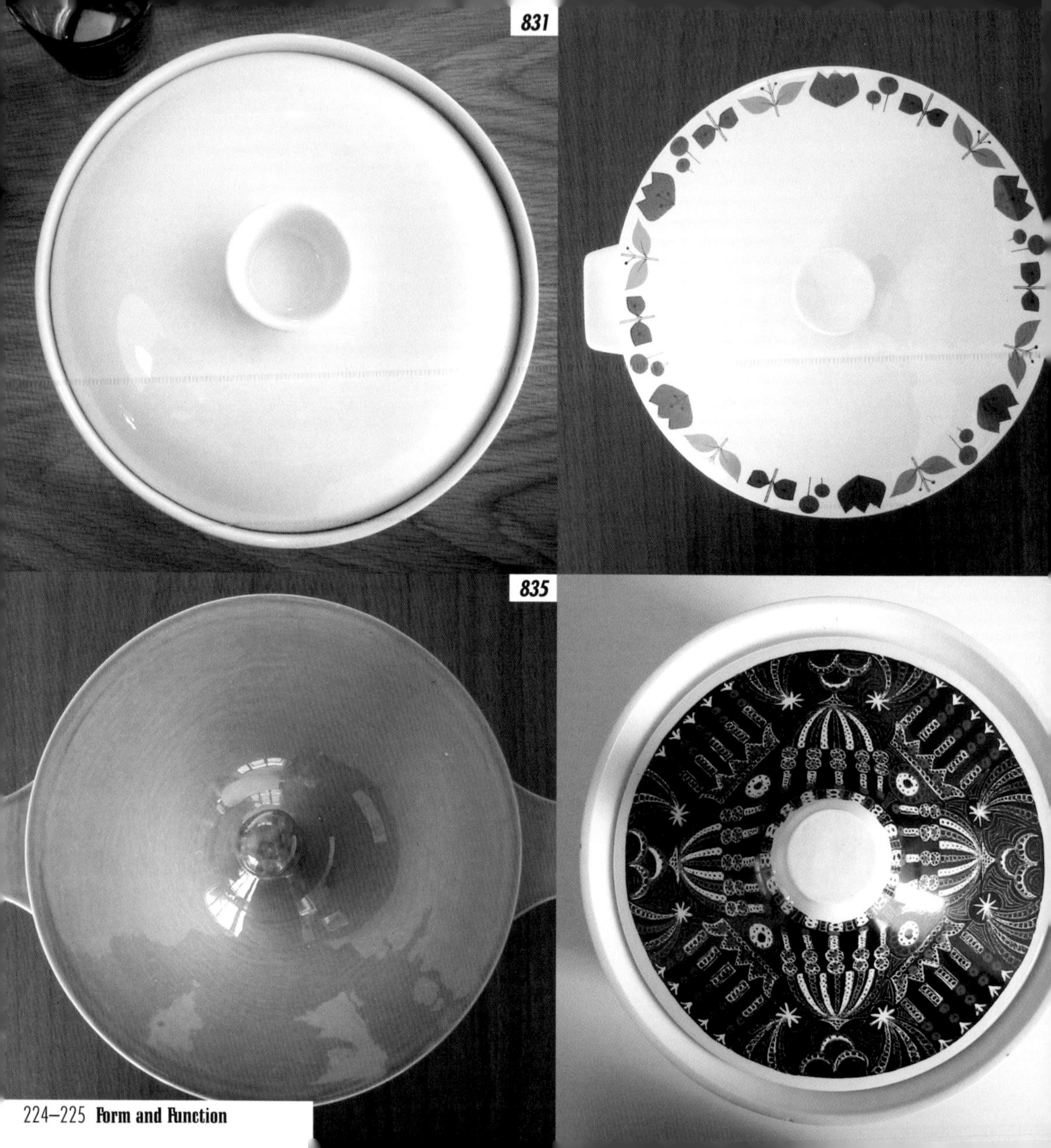
831
835

833

834

837

831, 832, 835, and 836 *A selection of tureen lids.*
833 *Groups of old glass bottles can be decorative.*
834 *The StopIt chair, designed by Redstr/Collective, US, uses a repetition of rubber stoppers in place of traditional cushions and fabric. Its minimalist form is a result of an exploration and abstraction of upholstered furniture. Retailed by The Future Perfect, New York, US.*
837 *The traditional wine cork is now being replaced with synthetic alternatives.*

Spirals

Although it isn't a pure circle, the spiral is a variation on a circular design, and deserves mention for its versatile combination of form and function. Spirals exist in the natural world as protective shells, coiled animal horns, and dynamic whirlpools. Coiled leaves can help a plant capture scarce rainfall. In architecture and design, the spiral offers a number of unique functions: a spiral ramp provides smooth, uninterrupted wheelchair access; spiraled springs offer support and flexibility; a spiral staircase can be both the most space-efficient and elegant solution for a building. The spiral's functional benefits should not detract from its esthetic beauty. Spirals have informed the architecture of Frank Lloyd Wright and the art of Henri Matisse. One of Matisse's later works, *The Snail*, is an energetic celebration of the spiral in geometric planes of vivid color.

Spirals can be delicately etched or robustly coiled and are associated with a diversity of themes and styles—from the elegance of ionic volutes to the violence of swirling tornados. Mysticism and spirituality are often communicated through the spiral and it is possibly one of the oldest religious symbols, found engraved into ancient rocks, perhaps referencing the sun. The triple spiral, found on Celtic tombs, has particular significance as it displays three spirals drawn in one continuous movement, suggesting the cycle of birth, life, and resurrection.

838 *Lewis Moberly, UK, used decorative spirals in the identity and packaging for the Panini Italian restaurant in the Grand Hyatt, Dubai.*
839 *A Danish pastry.*
840 and 842 *Spiral staircases are both space saving and beautiful.*
841 *Photographer, Mark Menzies captured the natural beauty of this snail's shell.*
843 *The mystical spiral—a sculpture outside the school of fine art, Ulaan Baatar, Mongolia, spotted by Jannie Armstrong.*
844 *Elegant spiral design cups by Rimmington Vian, UK.*

839
840
841
842
843
844

Holes and Perforations

There are all sorts of reasons why you might design something with one or several holes. Firstly, holes enable light or air to pass through. They also rid an object of excess material, so it's cheaper to produce, and make it lighter, so it's cheaper to transport. Moreover, holes look fun too—Swiss cheese and Lifesavers are both characterized as slightly quirky products because of their holes.

We tend to think of holes as circles—it's the optimal shape for the job. When engineers have to tackle underwater damage on an oil-drilling rig, such as rust or erosion, divers cut a circular piece out to remove the damaged area (as opposed to any other shape) because the circle has no pressure points of excess strain that would cause further rupture. →

845 *The holes in these children's balls make them lighter and more fun looking.*
846 *The Bokka Lamp, designed by Karim Rashid, US, for Kundalini.*
847 *The hole in this Swivel PT7 chair, designed by Lebello, US, gives it an added sculptural quality.*
848 and 849 *Witty and functional—the Swiss door wedge, designed by Andrew Stafford, distributed by Worldwide Co, UK.*
850 *Holes offer lightness and elegance to this Ionic screen by Moxbox, US, made of amber bamboo panels in a brushed stainless steel frame.*

846
847
848
849
door wedge
Swiss
850

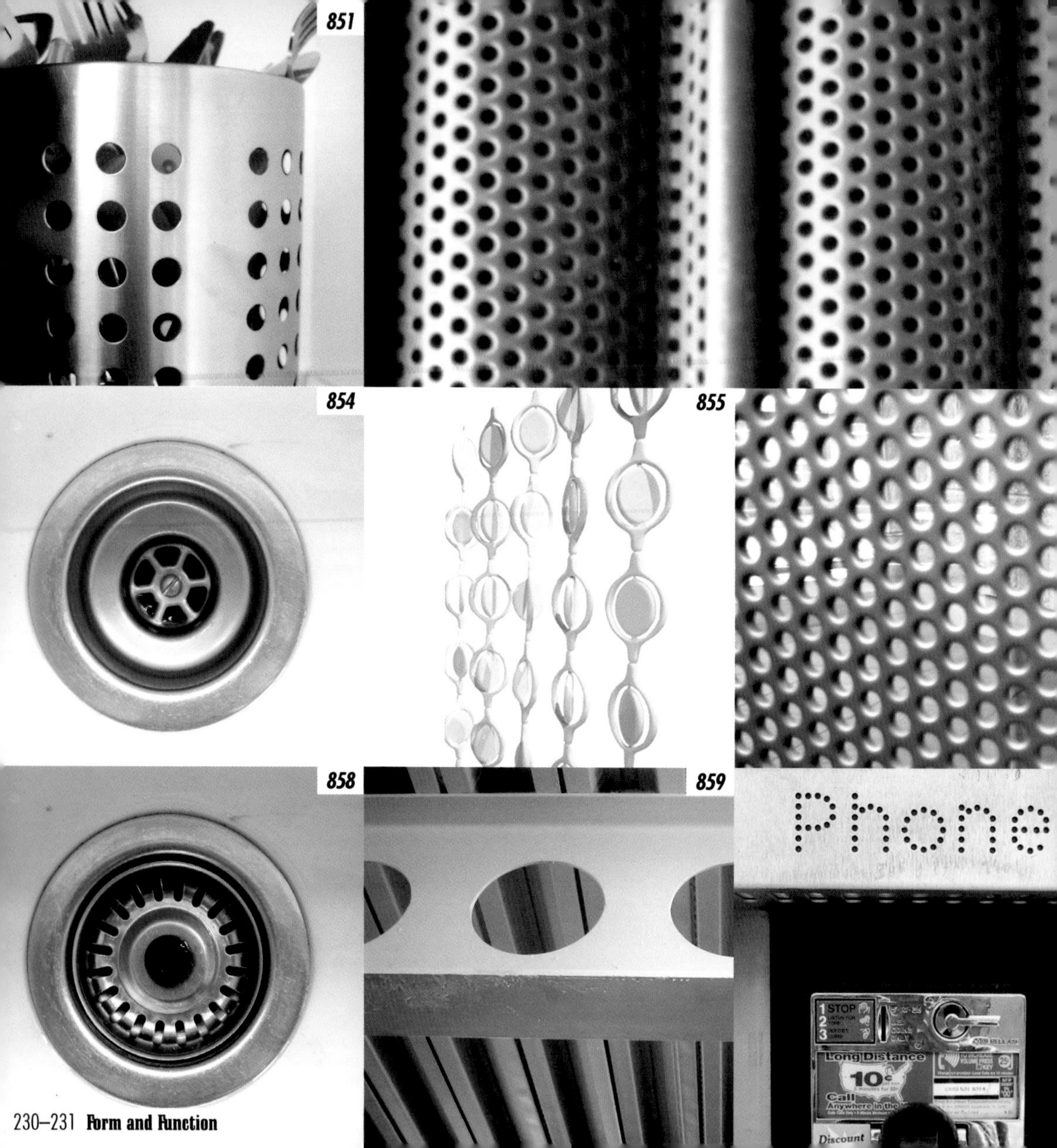

851

854

855

858

859

851 A cutlery holder with decorative holes.
852 and 856 Perforated metal screens.
853 Drain holes are useful in kitchen utensils—the Silica range by Habitat, UK, is silicone coated for extra ease of use.
854 and 858 Plug holes.
855 Blow is an indoor/outdoor modular screen made of cast polyurethane, designed by Elizabeth Paige Smith.
857 Public announcement speaker.
859 The holes in this steel girder make it lighter, without compromising on strength.
860 Holes forming signage.
861 Peg board—popular in traditional hardware stores.
862 The familiar perforations of a postage stamp.
863 Junior Philatelists of New York logo by Lance Wyman, US.

→ Perforation is the result of many tiny holes being punched out of paper, metal, plastic, or fabric. The chief benefits of perforation are lightness, flexibility, and a degree of translucency, all without compromising on strength. Sheets of stamps are perforated to allow them to tear easily, leaving each stamp with a distinctive border of semicircular serrations, the basis of Lance Wyman's logo for Junior Philatelists of New York. Little holes are useful for straining and draining water, emitting sound from loud speakers, and circulating air through vents. Dot-like holes can be formed into letters punched out of metal, sometimes seen as signage on phone booths. The many regular holes of pegboard make it an extremely serviceable material for displaying products. Particularly prevalent in old-fashioned hardware stores, modern variants of this flexible system are being explored by retail designers as a more stylish alternative to slat wall.

Performance fabrics utilize tiny holes to create a breathable membrane and technology is constantly being pushed to create ever more high-tech solutions—like Stomatex®, a technical fabric that replicates the way that the leaves of plants transpire, maintaining a perfect microclimate between the skin and the fabric at any level of physical activity.

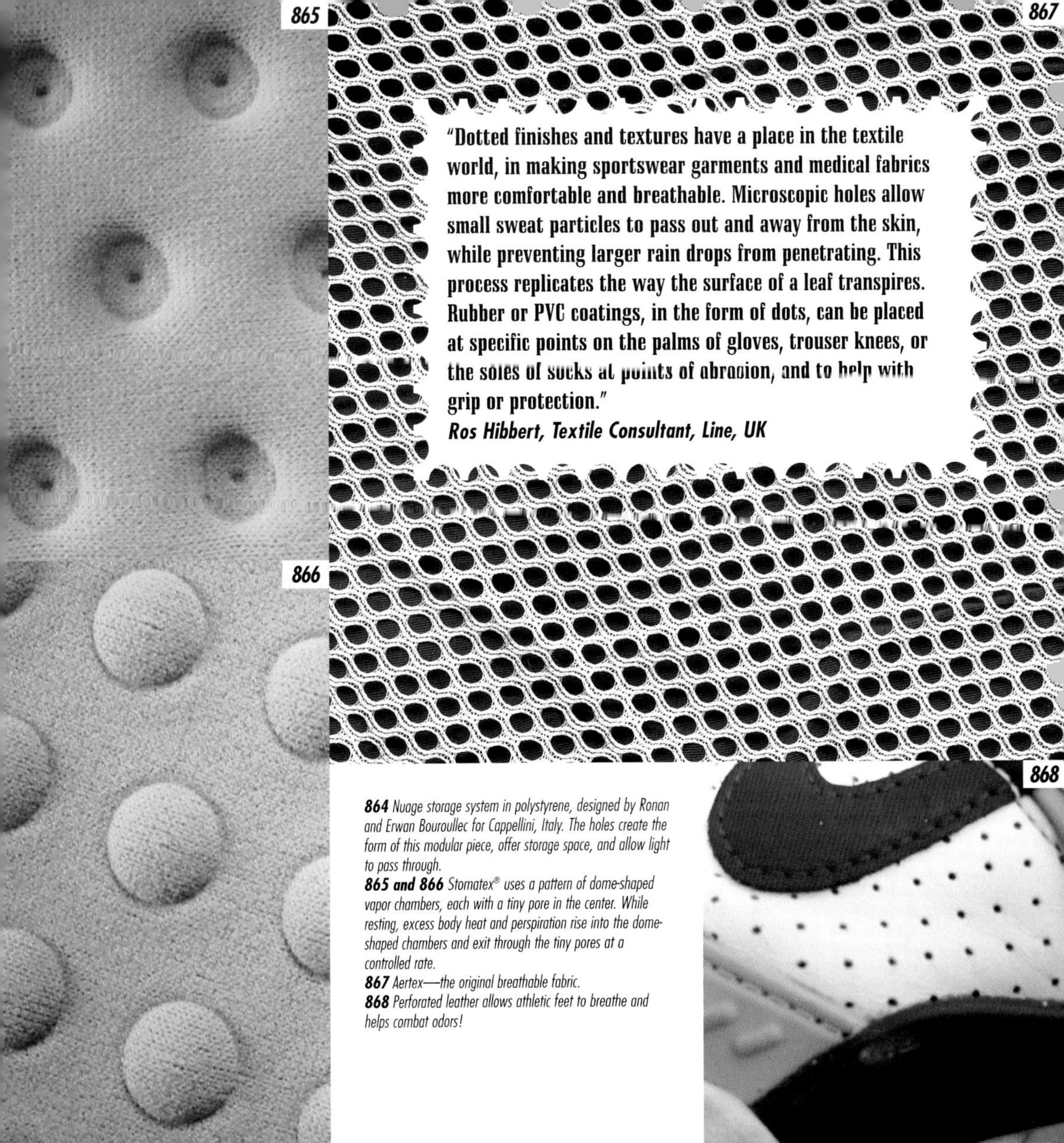

865

866

867

“Dotted finishes and textures have a place in the textile world, in making sportswear garments and medical fabrics more comfortable and breathable. Microscopic holes allow small sweat particles to pass out and away from the skin, while preventing larger rain drops from penetrating. This process replicates the way the surface of a leaf transpires. Rubber or PVC coatings, in the form of dots, can be placed at specific points on the palms of gloves, trouser knees, or the soles of socks at points of abrasion, and to help with grip or protection.”

Ros Hibbert, Textile Consultant, Line, UK

868

864 *Nuage storage system in polystyrene, designed by Ronan and Erwan Bouroullec for Cappellini, Italy. The holes create the form of this modular piece, offer storage space, and allow light to pass through.*

865 and 866 *Stomatex® uses a pattern of dome-shaped vapor chambers, each with a tiny pore in the center. While resting, excess body heat and perspiration rise into the dome-shaped chambers and exit through the tiny pores at a controlled rate.*

867 *Aertex—the original breathable fabric.*

868 *Perforated leather allows athletic feet to breathe and helps combat odors!*

Buttons

There is a well-documented phobia of buttons, which forces sufferers to look for alternative clothes fastenings, such as zippers and Velcro. Pity them because, unlike other more prosaic fastening devices, buttons are both functional and decorative, holding things together at the same time as they embellish a garment. There is no recognized condition for button aficionados, but they are out there—none more vehement in their devotion than designer, Gini Coates. Her fascination for buttons stems from an interest in all things circular and she uses them in her installation and design work, along with other found and reclaimed materials, creating something new and unexpected in the mix.

Fashion brands use buttons as another medium to carry their logo and this is particularly prevalent in denim labels. As well as being embossed with the brand name, the location and configuration of brass buttons and rivets can be part of the brand's equity. When Levi's reintroduced the button fly 501 in the 1980s, it caught the demand for authentic original denim products, boosting sales and brand image.

London's Pearly Kings and Queens are a group of families who for 125 years have kept up a tradition of adorning their clothes with mother-of-pearl buttons, in honor of Henry Croft and his band of benevolent costermongers who fundraised for hospitals and orphanages, dressed in this button-clad garb. →

"Finding a rusty tin of old buttons at the back of a junkshop is like discovering treasure. They are like giant hundreds and thousands for grown-ups and I'm convinced they are used in certain parts of the country as currency. Circles and dots should embellish the world as they are unquestionably the most esthetically pleasing and truly satisfying shape."

Gini Coates, Artist and Designer, UK

869 and 870 *Lines to Somewhere 2004–2005 by Gini Coates, UK. The project was inspired by 1980s angular print designs. Using a combination of different materials and processes, including screen printing, upholstery, buttons, foiling, and wallpaper, patterns run from one texture to the next. The 1950s kitchen cabinet is a key element in the graphic interior installation piece which also includes embroidered paneling, a school chest, printed mirror, and upholstered signage.*

871 *A classic button.*

872 *An industrial, rivet-style metal button.*

873
LEVI'S 501
£39:99*
*SELECTED STYLES ONLY

873 *Point-of-sale material for Levi's, designed by Nextbigthing, UK, makes a virtue of the branded button—a key element of the classic button-fly 501 model.*

874 and 876 *Branded metal buttons from both ends of the fashion spectrum.*

875 *The tradition of Pearly Kings and Queens started among London's market barrow-boys. Each borough of London would appoint members of this "people's monarchy." The Kings do all the designing and sewing, and costumes come in two types—a Smother Suit which is entirely covered in buttons and a Skeleton Suit like the one shown here. Many tens of thousands of buttons can be used on one suit, weighing 66lb (30kg) or more.*

877 *The Pearly Queen jacket by Social Suicide, UK, reinvents the pearly tradition. Expect to be treated like royalty if you're bold enough to wear it.*

TELEPHONE

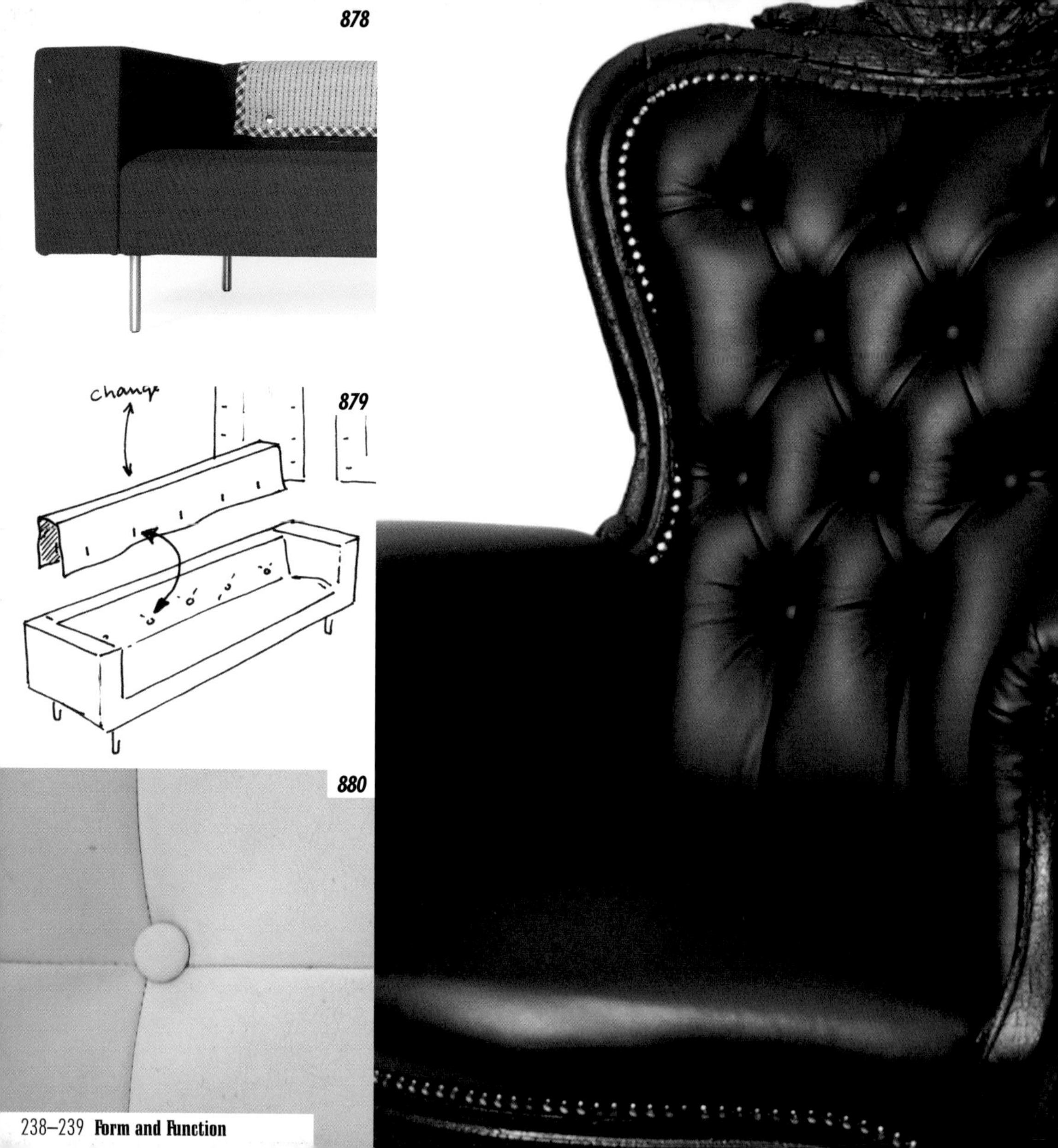
878
change
879
880

p-buttoned upholstery stands for luxury. ıptuously padded and buttoned leather sterfield sofas are traditionally reserved for denizens of gentlemen's clubs, but as the ırious look is reinvented by contemporary ;gners, more and more buttoned furniture ıaking it into stylish modern interiors.

button is not just about clothing and ıiture. We push buttons to ascend in the vator, start the spin cycle, and obtain a king permit. The push button is shorthand ease and convenience in an increasingly omated world.

8 and 879 *The Bottoni sofa by Marcel Wanders for ɔoi, the Netherlands, allows the user to attach a variety of erent fabrics, secured by the upholstery button in its back.*
0 Detail of vintage buttoned leather chair.
1 Smoke chair by Maarten Baas for Mooi, the Netherlands, ates the traditional buttoned chair in slick black leather and ny burnt wood frame.
2 Functional buttons on an entry system.
3–885 *Push buttons switch on electrical equipment and ke public machinery function.*
6 Push buttons to operate a crane.
7 An emergency stop is most speedily effected by pushing utton.

Architecture

In architectural terms, the circle makes an appearance in both the simplest and grandest structures—with the boxy rectangle occupying the mediocre space in between. The humblest dwellings are often circular—the Native American tepee and the Mongolian ger are both examples of traditional shelters that make use of the circular form. At the other end of the scale, there's the dominating dome of Sir Christopher Wren's St Paul's Cathedral, London, or the spectacle of Roman amphitheaters like the Colosseum in Rome.

This duality is typical of the circle: it can be simple and elemental as well as exuberant and grand. The circle has always played a part in the engineering aspect of architecture—the arch, for all its beauty and grace, is essentially a structural solution, a way of creating strength, and a means of support. It enabled the building of vast cathedrals, bridges, and viaducts. The dome can be considered an arch that has been rotated around its vertical axis—again, strength and stability are offered by the circular form. →

888 and 889 *Both interior and exterior of the Sage music center, Gateshead, UK, use circular forms in their design.*
890 and 894 *The sculptural beauty of Klein Dytham Architecture's Leaf Chapel, in the grounds of the Risonare Hotel in Kobuchizawa, Japan, is formed by two leaves—one glass, one steel—which have seemingly fluttered to the ground. Photographs by Katsuhisa Kida.*
891 *The Auckland Sky Tower, New Zealand.*
892 *The identity for London's Wembley Stadium by UK brand consultants, Identica, incorporates the circular form of its arena and the arch that is set to dominate the London skyline.*

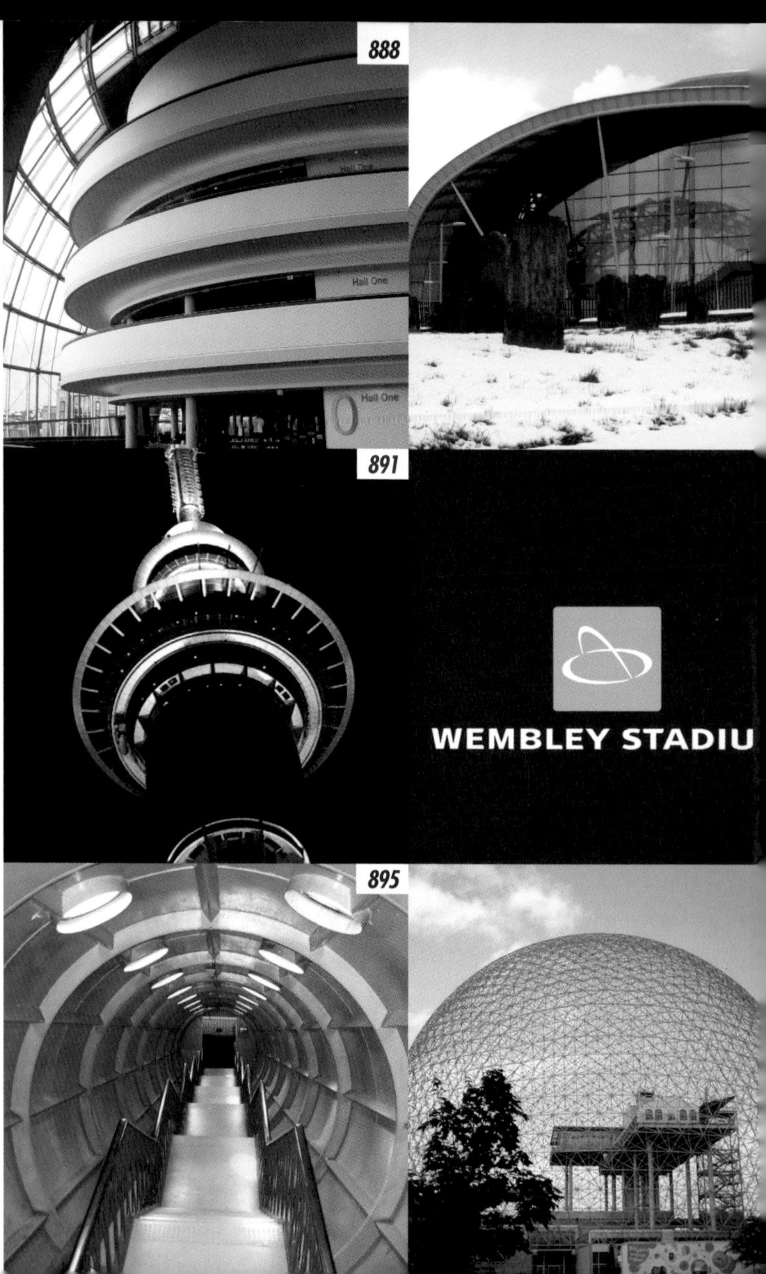

893 *Love it or hate it, London's Millennium Dome, built on the Greenwich Peninsular, is a remarkable feat of engineering.*
895 *This tunnel-like staircase rises up through one of the legs of the Atomium in Brussels, Belgium.*
896 *Biosphere, Montreal, Canada, designed by R. Buckminster Fuller for Expo 1967.*
897 *A traditional Mongolian ger captured at the Malar camp at dawn by Jannie Armstrong*

→ Given the circle's functionality, it is odd that the use of curves, arches, and domes is considered so daring in modern architecture. It has become "statement" architecture. Much of this is down to improvements in engineering. London's new Wembley Stadium features a 436 foot (133m) tall arch that can be seen across London's skyline. Not only does the arch support 11 million pounds (5,000 tonnes) of roof structure, eliminating the need for obtrusive pillars in the stadium, but also it is the key icon for the stadium, exploited in the powerfully simple logo by Identica, London.

898 *A London domed skyline, featuring St Paul's Cathedral in the background.*
899 *An ornate glass domed ceiling.*
900 *The interior of the dome of the Illinois State Capital Building in Springfield, Illinois.*
901 *Trompe l'oeil paint techniques make this dome in the Palace of Versailles, France, appear higher than it is.*
902 *The circular skylight in the entrance to the Tate Gallery, St Ives, UK.*
903 *An impressively painted dome.*
904 *The delicate glass dome of a Victorian palm house.*

900

Architectural Details

Look closely at any building facade and you will see a wealth of circles in the form of door bells, knockers, knobs, keyholes, and a host of other decorative embellishments. These items come under the banner of "door furniture" and act like jewelry for buildings. In painted cast iron or gleaming brass, they add the finishing touches and allow the owner to express their individuality. Rivets and screws are less likely to be considered decorative features, but can, nonetheless, add to the allure of a building by adding either rustic shabbiness or a crisp industrial edge.

Round windows work in sharp contrast to the right angles of most traditional buildings and are often used as feature elements. Aside from esthetics, there are theories as to why architects would go to the trouble of designing the more challenging round window. These theories include the practicalities of strength (ships and airplanes traditionally use round windows to avoid fracture points) and the more romantic notion that the round window mimics the human eye and is therefore an expression of the building's inner soul.

905–907 and 914–916 *Doorbells and elaborate knocke announce visitors and embellish the front of your home.*
908 *A decorative inset plaque displays a classical scene.*
909 *Traditional wooden peg joints.*
910 *Chunky bolts give an industrial feel.*
911 *A substantial door knob.*
912 *Screw Tables by Eero Aarnio, Finland.*
913 and 917 *Screw head and keyhole.*
918 *Rivets with the patina of age.*

914

915

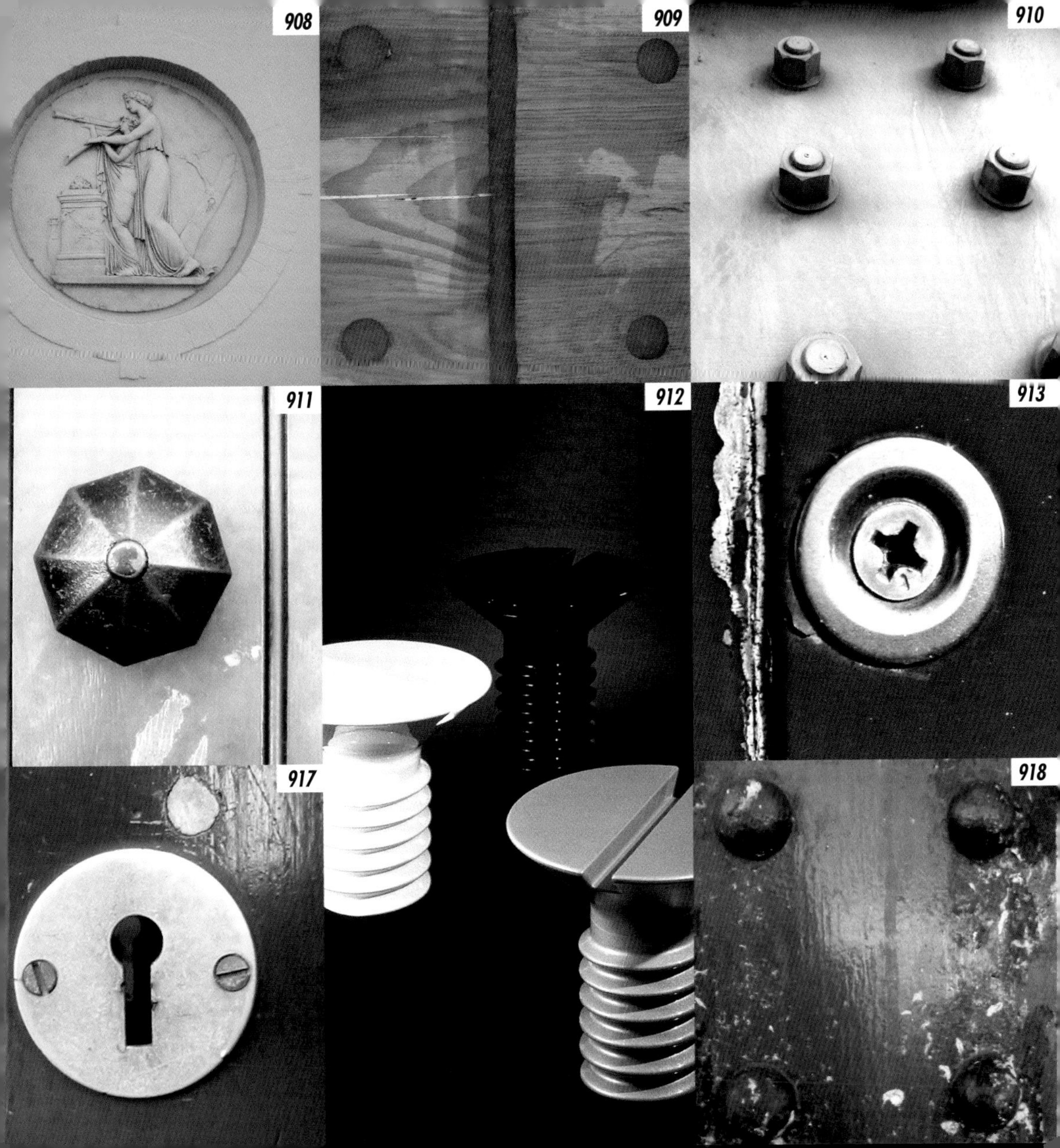
908
909
910
911
912
913
917
918

919
920
922
923
925
926

919–922 and 924–927 *Round windows make an elegant feature on a building's facade and are often considered more romantic than their square counterparts.*

923 *This circular pattern in the glass dates back to early glassblowing methods. The bobble was left by the blowpipe. Nowadays, these "bullseye" windows are reproduced to give old-world character to modern buildings.*

928–930 *A modern take on round windows: Klein Dytham Architecture's R3 building in Akihabara, Tokyo. The circular windows randomly pierce a tent membrane which has been erected in front of the existing building—this offers privacy from within but allows light into the interior. Photography by Daici Ano.*

Appendix

Index
Contributors
Photography Credits
Acknowledgments

Index

Contributors

Featured Designers and Suppliers

Absolute Zero°
www.absolutezerodegrees.com

ACID Anti Copying In Design
www.acid.uk.com

Airside
www.airside.co.uk

Alex Turner
a.turner.design@dsl.pipex.com

All Zones
www.allzones.com

Amazed
www.amazed-rugs.co.uk

Amy Ruppel
www.amyruppel.com

André Klauser
www.andreklauser.com

Audrey Hayes
auds@singingforlarks.co.uk

BT
www.bt.com

Bahari
moo@baharithailand.com

Ball-Nogues
www.ball-nogues.com

Barnaby Barford
www.barnabybarford.com

Bauerware
www.bauerware.com

Big Lottery Fund
www.biglotteryfund.org.uk

Biojewellery
www.biojewellery.com

Blue Source
www.bluesource.com

Cabin project
www.motherbrand.com

Calvin J. Hamilton
www.solarviews.com

Cappellini
www.cappellini.com

Chris Cain
christophercain@hotmail.com

Chris George
herennow@hotmail.co.uk

Daniel Buren
www.danielburen.com

Darren Chandler
darren20@fsmail.net

dragdesign
www.dragdesign.it

Donna Wilson
www.donnawilson.com

Doshi Levien
www.doshilevien.com

Douglas Homer
www.douglashomer.com

Dulux
www.dulux.co.uk

Eero Aarnio
www.eero-aarnio.com

Eleventwentyfive
www.eleventwentyfive.com

Elizabeth Paige Smith
www.epsdesign.com

Ella Doran
www.elladoran.co.uk

Emily Clay
em_clay@hotmail.com

Fashion Targets Breast Cancer
www.fashiontargetsbreastcancer.com

Ferlea
www.ferlea.com

Fold Bedding
www.foldbedding.com

Free Spirit Spheres
www.freespiritspheres.com

Gini Coates
www.ginicoates.com

Graham & Brown
www.grahambrown.com

Graphiculture
www.graphiculture.com

Habitat
www.habitat.net

Helen Waites
pogaloo@yahoo.co.uk

Hemingway Design
www.hemingwaydesign.com

Hotel Pelirocco
www.hotelpelirocco.co.uk

I.D.
www.idonline.com

Identica
www.identica.com

Innocent
www.innocentdrinks.co.uk

Intoto
ww.intotonyc.com

Intro
www.introwebsite.com

Jemma Lumber
www.jemfurnituredesign.co.uk

Jonathan Adler
www.jonathanadler.com

Joseph Joseph
www.josephjoseph.com

Josh Owen
www.joshowen.com

Julie Nelson
jfNelson1@aol.com

Karim Rashid
www.karimrashid.com

Karl Fritsch
schmuckfritsch@mac.com

Klein Dytham
www.klein-dytham.com

Lambie Nairn
www.lambie-nairn.com

Lance Wyman
www.lancewyman.com

Lara Bohinc
www.larabohinc107.co.uk

Leanne Doherty
lea_doherty@yahoo.co.uk

Lebello
www.lebello.com

Lewis Moberly
www.lewismoberly.com

Lisa Stickley
www.lisastickleylondon.com

Line
www.lineconsultants.co.uk

Lost Found Art
www.lostfoundart.com

M Worldwide
www.m-worldwide.co.uk

M&A (Materials & Applications)
www.emanate.org

Matthew Harding
www.matthewharding.com.au

Mark Titchner
marktitchner@yahoo.co.uk

Mary Rose Cook
mary_rose_cook@hotmail.co.uk

Matt Cooper
matt@trademarkarts.com

Michael Young
www.michael-young.com

Minale Tattersfield
www.mintat.co.uk

Mobi
www.mobi-usa.com

Moooi
www.moooi.nl

Moxbox
www.moxbox.net

NSPCC
www.nspcc.org.uk

Nextbigthing
www.nextbigthingcreative.co.uk

Niche Modern
www.nichemodern.com

Nic Fraser
nic_the_fraser@hotmail.com

One World Alliance
www.oneworldalliance.com

Pare*Umbrella
www.pareumbrella.com

Paula Hayes
www.paulahayes.com

Pentagram
www.pentagram.com

Peter Jones
www.lineardesigns.co.uk

People Will Always Need Plates
peoplewillalwaysneedplates.co.uk

Places and Spaces
www.placesandspaces.com

Pout
www.pout.co.uk

Random House
www.randomhouse.com

Random International
random-international.com

Redstr/Collective
www.redstr.com

Rena Tom
www.renatom.com

Rimmington Vian
www.rimmingtonvian.co.uk

Rockit
www.rockit.co.uk

Ronan & Erwan Bouroullec
www.bouroullec.com

Rupert Clamp
www.rupertclamp.com

Scabetti
www.scabetti.co.uk

Schafline/Pinsharp 3D
www.pinsharp3d.co.uk

Scott Wilson
www.studiomod.com

Sesame Letterpress
www.sesameletterpress.com

Sharon Elphick
www.sharonelphick.com

Shelley Fox
www.shelleyfox.com

Simon Sheeran
simonsheeran@hotmail.com

Slick Design
www.slickdesign.com

Social Suicide
www.socialsuicide.co.uk

Start
www.startcreative.com

Steve Alexander
www.temporarytemples.com

SUCK UK
www.suck.uk.com

Sun and Doves
www.sunanddoves.co.uk

Swarovski
www.swarovski.com

Sybarite
www.sybarite-uk.com

Tabletop Group
www.ttctabletop.com

Tai Ping Carpets
www.taipingcarpets.com

The Future Perfect
www.thefutureperfect.com

The Team
www.theteam.co.uk

The Public
www.thepublic.com

Thomas Paul
www.thomaspaul.com

Tom Dixon
www.tomdixon.net

Totem Design
www.totem-uk.com

Transport for London
www.tfl.gov.uk

Twenty2
www.shoptwenty2.com

Velocity Art and Design
www.velocityartanddesign.com

Wendt design
www.wendtdesign.dk

Worldwide Co
www.npw.co.uk

Zip Design ltd
www.zipdesign.co.uk

Photography Credits

By image number

Cover
For photography credits see repeated image numbers:
Back cover L/R: **304, 524, 773, 721, 370, 476, 631, 539.**
Spine: **845.**
Front cover L/R: **241, 151, 065, 697, 204, 216, 394.**

Title page
For photography credits see repeated image numbers: L/R: **122, 307, 908, 871, 709, 259, 845, 143, 624, 773, 458, 104.**

Contents
For photography credits see repeated image numbers: L/R: **271, 564, 126, 053, 543, 470, 697, 712, 049, 361, 279, 398, 595, 033.**

Introduction
001 Henry Bourne

Life Circles
002, 006, 011 Keith Stephenson
003 and 019 Leo Reynolds
004 Carol Cotter
007 NASA
008 Jannie Armstrong
009 Thom Watson
010 Calvin Hamilton www.solarviews.com
013 NASA
014, 015, 017, 018 Keith Stephenson
022–026 Mark Strozier
028 William Helsen
029–031 Mark Strozier
033 Brian Murdock
037 Karol Miles
038 NASA
040 NASA
041 NASA
043 Plasma Slug in NY
045 and 046 Leo Reynolds
047 Hilde Bakering
048 Sam Judson
049–051 Steve Alexander
052 NASA
053, 057, 058 Keith Stephenson
054 Bret A. Salmons
056 Tom Chudleigh
063 Leo Reynolds
064 Robin A. F. Olson, Ultra Maroon Design
066 Thom Watson
067 Mark Hampshire
069 and 076 Keith Stephenson
074 Adam Miller
075 Leo Reynolds

Membership and Identity
077 Brian Winters
078, 079, 083 Keith Stephenson
080 Aaron Booth
082 Leo Reynolds
084–088, 090, 094 Leo Reynolds
092 Paul Francis
095 Veronica Lynne
096 Thom Watson
097 Mark Hampshire
098 Mirjana Vucic
099 and 101–108 Leo Reynolds
100 Laura Bell
109–118 Keith Stephenson
119 and 122 Ashley Cameron
120 and 123 Leo Reynolds
121 Paula Bailey
124 Thom Watson
126–130, 132, 135 Leo Reynolds
131 Ashley Cameron
136 and 138 Keith Stephenson
137 Lance Robotson
139 Felix Molter
140 Julia Franz
141 James Preiss
142 Os Osment
143, 169, 170 Leo Reynolds
144 Charlie McRae
151, 152, 162 Mark Strozier
171 Mark Menzies
172–177 Keith Stephenson

Themes and Moods
178 Heather Sorrells
179 Thom Watson
180 Colin Palmer www.ColinGregoryPalmer.net
181, 185, 188, 191, 201 Keith Stephenson
182 Brandy Shaul
184 Patrick Benny www.chipple.net
186 Raffy Dakessian
187 Jim Randolph
189 and 190 Hilde Bakering
192 Esther Simpson
202 Lisa Brockmeier
207, 208, 210–212 Keith Stephenson
213 Sarah Norris
216 Steve Jurvetson
218 William Helsen
219 Steve Jurvetson
220 Sam Judson
226 Keith Stephenson
229–232 Raffy Dakessian
233 John Hutchinson
241 and 243 Keith Stephenson
245 Stephane de Bougies
247 Keith Stephenson
249 and 250 Hilde Bakering
252, 253, 254 Hilde Bakering
255 and 256 William Helsen
258 and 259 Keith Stephenson
261 Thom Watson
262 Ian Rippington
263 Hilde Bakering
264 Mark Strozier
265 Benjamin Ball
266 Hilde Bakering
267 Keith Stephenson
268 Courtesy of Materials & Applications
269 Oliver Hess
270 Sharon Elphick
271 and 273 Keith Stephenson
274, 275, 280 Julie Nelson
277 Julie Nelson
278 and 279 Keith Stephenson
281 Hilde Bakering
282 and 284 Mark Strozier
285 Mark Menzies
286 and 290 Keith Stephenson
291 Paul Francis
292 Leo Reynolds
293 Paula Bailey
294 and 295 Keith Stephenson
296–297 and 299 Leo Reynolds
300 and 301 Keith Stephenson
302 Thom Watson
304 Paula Bailey
305 and 306 Leo Reynolds
307 and 308 Keith Stephenson
309–311 Leo Reynolds
312, 313, 315 Keith Stephenson
314 Mark Strozier
316 and 323 Leo Reynolds
317 and 319 Keith Stephenson
322 Ashley Cameron
325 Katsuhisa Kida
326, 329, 330 Keith Stephenson
334 Ashley Cameron
340 Stephane de Bougies
343 José Maria Sotomayor
348 Mark Strozier
350 Anne van der Vaart
351 Maya Nikin
352 Mark Hampshire
353–355 Keith Stephenson
357 Jim Randolph
358 Bryan Howard
359 Timmy Perez
361 Keith Stephenson
362 Paul Duree
363 and 364 Mark Menzies
365 Keith Stephenson
366 Bo R. Wells
368 and 369 Mark Menzies
370 Keith Stephenson
372 Mark Menzies
377 Muhammad Ghouri
379 Hilde Bakering
380 Leo Reynolds
381–383 and 385 Lisa Brockmeier
384 Leo Reynolds
386 Mark Menzies
387 Tina Lee
389 Keith Stephenson
390 Abigail Chicken
391 Teresa Lenihan
393, 394, 396 Lisa Brockmeier

397 and 398 *Keith Stephenson*
399 *Hilde Bakering*
402 *Paula Bailey*
403 *Mark Strozier*
404 *Paul Francis*
405 *John Williams*
406 *Keith Stephenson*
408 *Paul Francis*
410 *Keith Stephenson*
411–420 *Thom Watson*
421 *Charlie McRae*
422 *Karol Miles*
423 *Paul Francis*
424 *Keith Stephenson*
426 *Leo Reynolds*
427 *Charlie McRae*
428 *Thom Watson*
429 *Leo Reynolds*
430 *Thom Watson*
433 *Karol Miles*
434 *William Helsen*
435 and 439 *Keith Stephenson*
442 *Mark Hampshire*
445 *Amanda Rhode*
450 *Keith Stephenson*
455 *Stephane de Bougies*
458, 459, 465 *David Grant*
460 *Dorin Nicolaescu*
461 *Todd Ehlers*
466 *Maarten van Houten*
467 *Keith Stephenson*
468 *Paul Francis*
470 *Jerrick Haddad*
472 *Maarten van Houten*
474–476, 478, 479 *John Ross*
480 *Chris Gladis*
481 *Henry Bourne*
483 *Keith Stephenson*

Signals and Information
485, 488, 489 *Keith Stephenson*
486 *Thom Watson*
487 *Leo Reynolds*
491 *Sam Judson*
492 *Mark Stroup*
493 *Keith Stephenson*
494 *Abigail Chicken*
495, 496, 497, 507 *Keith Stephenson*
498 *Ashley Cameron*
499 *Kristofor Westermeyer*
500 *Shari Sakahara*
501 *Patrick Quinn-Graham*
504 and 505 *Chris Moore*
506 *Stephane de Bougies*
512 *Ashley Cameron*
514 *Joakim Syversen*
522, 531,535–542, 544
Keith Stephenson
543 *Mark Strozier*
546 *Leo Reynolds*
547 *Sam Judson*
549, 550, 552, 553, 556
Keith Stephenson
554 *Paula Bailey*
557 *Charlie McRae*
558 *Mark Strozier*
559 and 560 *Keith Stephenson*
561 *Amanda Rhode*
www.designtangents.com
562–564 *Leo Reynolds*
565 *Hector Loudon*
566 *Elizabeth Lee*
567–570 *Sam Judson*
571–577, 586, 588, 589,
593, 596 *Leo Reynolds*
587 and 592 *Brian Everitt*
590 *Frank Lynch*
591 and 595 *Mark Hampshire*
594 *Paul Francis*
607, 608, 611, 613 *Leo Reynolds*
610, 616, 621 *Keith Stephenson*
612 *Mark Menzies*
614 *Mark Laforet*
615 *Lisa Brockmeier*
617 *Stefan Klein*
622 *Leo Reynolds*
623 *Jannie Armstrong*
624, 626, 630 *Keith Stephenson*
625 *Paula Bailey*
627 *Holly Laury*
628 *Ken Douglas*
631 and 633 *Leo Reynolds*
634 *Henry Bourne*
635–639 and 642 *Keith Stephenson*
641 *Ashley Cameron*
643 *Leo Reynolds*
645 *Lisa Brockmeier*
646 *Thom Watson*
647 and 648 *Keith Stephenson*
652 *Mark Menzies*
653, 654, 666 *Leo Reynolds*
655 *Keith Stephenson*
657 *Duncan Walker*
www.walker1890.co.uk
658–660 *Leo Reynolds*
661 and 665 *Heather Sorrells*
662 *Ashley Cameron*
663 and 667–669 *Keith Stephenson*
672 *Leo Reynolds*
674 *Dulux*
684 *Leo Reynolds*
691–702, 704, 705
Steve Alexander
709 *Andrew Walsh*
710 and 711 *Keith Stephenson*
712 *Nicholas Tang*
713 *Paul Watson*
722–727 *Leo Reynolds*
729, 730, 738 *Mark Hampshire*

Form and Function
740 *Leo Reynolds*
741–743 *Keith Stephenson*
744, 752, 755 *Leo Reynolds*
746 *Mark Phillips*
747 and 750 *Keith Stephenson*
748 *Karol Miles*
751 *Mark Menzies*
749 *Mark Strozier*
753 *Keith Stephenson*
754 *Paula Bailey*
756–761 and 764–769 *Thom Watson*
762 and 763 *Keith Stephenson*
770 *Hilde Bakering*
772 *Paula Bailey*
773 *Charlie McRae*
774 *Mark Strozier*
775 *Paul Francis*
776 *Paula Bailey*
777 *Karol Miles*
778 *Paul Francis*
782 *Stuart Boreham*
783–785 *Keith Stephenson*
786 *Paul Francis*
787 *Mark Menzies*
788, 789, 794 *Leo Reynolds*
791 *Karl H. Schön*
793 and 795 *Keith Stephenson*
796–798, 800, 801
Ashley Cameron
799 *John Ross*
803 *Paula Bailey*
806 *Leo Reynolds*
807 *Thom Watson*
808 *Keith Stephenson*
809 *Henry Bourne*
810 *Jonathan Clapper*
811 *Debbie Stickl*
812 and 813 *Katsuhisa Kida Photography*
4-20-12-101, Sakuradai, Nerima-ku,
Tokyo, 176-0002, Japan
Tel +81-3-5999-7390
www.katsuhisakida.com
814 *Stephane de Bougies*
816 and 817 *Kozo Takayama*
818 and 819 *Thom Watson*
820 and 821 *Keith Stephenson*
823 *Gini Coates*
824–828, 830, 839 *Leo Reynolds*
829 and 831 *Keith Stephenson*
832 and 835–837 *Mark Hampshire*
833 *Mark Strozier*
840 *Marina Kukso*
841 *Mark Menzies*
842 *Paul Francis*
843 *Jannie Armstrong*
844 *Ashley Cameron*
845 *Tina Loo*
851 and 852 *Keith Stephenson*
853 *Henry Bourne*
854, 856–862, 865–868, 871,
872, 874, 876 *Keith Stephenson*
875 *Matthew Thompson*
880 and 882 *Keith Stephenson*
881 *Erwin Olaf*
883 *Thom Watson*
884 *Lisa Brockmeier*
885 *Leo Reynolds*
886 *Keith Stephenson*
887 *Thom Watson*
888 and 889 *Sam Judson*
890 *Katsuhisa Kida*
891 and 910 *Paul Francis*
893 *William Helsen*
894 *Katsuhisa Kida*
895 *Werner Watten*
896 *Adair Broughton*
897 *Jannie Armstrong*
898 *Keith Stephenson*
899 *Thom Watson*
900 *Marina Kukso*
901 *Charlie McRae*
902 *Mark Hampshire*
903 and 904 *William Helsen*
905, 908, 909, 911
Keith Stephenson
906, 907, 913, 914 *Leo Reynolds*
915–919 and 923 *Keith Stephenson*
920–922 and 926 *Leo Reynolds*
924 *Paula Bailey*
925 *Thom Watson*
927 *William Helsen*
928–930 *Daici Ano, FORWARD INC,*
3-3-17-202
Higashi Nihonbashi, Chuo-ku, Tokyo
103-0004. Tel 0081 3 3668 7722

Acknowledgments

Writing this, our second book in the series, has been made enjoyable through the help and cooperation of the (often patient) team at RotoVision—thanks to Chris, April, Jane, and Tony. Thanks, as ever, to Spike at Spike Ink for all his support.

We owe a debt of gratitude to all the artists, designers, and makers for contributing their work and quotes, along with the helpful souls in consultancies who have secured permission, sourced images, and cajoled colleagues. Among them: Jenny Brown at KDa, Ginny Wain at Habitat, Brendan Martin, Nicola Shellswell, Saskia Boersma at All Zones, Marcello Minale, Peter Chadwick, Wayne and Gerardine Hemingway, Alice Keens-Soper, Sharon Elphick, Simon Mitchell, Tom Dixon, Katie McInnes, Swarovski, Michael Erdmann and The Cabin Project, Steven Bateman, Michael Young, Matthew Harding, Lance Wyman, Eugenia, Laura at Places and Spaces, David at The Future Perfect, Ros Hibbert, Karim Rashid, Elizabeth at FTBC, Kyra and Gary at Lambic Nairn, Janet and Joe Doucet at inlulu, Gini Coates, Josh Owen, Julie Nelson, Julie Lasky at I.D.Magazine, Grace at design*sponge, Calvin J. Hamilton, NASA, Ali Hanan and her book *Colormatch*, Mark Dodds, Glenn Harrison, Margaret Cooney, Caren Crangle, Anne Brassier, Tessa Herbert at NSPCC, Jane Slater at the Pelirocco, Trevor Pitt, and Mark Titchner.

Finally, thanks to the brilliant photographers who contributed their work for publishing—particularly: Ashley Cameron, Henry Bourne, Stephane de Bougies, Katsuhisa Kida, Daici Ano, Kozo Takayama, John Ross, Leo Reynolds, Thom Watson, Paul Francis, Steve Alexander, Charlie McRae, Hilde Bakering, Lisa Brockmeier, Mark Strozier, Mark Menzies, and Jannie Armstrong.